UNDERSTANDING EXPORTING IN THE SMALL AND MICRO ENTERPRISE

UNDERSTANDING EXPORTING IN THE SMALL AND MICRO ENTERPRISE

DENSIL A. WILLIAMS

Nova Science Publishers, Inc.
New York

For permission to use material from this book please contact us:
Telephone 631-231-7269; Fax 631-231-8175
Web Site: http://www.novapublishers.com

LIBRARY OF CONGRESS CATALOGING-IN-PUBLICATION DATA

Williams, Densil A.
Understanding exporting in the small and micro enterprise / Densil A. Williams.
p. cm.
Includes bibliographical references and index.
ISBN 978-1-60692-733-5 (hardcover)
1. Exports--Jamaica. 2. Small business--Jamaica. I. Title.
HF3346.5.W55 2009
658.8'4097292--dc22

2008052992

Published by Nova Science Publishers, Inc. ✦ New York

DEDICATION

To Claris Thobourne-Brown and Tracy Ann Henry-Williams

CONTENTS

LIST OF TABLES AND FIGURES

PREFACE

All firms, especially those from small, open developing economies will have to engage in international business to ensure their future survival. It is no secret that globalization has brought with it increased competition, thus forcing firms to seek new customers outside their domestic market. This pressure is even more severe for firms in small, open economies. The markets in these economies are too small to ensure the survival of all firms that operate there. Therefore, these firms have to seek business opportunities outside of their domestic market in order to grow and survive. The majority of firms in these economies are very small by international standards. Further, because of their resource constraints, these small firms generally seek new business abroad by exporting a portion of their sales. They do not always have the resources to engage in other forms of international business such as mergers or foreign direct investments. Exporting becomes an important growth pole for these firms and by extension the local economy.

Economies around the world have highlighted the benefits they derive from having their firms engaged in exporting. These benefits are not unique to an individual country. All economies, especially those small, open developing locations that are trying to integrate in the global economy, should encourage more of their firms to become engaged in exporting. The future survival of these economies will no doubt rest on the successful engagement of their firms in exporting and international business in general.

Despite the tremendous benefits that are derived from exporting, a large number of small firms are not engaged in the activity. It is still unclear why this is the case, especially in small, open economies where globalization has significantly reduced the size of the domestic market. This book investigates the issue by answering the question: *why, of the population of small and micro firms, some choose to sell a portion of their sales abroad while seemingly similar others, facing similar market conditions, remained focused on their domestic market?*

Small firms represent a significant portion of all enterprises in most economies, but yet they account for the lowest level of exports from these economies. If most economies are to benefit from exports, more of their small firms will have to be engaged in exporting. Those small firms that are already exporting will need to increase their volume, while at the same time, those that are not engaged in exporting need to start the activity. Market integration and technological evolution are not showing any signs of slowing down much less reversing. Therefore, firms, especially small ones; will have no option but to get involved in exporting. This is even more pertinent for firms from small, open economies. Importantly, the state in these economies will have to play a major role in helping these firms to engage in exporting.

Public policymakers and managers in small firms need to better understand why some firms export while others do not if they are to stimulate more of these firms to engage in exporting. An extensive literature covering the *export behaviour of the firm*, *internationalization process of the firm* and *international entrepreneurship* have provided some explanations for this seemingly obvious problem. However, the literature is generally fragmented, inconclusive and, limited in geographical scope. The majority of studies focus on US or European firms. Moreover, despite this large body of work, only a limited number addresses the issue from the perspective of the small firm. This therefore leaves a gap in our knowledge regarding the export behaviour of these firms, especially those from small, developing countries. By extending the empirical literature in this area using a study that is focused on Jamaican firms, this book has made a significant contribution to the field. Although all firms will face similar challenges in entering export markets, small firms, especially those from small economies will have added disadvantage because of their smallness and the weak enabling environment in the economies from which they emerge. Therefore, a book dedicated to this subject using perspectives from a small economy, is quite timely.

This book highlights a SOR model which focuses on the export behaviour of small firms from a small, developing economy, Jamaica. The model is theoretically rigorous but parsimonious. It draws on theoretical insights from the *resource-based theory of the firm, process theory of internationalization, network theory, entrepreneurship theory and, international new venture theory* among others, to provide a strong theoretical foundation for the development of its thesis. The basic interpretation of the model is that the decision to initiate exporting is a function of stimuli *(latent or manifest)* inducing entry into international markets. However, stimuli alone cannot result in firms becoming an exporter. The resources *(absorptive capacity)* which the firm possess will determine how it interprets these stimuli when deciding on export initiation. Importantly, in the small firm, there is a strong link between the owner/entrepreneur and the firm. In other words, you cannot separate the owner from the firm. It is argued correctly by many other researchers that the entrepreneur is at the heart of any decision making in the small firm. Therefore, the resources that are analysed in this model reflect the human capital resources that are embodied in the owner/entrepreneur.

To empirically validate the theoretical model, data were collected from small firms that are engaged in exporting *(exporters)* and those that are not exporting *(non-exporters)*. These firms were drawn from the manufacturing and agricultural sectors in Jamaica. The data were analysed using quantitative techniques and descriptive mini-case studies. The quantitative techniques involved econometric models of the qualitative genre *(logistic regression)* and parametric and non-parametric statistics. Mini-case studies were also used to provide further empirical validation to the findings based on the qualitative responses gained through in-depth interviews with a selected number of small firms.

The results from the analyses indicate that the model matches well with the empirical data. Firms possessing the following profiles: *a standardized product, a high quality product, entrepreneurs with a high level of foreign travel experience and previous professional experience in the export sector,* are more amenable to initiate exporting. Firm size is also found to be a significant factor when deciding on export initiation. Further, the results reveal that non-exporters, although collectively they are not engaged in exporting, are not a homogeneous group. Three types of non-exporters were identified in this study. There is one set of non-exporters that have exported before but have withdrawn from the export market these were labelled *experienced non-exporters*. Another set of non-exporters which are not exporting at present but are actively looking for export opportunities and plan to engage in the export trade in the near future were labelled *international business seekers* and, there is still another set of non-exporters that do not have an interest in becoming exporters, there were labelled *uninterested non-exporters*. Collectively, the most common reason for these non-exporters not being involved in exporting is their preoccupation with their domestic market. They also have a strong perception that their product is not for sale in the export market.

The work presented in this volume has definitely extended the empirical work in the area of the export behaviour of the firm, especially small firms from small economies. The development of the integrated SOR model and its empirically validation using data from a small, developing economy, will serve as an important step in advancing a general theory on the export behaviour of the firm. This book has provided new insights that can help theorists to develop a general theory on the export behaviour of the firm. Further, the work also provides strategies to export policymakers and managers in small firms on how to motivate more of these firms to enter into exporting.

Densil A. Williams
Department of Management Studies, UWI Mona

FOREWORD

> *"I have referred a couple of times to the process of crossing the divide from thinking only about the physical opportunities to thinking about what goes on in someone's head. Once we do that more systematically, we can begin to understand the choices that individuals and societies make about growth... What we need to know is why individual and collective decision procedures... keep them from implementing (the) policies."* (Paul Romer, quoted in Snowdon & Vane, 1999, p.16).

A small business everywhere is a lonely enterprise. A small business in a developing country is a particularly audacious endeavour. A small business that exports is dangerously close to hubris in this highly competitive, globalised world. Yet, during the last decade, in particular, the explicit prescription for growth has emphasised the need for export – led growth (Harris, 1997), with the expectation that small and medium- sized enterprises (SMEs), would lead this growth.[i] There is insufficient evidence, however, that the framers of policy have been sufficiently attentive to the practice of the real people who must behave in entrepreneurial ways if real results are to be achieved. This work, *Understanding Micro, Small and Medium Enterprise (MSME) Exporting Firms*, represents a significant contribution to addressing this gap.

The failure of the developing world to develop, whatever epistemological construct is brought to the notion of development, is a matter of concern among its citizens, the development community, academics, and designers of policy. Jamaica's failure to grow has been particularly stark and is especially poignant when compared, not with the developed world, but with its neighbours in the Caribbean. This failure of the Jamaican economy to grow has had profound repercussions on the lives and future of the people of the country, a situation where they find themselves in "the dark tunnel of underdevelopment" (Adjibolosoo, 1999). The contribution to an understanding of the reasons for that failure by focusing on what makes small exporting firms tick has significant meaning for the lives of real people. It

---

[i] "Small independent firms have long been heralded as the great hope for economic growth in the developed economies...But whilst some small firms grow rapidly, the vast majority either languish in the doldrums, or fail altogether...Most SMEs employ no one but the owner themselves (DTI 1997). And most surviving SMEs don't grow. One research study (Storey, 1985) concluded that significant growth is confined to fewer than 4 percent of owner-managed firms. This view is supported by other studies in America (Reynolds and Miller, 1988), and elsewhere." (Barrow, 1998: p.1)

is within this larger context of Jamaica's development that I would like to applaud Dr. Williams' work.

Viewed from the perspective of small exporting firms, what is really going on in the development and growth of the Jamaican economy? What is the theoretical construct within which their perceptions and actions might be considered? The literature calls attention to a number of significant characteristics in this sector: failure is concentrated among the smallest and youngest firms; owner personality has an impact on success as do strategic planning, the impact of market structure, and export orientation. Success, in turn, is said to be attributable to the degree of focus; the customisation of market offerings; and the competitive landscape, inclusive of its home territory, that makes up the arena in which the small firm plays (Hall, 1995). This book extends the extant work by looking at a much wider range of variables which allow the development of testable models.

Research on exporting firms in Jamaica has hitherto emphasised managerial mindset (Garvey 2002; Wint 1997) in relation to the specific concerns of the firms – competitiveness, technology and innovation, for example - but has not identified the sophisticated awareness that players have of the overall environment in which they operate. By paying attention to the processes that underlie the decisions of exporting firms; this work adds a dimension where the experiential knowledge of the small firms is included in the models which emerge from the research. This has implications for the firms' response to the environment in which they are located. These actors will not be inclined to engage in risk – taking activity unless their scan of the entire ecology suggests that there is a reasonable chance of realising profitable outcomes, within acceptable levels of uncertainty.

The issues that lead to the growth and prosperity of societies, especially societies in the developing world, are extremely complex and the variety of analyses and consequent prescriptions highly nuanced. The varying stances of the participants suggest that if economic growth and development depend on the intentional choices and actions of a wide variety of actors, explicit attention needs to be paid to the ways in which different stakeholders apprehend the policy environment in which they are located. The book contributes to our improved understanding of the elements which small firms take into consideration as they make their decisions to export or not.

The book helps to reveal what it means to respond as a small firm to an environment which is not always enabling. The insight which is gained is into the lived experience of firms and their principals as they try to be competitive and survive in the policy shoals, made treacherous by so many undercurrents. The opportunity which the book presents is to discover, through careful analysis, the realities of small firms that export. The outcome of the book's quest is an extension of the discourse which results from its consideration of some of the subtle, implicit and complex forces, not captured hitherto, which tell the story of small exporting firms. The expectation is that this research will lead to a clearer revelation of the frameworks that guide the actions of the firms. The reward is the uncovering of the actual practice of the firms, enabling the development of deductive models that have the capacity to guide policy, with implications for economic growth. The hope is that the contribution to bridging the gap between earlier work and new knowledge will enhance Jamaica's capacity for growth, led by the small exporting firms. The deep desire is to see better policy and more profitable entrepreneurial choices.

Dr. Beverly J. Morgan
Head, The Competitiveness Company

ACKNOWLEDGEMENTS

This scholarly work would not have been possible without the input of a number of persons. It is therefore incumbent on me to offer my sincere gratitude to these individuals.

This book results from the extensive work that was carried out over the course of my doctoral studies at the Manchester Business School in the U.K. During this period, I met and worked with Dr. Graham Hall, who skillfully supervised my doctoral work. I am indebted to Graham for his insightful comments on the work and also his insistence that I publish the output from my extensive research.

My deepest gratitude goes to my mother: Claris Thobourne-Brown; father: Ranold Williams; sisters: Valerie and Patricia; brothers: Delroy, Donavan and Dwayne; and my nieces and nephew for their emotional support. This support proved invaluable in putting this book together. Without it and their encouragement, this work would not have been possible.

My gratitude also goes to my friends from both sides of the Atlantic. Those of you who have always been interested in my work and provided a forum for me to discuss my progress, I thank you immensely. You are too many to be mentioned by name, but you know who you are, a big thank you to all of you.

It would be remiss of me however, not to give special mention to Dr. Boumediene Ramdani who sat with me in the evenings during the writing phase for this book and provided a sounding board for my ideas. He has also provided useful advice on editorial matters. Respect, Ben. Dr. Jonathan Murray and his family played very good host to me over the summer while I was writing this book in the U.K. Special thanks to them as well.

I must also thank the Commonwealth Scholarship Commission for their financial assistance during the initial phase of the research for this book. The University of the West Indies, through the Office of the Principal and the Department of Management Studies also provided financial assistance for me to complete the writing of the manuscript. I owe a big debt of gratitude to this illustrious regional academic institution.

I am also grateful to Mr. Frank Columbus and his team from Nova Science Publishers for their professionalism throughout the publication process. I thank you, Frank for contacting me about a book idea and eventually publishing this book. I look forward to future collaboration with you and your team.

I have to thank the Almighty for spiritual guidance and a source of inspiration during the research and writing phase for this book. Without these, possibly I would not have had the strength to carry on each day.

Finally, I will save the best for last, so I express deep appreciation to my wife, Tracy-Ann for her dedication and understanding during the difficult period of the research for this book. She has been a tower of strength to me and is a collaborator in all my ventures. I dedicate this book to her and my mother, Claris

Although a number of persons contributed to getting this book published, I am solely responsible for all errors. All lacunae are mine.

ABBREVIATIONS

EPA……..……………….........	Economic Partnership Agreement
ASEAN…………………………	Association of South East Asian Nations
BOJ……………………………..	Bank of Jamaica
CARICOM……………………..…	Caribbean Community
CRNM…………………………..…	Caribbean Regional Negotiating Machinery
CSM……………………………..…	Caricom Single Market
CSME…………………………..…	Caricom Single Market and Economy
EU……………………………….	European Union
FTAA…………………………….	Free Trade Area of the Americas
GATT…………………………...	General Agreement on Tariffs and Trade
GDP……………………………..	Gross Domestic Product
HACCP………………………….	Hazard Analysis Critical Control Points
ILO……………………………...	International Labour Organization
ISO……………………………….	International Organization for Standardization
JTI……………………………….	Jamaica Trade and Invest
JBDC……………………………	Jamaica Business Development Centre
JMA……………………………..	Jamaica Manufacturers Association
MERCOSUR…………………….	Southern Common Market
NAFTA………………………….	North American Free Trade Area
PIOJ……………………………..	Planning Institute of JamaicA
PSOJ…………………………….	Private Sector Organization of Jamaica
SBAJ…………………………….	Small Business Association of Jamaica
STATIN………………………….	Statistical Institute of Jamaica
SRCJ…………………………….	Scientific Research Council of Jamaica
UNCTAD……………………….	United Nations Conference on Trade and Development
WTO…………………………….	World Trade Organization

INTRODUCTION

Should small firms[2] export? What can they export? Where should they export? To whom should they export? These are some of the questions that are posed by a number of persons when the topic of exporting from the small firm is being discussed. These questions become louder when the subject is discussed in the context of small firms from small, open developing economies[3]. The fact that the firms in these economies are so small by international standards[4] puts doubt in a lot of entrepreneurs mind as to whether or not they should get into exporting. However, the extant reality of the international economic system obliges all firms to take part in international business. It is not sufficient for any firm, irrespective of size, age or industry sector, from small economies to remain local if they are to guarantee their long term survival. With increased competition from the integration of markets and the limited market size of small economies, the survival of firms in these geographical locations will depend heavily on their involvement in international business. For the small firm, the most feasible form of international business activity is exporting. This is partly due to their limited resource stock. One of the aims of this book is to provide an understanding of how these firms can successfully engage in exporting.

There is no doubt that small firms are finding it easier to expand internationally, thanks to the globalization spurred on by the advances in transportation and communication technologies, reduction in trade barriers and the creation of economic trading blocks (e.g., EU, NAFTA, MERCOSUR, ASEAN, CSM etc.). However, what is not clear is how smaller firms from small, open developing economies are internationalizing. This is a subject that is not well researched among these economies. This book attempts to address this issue by focusing on the question: *"Why, of the population of micro and small firms, some choose to sell a portion of their sales abroad while seemingly similar others, facing similar market conditions, remained focused on their domestic market?"* Data from the experiences of

---

[2] There is no doubt as to the controversy that surrounds the definition of a small firm. The literature is replete with arguments about a suitable definition. For a comprehensive treatment of this debate see Storey, 1994. However, in this book, small firms are defined by their number of employees and comprise those entities with 100 or less fulltime employed personnel. Micro firms are those that have 1- 10 employees. Throughout the book small firm is used interchangeably with micro and small firms.

[3] Small economies can be defined in a number of ways. However, for the purpose of this book, the definition adopted is based on population size and, consists of those with population of five (5) million or less. Further, for openness, trade to GDP ratio must be more than 100 percent.

[4] Bernal refers to these firms as Nano- Firms because of the huge difference in size between all Caricom firms and their international counterparts. For a full treatment of the concept, see Bernal, R. (2006) Nano-Firms, Regional Integration and International Competitiveness: The Experience and Dilemma of the CSME, Production Integration in Caricom pp. 90- 115.

Jamaican small and micro enterprises are used to shed light on the issue. The aim is to utilize the experiences of these enterprises to provide lessons for export development in enterprises of similar structure and characteristics from other geographical locations.

Many studies on internationalization, export behaviour and international entrepreneurship have focused on exporting in small firms but, their arguments do not always take into consideration, the idiosyncrasies of firms from small and developing economies. Indeed, firms from small, developing economies will confront some of the same challenges that firms from developed and larger developing economies face when developing their export business. However, firms from small, developing countries face the double-edged sword of being domiciled in a small country and having an unsophisticated enabling environment[5]. Therefore, the traditional frameworks used in developed economies for explaining exporting in their small firms may not be applicable in these small, developing economies. To understand exporting in the micro and small firms from small, open developing economies, new models and method of thinking will be required to reframe the question about how these firms develop their export business.

This book proposes a new model that can be used to explain the export behaviour of firms in these geographical locations. Using theoretical arguments from the: Resource-Based View Theory, Process Theory of Internationalization, New Venture Theory of Internationalization and Network Theory, the model captures the complexity of small firm's export development process. It looks at stimuli (internal and external to the firm) that are responsible for inducing the decision to initiate exporting and further argues that the presence of stimuli alone cannot lead to firms becoming exporters but, the resource endowment of the firm is also necessary to effectively activate these stimuli (latent or manifest) before the firm can operate in the international marketplace. In other words, the firm will have to possess some capabilities (absorptive capacity) in the local market before it can engage in international business. Indeed, this framework will complement a lot of the other conceptual frameworks put forward when explaining exporting from small firms. Further, it will give future researchers the chance to carry out additional cross country empirical research on the subject. The full details of this model are presented in chapter 2 of the book.

BACKGROUND TO THE RESEARCH

Over the last four decades, an extensive body of work has surfaced on the internationalization of the firm[6], export behaviour of the firm and recently, international

[5] The small size of the domestic market in these small economies limits the amount of physical resources that these firms can acquire and therefore, they will not have sufficient resources to build the absorptive capacity needed to enter exporting. The importance of having absorptive capacity in the local market before going international is captured appropriately in Deng, P. (2008) Resources, Capability, and Outbound FDI from Chinese Companies in Ilan Alon and John R. McIntyre (ed) Globalization of Chinese Enterprises, Palgrave Macmillian: New York. Further, unlike developed countries, small developing economies generally have poor infrastructure such as sea-ports, telecommunications, roads etc., macro economic instability (high interest rates, unstable exchange rate, high inflation) which make enabling environment for export development very difficult.

[6] Implicit in the export literature is the assumption that exporting is synonymous with internationalization. This however is not always true. Internationalization encompasses much more than exporting (Rialp & Rialp, 2001, Jones, 1999). Exporting is one mode by which the firm internationalizes. Other modes include: licensing, franchising, direct investment etc. However, to understand internationalization, it is advised that the different

entrepreneurship[7]. The majority of the literature however, narrows down to a focus on the export behaviour and performance of the firm (Coviello & Jones, 2004).

The emergence of the international entrepreneurship literature broadened the research focus in that, it looks beyond exporting and focuses on other aspects of the firm's international mode of entry and also incorporates both international business and entrepreneurship issues (Jones, 1999; Coviello & Jones, 2004). Still, the bulk of this literature is heavily focused on factors stimulating the decision to initiate, develop and sustain exporting (e.g., Leonidou, 1995a; Bilkey & Tesar, 1977; Bilkey, 1978; Leonidou & Katsikeas, 1996 etc.); barriers hindering entry into exporting; the ability to develop and sustain exporting (e.g., Ifju & Bush, 1993; Shaw & Darroch, 2004; Morgan & Katsikeas, 1997; Leonidou, 1995b, 2004 etc.) and, firm and managerial characteristics which discriminate between exporters and non-exporters (e.g., Obben & Magagula, 2003; Hall & Tú, 2004; Leonidou et al., 1998; Andersson et al., 2004 etc.). Despite this extensive literature, there is still comparatively limited information and inconclusive findings as to the factors which motivate the small and micro firms to export goods or services abroad (Westhead, 2005; Westhead et al., 2001; Jones, 1999). After reviewing 55 studies on the export behaviour of the firm; Aaby and Slater (1989) remained unclear as to why two firms operating in the same industry with similar characteristics took contrasting decisions regarding issue of export initiation. Other researchers have also concurred. For example, in their analysis of the internationalization of new and small firms in Britain, Westhead et al., (2001 pp. 334) state that: "despite the volume of research focusing on the factors associated with the ability of firms to export goods and services abroad, there is still insufficient knowledge about the internationalization of new and small firms". Further, Andersson et al., (2004) after conducting research on Swedish small firms, concluded that internationalization theories such as the process model do not explain why some small firms start to internationalize while others remain in the domestic market.

These inconclusive findings can be attributed to factors such as difference in methodology, difference in operationalization of constructs and, difference in study context (Westhead et al., 2001; Leonidou et al., 1998; Coviello & Jones, 2004). Of critical importance is the study context. Most studies are focused on export development of firms in the developed world (e.g., Westhead et al., 2004; Jones, 1999; Mittelstaedt et al., 2003 etc.) thus leaving a gap in our knowledge regarding export development of small and micro firms in developing countries, especially small, developing countries. This has elicited calls from scholars (e.g., Fillis, 2001; Shaw & Darroch, 2004; Katsikeas & Piercy, 1993; Oviatt, 2005 etc.) for a replication of studies from developed countries into developing countries in order to aid in formulating a general theory on export development in the small firm. Importantly, country specific studies will help policy makers and practitioners to design better programmes to stimulate exporting from the small and micro firm sector in their economy.

---

modes be studied (Welch & Loustarinen, 1988). Because most small firms have limited resources, their major form of international involvement is through exporting (Westhead, 2005, Hatten, 1997, Philp, 1998). This therefore provides the basic rational for the focus on the export behaviour of the micro and small firms in this book.

[7] For a review of these literatures see for example Coviello & Jones, 2004; Jones & Coviello, 2005; Dana, 2004; Dimitratos & Jones, 2005; Rialp et al., 2005; Miesenbock, 1988; Leonidou et al., 1998; Leonidou, 1998; Leonidou & Katsikeas, 1996; Aaby & Slater, 1989; Caviello & McAuley, 1999; Oviatt & McDougall, 1994; Zou & Stan, 1998 etc.

Previous works do not address the conditions of smallness and a weak enabling environment, which often characterize small, open developing economies. The importance of this book is therefore derived from providing a new framework to conceptualize the export development of small and micro firms in these economies. This framework is anchored on the main question as to why some small firms seek opportunities abroad while similar others remain focused on their domestic market. To operationalize this question, the book will try to shed light on the following issues:

1) Is export initiation a systematic investigation of foreign market opportunities or is it a result of fortuitous circumstances?
2) What resources (absorptive capacity) are needed to enhance the firm's ability to enter export markets?
3) Can the process (stage) theory of internationalization help us to predict where micro and small firms will start their exporting after their positive response to export stimuli?
4) What are the perceived factors which prevent small non-exporting firms from seeking and exploiting opportunities in the international market?
5) What are the implications of the findings from this research for: government policy makers, managers in small firms and future researchers?

By investigating the above questions, this book hopes to achieve the following objectives:

1) to propose a model that can be used to predict which micro and small firms are likely to become exporters.
2) to determine what stimuli are most important in motivating micro and small firms from a developing country to initiate exporting.
3) to assess the usefulness of traditional theoretical models (e.g., stage theory of internationalization) in predicting where small firms from a developing country will start their exporting activity after deciding to get involved in exporting.
4) to identify from the perspective of the non-exporters, what perceptual barriers hinder them from becoming exporters.

RESEARCH RATIONALE

The rationale for carrying out this research is twofold. There is an academic rationale and a practical rationale. Although they are non-mutually exclusive separate attention will be paid to them in this discussion.

The extant literature identifies a number of studies which focus on the export behaviour of the firm with a limited number, until recently, paying attention to the micro and small firm[8]. This literature however, is replete with inconclusive findings regarding the motivation for these firms to initiate exporting. For example, some studies argue that it is a calculated

[8] See, for example, : Bilkey, 1978; Miesenbock, 1988; Leonidou & Katsikeas, 1996; Aaby & Slater, 1989; Westhead et al., 2001; Westhead et al., 2004 for a review of some of these studies

effort by decision makers to seek business in the international market (e.g., Leonidou, 1998; Garnier, 1982 etc.) while others argue that it results from forces external to these firms such as unsolicited order from foreign customers (e.g., Cavusgil, 1984a; Joynt, 1982 etc.). These inconclusive arguments have left a gap in our knowledge as to the factors that motivate micro and small firms to export their products and services abroad. As such, it becomes difficult for theorists to develop a robust theoretical framework that can sufficiently capture the increased internationalization trend that is being observed in the micro and small firm.

It is this gap that has motivated the research in this book. The book will shed new light on the subject from a new and unique geographical context that is, small, developing economies. This will help to complement the existing North-American and European explanations for the phenomenon of increased export involvement of micro and small firms. Using theoretical contributions from the Resource-Based View literature (e.g., Barney, 1991), Internationalization literature (e.g., Johanson & Vahlne, 1977) and Entrepreneurship literature (e.g., Covin and Slevin, 1991), a conceptual model that captures the complexity involved in understanding the internationalization behaviour of micro and small firms from a developing country is proposed. Indeed, the literature calls for replication of export behaviour studies in developing countries in order to better aid in theory development of small firms' internationalization behaviour (e.g., Fillis, 2001; Westhead et al., 2001 etc.). The research in this book has answered that call.

There is also a practical rationale for the research reported in this book. The research is relevant to Jamaica, a small, open developing economy. Since its "golden" era of economic growth and export boom of the 1950s-1960s, the country has been experiencing dismal performance in its export trade. More importantly, it is the country's merchandise exports that have under performed over the last decade. Figure 1 captures this performance for a 10 year period.

The graph reveals that while the world's export was growing, Jamaica's performance was declining. This poor export performance is also reflected in the country's balance of payments which has shown a deficit since 1978 when it last recorded a surplus. The continued negative trade balance has had adverse implications for the strength of the country's enabling economic environment[9]. Recognising the seriousness of a poor balance of trade performance, both private and public sector leaders called on firms to improve their export volume and for export capable firms to enter into exporting (PSOJ, 2004). To assist these firms, incentives and trade support schemes have been put in place to encourage them to improve their export performance, international competitiveness and by extension the country's balance of trade performance[10].

However, despite efforts to provide incentives and assistance for improved export performance, there are still a large number of firms that are not engaged in exporting. This

[9] A balance of trade deficit leads to devaluation of the local currency, high inflation, high interest rate, unsustainable external balances which are all conditions for macroeconomic instability. These will all weaken the country's enabling environment for doing business. It is not surprising therefore why the Jamaican economy has not been able to achieve sustained macro economic stability over the last 30 years.

[10] A number of initiatives aimed at improving the export competitiveness of Jamaican firms have been taking place over the last five (5) years. These include but are not limited to cluster development programmes, business incubators, increased access to financing etc. Some of the organisations that are driving these activities are: Jamaica Business Development Centre, Jamaica Trade and Invest through the Private Sector Development Programme funded by the European Union, The Competitiveness Company, A subsidiary of the Jamaica Exporters' Association.

appears to be the result of poor or inappropriate motivation (Seringhaus & Rosson, 1990). Clearly, the stimuli provided did not motivate them to export. A systematic analysis of the relevant stimuli that motivate micro and small firms in the economy to get involved in exporting is definitely needed. The research presented in this book has provided this analysis.

There are other studies which focused on the export performance of the Jamaican economy; however, they generally take a macroeconomic perspective (e.g., McIntyre, 1995, Nicholls et al., 1989 etc.). Further, those that focused on the firm level (e.g., Garvey, 2000; Ross, 1989; Harris, 1997 etc) did not pay specific attention to the micro and small firm. These studies tended to treat small and large firms as the same unit of analysis. A close interpretation of the literature showed that conflating both units of analysis will send the wrong signal to policy makers. Small and large firms are as different as a caterpillar to a butterfly (Storey, 1994), therefore specific attention must be paid to each group separately. The specific attention given to the small and micro firms is what makes this book distinct from others that have preceded it.

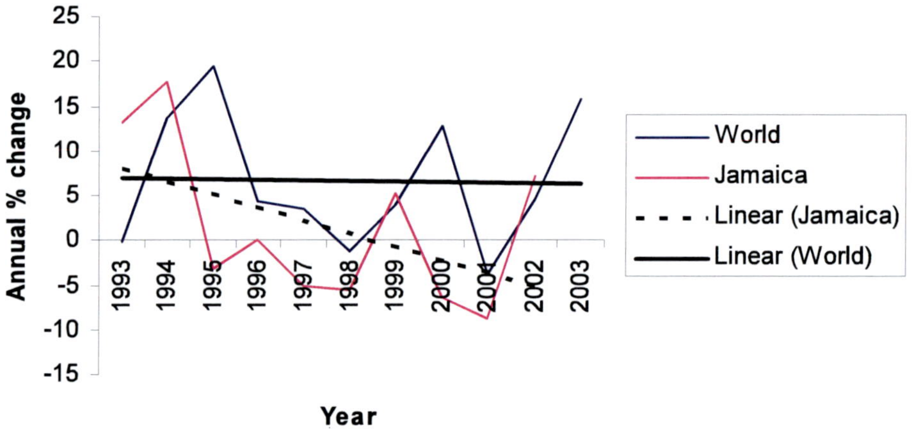

Source: WTO (2004), International Trade Statistics.

Figure 1. Jamaica's merchandise export performance.

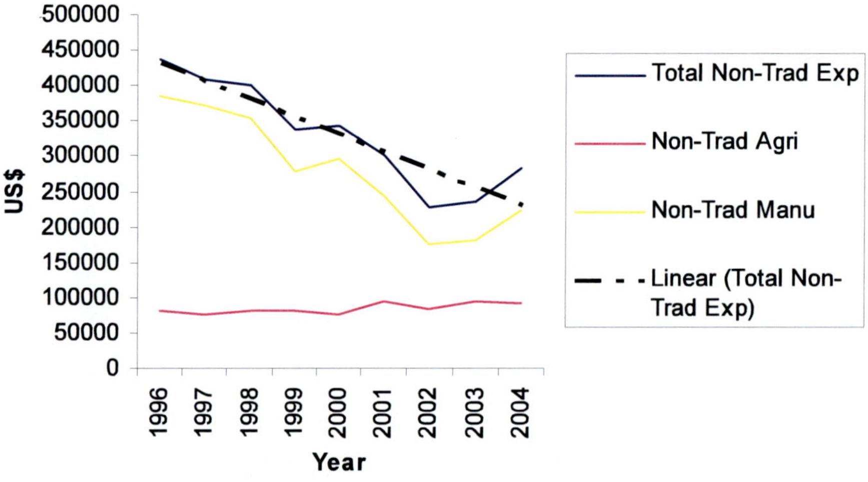

Source: PIOJ, (various issues), Economic and Social Survey Jamaica.

Figure 2. Performance of Jamaica's non-traditional exports.

Indeed, paying special attention to the export behaviour of the micro and small firms is very important because, the majority of firms in the Jamaica economy belong to this category (Harris, 1997). Further, most of these firms are also in the non-traditional export sectors[11]. It is these non-traditional exports that have been recognised as an important source for boosting the economic development of the country (Nicholls et al., 1989). They serve as a way of diversifying the export sector and alleviating the strain on the country's foreign exchange, as a result of the poor performance of traditional exports such as sugar and bananas; especially in light of the erosion of preferential treatment from Europe for these traditional exports. Figure 2 shows the performance of the country's non-traditional exports from the mid-1990s up to 2004.

Since 2002, it appears there have been efforts to increase non-traditional exports. The above picture shows that there is room for increasing exports from this sector. For example, in 2004 the United States imported US$1.8 billion worth of fish crustaceans from the world market. Jamaica, which is in close proximity to the United States and has fish crustacean as a non-traditional export could only manage to sell a paltry US$5.4 million or, less than one percent (.003%) to that market *(U.S. Department of Commerce, 2004)*. In fact, the country's share of the United States imports decreased by four percent between 2003 and 2004. There is no doubt that if more small firms can be engaged in exporting, this market share can rise and also Jamaica's export performance can be improved.

Implementing policies that stimulate more micro and small firms to export will have far reaching implications for the Jamaican economy. These firms have a more national appeal than large or multinationals firms. Therefore, increasing exports will lead to greater societal benefits such as employment creation in more areas of the country.

Organisation of the Book

There are many themes from the fields of International Business, Strategy, International Entrepreneurship and Economics that will permeate this book. The aim is to advance a multidisciplinary perspective and a richer explanation on why some firms export while others facing similar conditions do not. The remainder of the book is organized as follows:

Following this introduction, the book includes in chapter 1, an analysis of the export development and performance of the Jamaican economy. This chapter is important as it puts into context the practical rationale for this study. Further, the experiences from Jamaica's export performance can provide lessons for the export development process in other small, open developing economies.

Chapter 2 of the book presents the new model that was developed for explaining the export behaviour of micro and small firms from small, developing economies. The chapter will explain how the model was derived and also how it works. Among other things, it will highlight the key variables that need to be considered when testing the model empirically and

[11] See the PIOJ flagship publication; "Economic and Social Survey Jamaica" for a list of non-traditional exports from Jamaica.

also show how these variables are operationalized in order to ensure the reliability of the model. The remainder of the book revolves around testing and validating this model.

Chapter 3 will focus on the stimuli that motivate exporters to initiate exports. This chapter pays specific attention to stimuli (evokers, triggers cues, motivators etc.) which are critical in inducing the decision in the small firm to commence exporting. The chapter looks specifically at the first layer of the conceptual model presented in chapter 2. In this chapter, the full literature regarding export stimuli is reviewed and analysed. Export behaviour theories form the basis for conceptualization of major arguments.

Chapter 4 looks specifically at those factors owned or controlled by the firm (resources) which are critical in effectively activating stimuli and getting the firm to operate in the export market. In essence, it focuses on the absorptive capacity that micro and small firms need to possess in order to enter exporting. The resource-based view theory forms the basis for guiding the conceptualization and development theoretical arguments. Variables reflecting the firm's physical and human capital resources are used in a predictive logit model to test the likelihood of the firm becoming an exporter. This chapter along with chapter 3 will provide insights into why some firms export while similar others do not.

Chapter 5 pays attention to where the micro and small firms begin their export activity. After the decision is made to enter into exporting, managers will then have to make a decision regarding which export market to enter. The theoretical discussion regarding this phenomenon is highly inconclusive. The chapter will specifically test whether or not traditional theoretical concepts (e.g., stage theory of internationalization) can be used to predict how small firms from a small, developing country will behave when making international market entry decisions. Importantly, it will provide insights into the critical factors that influence where small firms will start their exporting after the decision to initiate the activity is taken.

Chapter 6 of the book looks at a group of small firms that have received very little attention in the export literature, that is, non-exporters. This book is one of the very few in the field that has dedicated an entire chapter to the perspective of these entrepreneurs when discussing exports from the small firm. By focusing exclusively on non-exporters, this chapter will help us to better understand the reasons; besides resource inadequacy, why these firms reject export stimuli and remain focused on their domestic market. This will provide policy makers with a better idea as to what factors to concentrate on when trying to motivate them to become exporters. This is especially important for small, open developing economies where a large number of their firms are not exporting or has never exported and limited resources are used to stimulate exporting in these firms.

Chapter 7, the final chapter in the book will bring together a discussion of the major findings. As befits a concluding chapter, it will present a summary of the findings from each chapter. Among other things, the chapter also entails a discussion on the implications of the research for managers in micro and small firms, government policy makers interested in stimulating micro and small firms to become engaged in exporting and, also future researchers interested in the export behaviour of micro and small firms.

Chapter 1

Jamaica's Export Development and Performance

Introduction

As market integration and multilateral trade liberalization deepen, economies in the global community are forced to shift their development strategies from a protectionist mode to an export oriented mode[12]. This shift in approach to development has placed increased emphasis on the role of the export trade as central to economic prosperity. Importantly, it is recognised in the new export oriented model that it is firms that trade not national governments (Porter, 1990). Therefore, the economic survival and prosperity of any nation will rest on the success of the firms within the economy. More importantly, the micro and small firms are critical to this prosperity since they form the bulk of enterprises in most economies; especially small, developing economies (Bernal, 2006). However, this emphasis on the role of the firm in economic development does not relegate the critical role and importance of policy, regulation, and macroeconomic management to second place since these factors are critical for the successful performance of the enterprise (Wint, 1998; Gumede, 2004).

There is no doubt that the issue of exporting from micro and small firms are of critical importance to the Jamaican economy. It was estimated that 75 per cent of new employment in any economy is provided by the small firm sector during times of economic contraction and restructuring (Roberts, 2000). Therefore, economies like Jamaica, which are restructuring to become more efficient and internationally competitive, need to pay close attention to this sector. During the decade of the 1990s, the Jamaican economy saw average rate of GDP growth of 0.1 per cent. For the period 1994-1999, the average GDP growth was -0.7 per cent, a clear sign of economic contraction (PIOJ, 2000). Over this same period, the rate of growth of exports was 0 percent (World Bank, 2000). For the period 2002-2007, average GDP growth was 1.6 per cent (PIOJ 2007). These unimpressive figures show that there is a

[12] Protections strategy is used here to refer to what development specialists call inward oriented strategy. This includes actions such as Import Substitutions Industrialization (ISI). Export oriented strategy is used here to refer to what the development specialists call outward oriented strategy. The evolution of these strategic shifts in the Jamaican economy is captured in King, 2001.

desperate need for the country to improve its export performance and take advantage of the tremendous benefits which can be derived from exporting[13].

The enhancement of the international competitiveness of the Jamaican economy must involve the participation of its enterprises in international business. The importance of these enterprises in driving the export-led growth and transformation of the Jamaican economy is well recognised. In the early 1980s when Anglo-American neo-liberalism became the model of choice for economic management, it resulted in a massive restructuring of the Jamaican economy[14]. This placed greater emphasis on the micro and small business sector to assume a greater role in economic development since it has the potential to absorb labour and also maintain existing jobs. However, the mere existence of these enterprises in any economy will not lead to economic prosperity. The challenge is for these enterprises to upgrade their processes to handle production of their goods and services for the international and domestic markets. The examination of Jamaica's export development and performance will indicate whether or not these enterprises have risen to that challenge.

The growth and survival of these micro and small enterprises and by extension the economy, will depend heavily on their interaction with the international market whether through exporting or other modes of internationalization. Jamaica is a small country, heavily liberalized and has a small market size. Therefore, the growth of its industrial sectors and firms will have to depend heavily on exports (PSOJ, 2004; Ocompo, 2002). As a result of the "liability of size", the country will have to develop a strong and effective export promotion programme so as to improve its export performance. In this campaign, specific attention will have to be paid to the small firm sector, since it consists of the bulk of enterprises in the country but accounts for the smallest portion of exports. This sector accounts for over 80 percent of firms in the economy but less than 10 percent of the country's exports (PIOJ, 2000). The economic structure of the Jamaican economy will have to be investigated in order to better understand why some firms export while others do not.

This chapter aims to provide a profile of the Jamaican economy in order to better position the empirical rationale for undertaking the research reported in this book. Among other things, the chapter will give a brief historical overview of the country's industrial pattern and development. This will be followed by a discussion on the importance of exporting to the economy. Here, the discussion will focus on the country's export potential and its achievements, that is, its export growth over the last half century. Further, there will be a discussion on the export incentive regimes in the country and the trade support networks which exist to assist Jamaican firms to get into exporting. The final section of the chapter will provide a summary of the major findings and give some conclusions.

Industrial Pattern and Development

In 1962, Jamaica became the first English speaking Caribbean colony to gain independence from British rule for over three centuries. Prior to independence, there was very

[13] Some of these benefits include increased foreign exchange earnings, economic growth etc. See Garvey, 2000 chapter 7 for a discussion on some of these benefits.

[14] A significant amount of work exists on the impact of structural adjustments on the Jamaica economy. This book will not engage in a debate on this subject. For an understanding of these policies see Davies and Witter (1989) and Witter and Anderson, (1991).

little industrial activity on the island. The level of industrial activity that took place was limited to the processing of primary products (mainly agricultural products) for exports and the manufacture of light consumer goods for the local market. After independence, the country promoted industrial development more aggressively. The work of development economist W.A. Lewis was highly influential in this period. His major line of argument was basically that Caribbean economies such as Jamaica have huge amounts of labour but lacked financial capital and entrepreneurial abilities which are critical for sustainable development. For these economies to grow he argued, they needed to attract foreign capital and entrepreneurial talents. To attract these scare resources it was suggested that incentives would have to be given to foreign investors (Lewis, 1954).

Incentives offered during this period included: tax holidays, cheap factory space, easy access to power, water and transportation (Davies et al., 1980). For the period 1960s- 1980s, investors were invited to produce for local consumption, not for export. This investment strategy was labelled Import Substitution Industrialization (ISI) as it focused on attracting firms that could produce locally, goods that would otherwise be imported (Davies & Witter, 1989). It is still argued that vestiges of this thinking remain in a lot of Jamaican enterprises thus negatively impacting the economy's international business performance (Garvey, 2000).

Given the drawbacks[15] of the ISI strategy owing mainly to economic liberalization, economic policy makers have shifted economic development strategy to an outward oriented framework. This new strategic thrust is akin to a Pro-Business model, where, the state's involvement in industrial activities is limited and private enterprises play the major role in the production process. These enterprises must also have an export orientation and not merely produce for the domestic market.

This export orientation strategy became prominent in the early 1980s and has continued since. Over the period 1980-2000, there was massive privatization of state owned enterprises, rapid liberalization of the country's trading regime, thus resulting in export promotion and trade taking on increasing importance. The increased importance of trade and export in economic development resulted in the formation of a number of trade support networks in both the public and private sectors. In the public sector, JTI has sole responsibility for export development and investment promotion in the economy. This rationalization of the public sector networks into a single organisation was aimed at reducing the public sector's role in industrial activities. Other players in the country's trade support network include the PSOJ, SRCJ, CRNM, JEA and JMA.

Compared to the pre-independence period and the early decade post independence, contemporary Jamaica has a more diversified manufacturing sector. Not only is the sector producing light manufactured goods but also sophisticated products such as, metals, chemicals and is heavily involved in the export trade. There is also a non-traditional export sector which sells products such as: processed foods, beverages, tobacco, minerals, animal and vegetable oils and fats, chemicals, and chemicals products to the export market. This sector accounts for a significant portion of the country's export revenues. In 2000, the non-traditional manufactured exports grew by 8.2 per cent which was the highest growth area in the manufacturing sector (PIOJ, 2000). However, its performance has been unimpressive since. This signals a need for more of the country's small enterprises to participate in the export trade.

[15] For a good treatment of the ills of the ISI strategy not only in Jamaica, but generally, see Wint, 1995.

The county's agricultural sector also became more diversified after independence. Besides the traditional export crops of bananas and sugar, there is also a non-traditional sector which produces crops such as: cucumbers, pumpkins, dasheens, sweet potatoes, cut flowers, fish crustaceans, and mollusc. The non-traditional crops recorded a 6 percent decline in export sales in 2000. Besides the natural causes from drought, this decline also reflects the reluctance of a number of small farmers to get involved in exporting. This book will explain the reasons for this and thus provide needed empirical evidence to formulate policies to stimulate these firms to get involved in exporting.

Despite the gains made since independence to diversify the country's economic sectors, there still exist serious challenges in growing the export sector. Although the data show that there is a growing demand for non-traditional manufactured and agricultural exports in the world economy (UNCTAD, 2004), Jamaica's export to GDP ratio continues to decline. Over the period 1996- 2004, the country's export to GDP ratio declined by 8.1 percent, in 2004 it stood at 16.0 percent (PIOJ, 2004). These figures show that although efforts are being made to improve export performance through the creation of trade support networks, the most relevant stimuli to trigger exporting in these firms are still not well understood. This book offers a better understanding of these stimuli in the Jamaican context.

It is critical to note that, while analysing the country's industrial development over time, no specific policy initiatives aimed at improving the international competitiveness of the micro and small firms were found. It is true that the scarcity of data on these firms makes it difficult to track their contribution to the country's industrial development and also to put forward a policy framework to improve their efficiency and competitiveness. However, the basic assumption that small and large firms are one and the same which policymakers adhere to when dealing with competitiveness policy at the firm level is dangerous. Special efforts need to be put in place to develop a national policy on the micro and small firm sector as a separate unit of analysis compared to larger and multinational firms. This national policy must have an element in it that is dedicated to stimulating exports among these firms. This is the only way that the economy can improve its export performance in any significant way.

Importance of Exports to the Economy

Jamaica, like many other countries in the world, can benefit tremendously from the export trade. The benefits to accrue from exports include but are not limited to the provision of foreign exchange; improvement in local firms' international competitiveness; provision of employment etc. (World Bank, 2000). These have been acknowledged by both practitioners and academics alike.

The small size of the Jamaican market makes exporting very critical for the growth and survival of its firms and economic sectors. The country has a population of 2.6 million peoples with per capita income in 2004 of J$89,600 (US$ 1,468). Unemployment stood at 9.4 percent in 2007. This is no surprise as employment over the decade of the 1990s showed a paltry 0.3 percent growth (World Bank, 2005). Adult literacy was 79.9 percent in 2004. The country's debt to GDP ratio was 133 per cent in 2003 with debt servicing taking up almost one third (32%) of GDP in 2003. The country's major export sectors are: Bauxite/Alumina; Agriculture; Tourism and Manufacturing (PIOJ, 2004). The economy is heavily import dependent purchasing significant quantities of consumer goods, raw materials and machinery from abroad. Imports as a percent of GDP stood at 44.8 per cent in 2004 while trade balance was US$2,516 million deficit, a 1.3 percent increase over 2003.

Clearly, to improve the country's competitiveness and by extension the survival of firms in the economy, firms must be encouraged to export. The revenue gained by firms from exports is critical to the local economy because of the multiplier effects it has. It serves to generate income and employment gains in the domestic economy as a result of the various other economic activities (both production and consumption) which firms depend on.

Exporting is also critical to the Jamaican economy because it provides a strong source of foreign exchange to stabilize the country's exchange rate with major trading partners. Owing to the high import dependency which characterises the economy, revenues from exports will make it possible to acquire from abroad the imports necessary to sustain critical production and consumption activities. It was estimated in 1994 that export earnings covered 92 per cent of the country's total import bill for goods and services (Harris, 1997). The gap was filled by factor incomes from abroad, private remittances and other transfers.

Besides the direct revenue benefits from exports, there are also other spill-over effects. For example, major export sectors such as bauxite and technology establish basic infrastructure such as roads, water, and telecommunications networks which enhance the country's infrastructure base thus increasing the sophistication of the enabling business environment. It can be argued that in various ways, exports constitute the basic driving force for growth and development of the economy. The export sector links various sectors in the economy thus creating a feedback effect for an all round growth in the economy. Just like the much trumpeted economic success of the economies east and south-east Asia, the Jamaican economy can gain similar feat with increased attention being paid to the export sector, especially exports from micro and small firms, which constitute the bulk of enterprises in the economy.

Export Growth and Competitiveness

There is absolutely no doubt that Jamaica's best period of export growth occurred during the period just before independence (1950s) and the first decade post independence (1960s). This period has been referred to by many commentators as the halcyon years for the economy (Harris, 1997). Analysing the comparative growth picture of Jamaica's merchandise exports with the rest of the world since the 1950s to 2005, the data confirm that Jamaica's best export growth was indeed in the 1950s. Over the decades of the 1980s and 1990s, the country's merchandise exports recorded average growth of 1.4 percent for the period 1981-2002 (World Bank, 2005). The decade of the 1990s was the worst period for the growth of merchandise exports. Growth averaged less than one percent (0.75%) for the period 1991 -2002 (ibid). Table 1.1 captures this picture over the review period.

Table 1.1. Comparative growth rate of merchandise exports for the period 1950- 2005 (Average annual percent)

Year	1950-1960	1960-1970	1970-1980	1980-1990	1990-2000	2000-2005
World	6.4	9.2	20.4	6.1	7.7	11.3
Developed Economies	7	10	19	7.6	5.7	9.4
North America	5.4	9	17.5	6	9.3	4
Europe	8	10.1	19.4	8.1	5	11.8
Developing Economies	3.6	6.7	25.8	3.2	12.2	14.1
Latin America & Caribbean	2.4	5.6	20.8	2.1	13.1	5.9
Africa	3.8	9.5	21.5	(2.5)	(3.5)	16.3
Selected Countries						
Barbados	3.4	4.8	18.1	(3.2)	2.7	4.8
Jamaica	14.6	5.2	12.4	0.7	1.2	3.4
Trinidad & Tobago	10.5	4.8	23.6	(9.9)	11	17.2
Dominican Republic	5	2.1	14.7	(2.1)	14.8	1.3

Source: UNCTAD (1996/97), Handbook of International Trade and Development Statistics.
WTO (2001), International Trade Statistics.
IMF (2002 & 1997), Balance of Payments Statistics Year Book Parts 2 & 3: World and Regional Tables.

During the period of the 1950s, Jamaica's growth rate of merchandise exports was equivalent to four times that of developing countries as a whole and twice that of the world. In the last decade of the century, this trend was reversed. For the period 1990-2000, merchandise export growth was 1.2 percent per annum, which was 10 times less than that of developing countries as a whole and six times less than the world's growth. Nevertheless, export growth improved slightly over the period of the 1990s for the first half of the decade of the 21st century. This increase however, was not significant enough to result in any massive improvements in the country's balance of trade position.

Export growth during the 1950s and 1960s could possibly be attributed to unique circumstances. The country is heavily endowed with natural resources such as bauxite and is also a large producer of agricultural commodities such as sugar cane and bananas. The period of the 1950s saw heavy growth in demand for bauxite from developed countries that were just recovering from the world war in the 1940s. There was also strong growth in demand for agricultural products. These increases in demand led to high prices for these commodities on the world market. As such, countries like Jamaica were able to enjoy a huge growth in exports over the period. However, in the 1990s, the price for these commodities fell sharply on the world market due mainly to reduced demand. This resulted in a reduction in export revenue and volume. The country did not take advantage of the growth opportunities in the non-traditional export sector.

Although merchandise exports performed poorly over the 1990s, the export sector realised some growth. The years of export growth during the 1990s was heavily driven by growth in the export of services, especially tourism. For the period 1991-2002, average growth rate of services was 5.65 percent compared to goods at 0.75 percent (World Bank,

2005). Traditional and non-traditional merchandise exports showed unconvincing performance for the same period. Table 1.2 summarizes the performance of the country's total export growth over the decade of the 1990s.

The growth in the services sector led to some respectable export growth in the country's total exports over the decade of the 1990s. The non-traditional export sector where the majority of micro and small firms operate, has performed poorly especially in the latter part of the decade. The data that are available for the first half of the 21st century show that the situation is quite similar. There have not been any marked improvements in the exports from this sector. Indeed, based on the data, it is clear that there is a need for improving the country's export performance by targeting the small firm sector.

Table 1.2. Growth of total exports for the period 1990-2000

Year	**1990**	**1991**	**1992**	**1993**	**1994**	**1995**	**1996**	**1997**	**1998**	**1999**	**2000**
Total Exports	7.1	(3.4)	2.1	8.2	7.7	15.2	(6.2)	0.5	(6.5)	(5)	3.7
Composition											
Merchandise	15.7	(0.6)	(8.4)	2.1	13.4	17.7	(3.1)	0	(5.1)	(5.5)	5.2
Traditional	26.2	(7.1)	(11.9)	-3.0	8.9	17.9	.07	3.8	-8.5	0.3	4.7
Non-Traditional	(11.7)	1.5	3.7	(16.6)	17.6	14.4	(8.75)	(6.1)	(2.1)	(16.7)	(3.1)
Re-exports	(1.1)	155.2	(75.2)	(22.3)	114.6	35.4	(17.17)	(18.8)	53.2	(31.1)	15.3
Services	(0.2)	(6.2)	13.1	13.4	3.3	13.6	0.3	6	4.2	11.7	2.3
Tourism	24.8	3.2	12.3	9.8	(2.5)	11.1	(0.3)	4.3	4.9	3.1	8.1
Other Services	(25.7)	(22.5)	15.0	21.2	15.1	17.9	2.9	9.7	(5.3)	33.9	(8.5)

Sources: PIOJ (various issues), Economic and Social Survey Jamaica, IMF (2004 & 2002), Balance of Payments Statistics Country Tables, WTO (2004), International Trade Statistics.

N.B. Figures represent percentage change from one year to the next. ( ) represents negative growth.

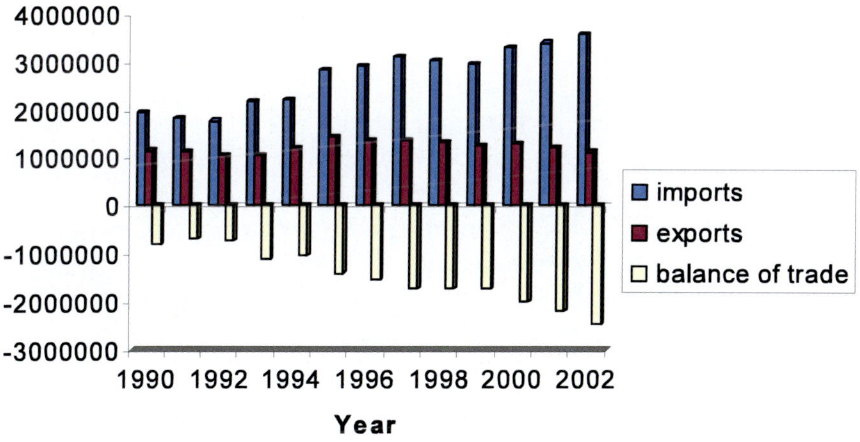

Source: STATIN (various issues), External Trade, BOJ (various issues), Balance of Payments. N.B. Figures relate only to merchandise trade.

Figure 1.1. Jamaica's balance of trade performance.

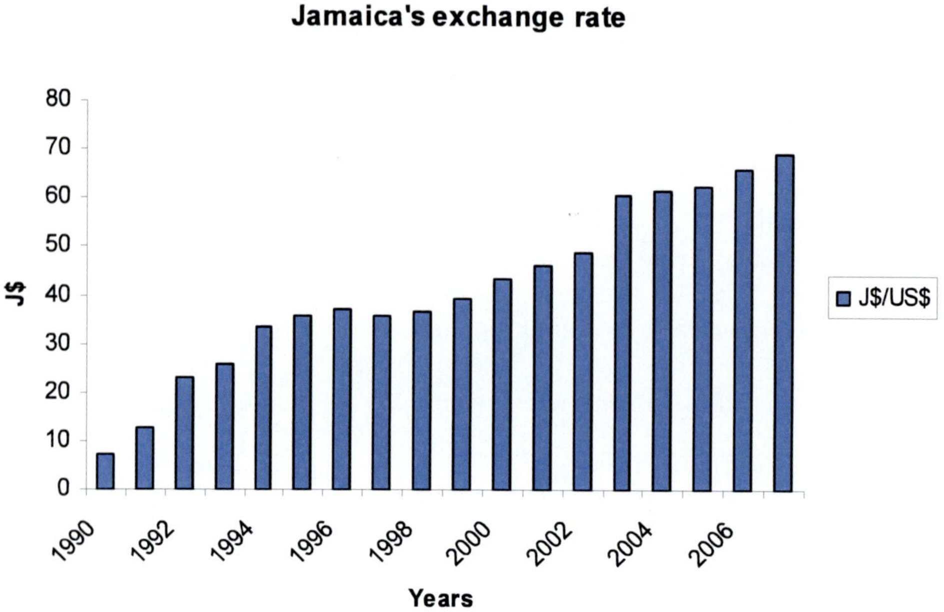

Source: BOJ (various issues), Economic Statistics.

Figure 1.2. Jamaica's exchange rate performance over the period 1990 -2004.

The country's unimpressive export growth has had implications for the management of its macro-economic policy. This is reflected in the impact on the balance of trade record and also the foreign exchange rate depreciation. Since 1977/1978, the country has not seen a balance of trade surplus. Imports have continued to outperform exports over the last decade. Figure 1.1 captures this performance over the decade of the 1990s.

Further, the country's exchange rate has become very unstable as well. Over the same period of its balance of trade deterioration, the country's exchange rate with its major trading partner, the United States of America depreciated by over 700 percent to stand at J$69.06 to US$1 in 2007.

This massive depreciation of the country's exchange rate is a reflection of its poor export and trade performance over the years. This has had serious ramifications for the export sector because of its high import dependency. It has also affected the country's level of macro-economic stability therefore; making the enabling environment more unfriendly for business operations. Indeed, with imports outpacing exports at this alarming rate, the only choice for Jamaica is to increase exponentially, its export offerings to the world. Although total exports in 2007 grew by 7.6 percent, this increase was not sufficient to reduce the trade deficit which stood at US$3,957 million in 2007.

Does Jamaica Have Anything to Sell to the World?

The questions that come to mind after looking at Jamaica's export performance, especially over the last decade are: a) Does Jamaica have any thing to export to the world?

and b) Will the world buy anything from Jamaica? These questions address both supply and demand issues regarding Jamaica's ability to export. To answer these questions, a critical analysis of the data on the composition of the country's export offerings and their destinations were undertaken. The data presented below focus on merchandise products which the country sells to the export market. Table 1.3 presents a comprehensive range of items which the country sells to the export market. The idea is to highlight Jamaica's diversified export portfolio and to determine if further diversification is needed.

Table 1.3. Composition of Jamaica's merchandise exports ranked by SICT Code

Year SICT	Section Name	2000	2001	2002	2003	2004	2005	2006	2007
00	Live animals for food	0.00	0.00	0.00	0.00	0.00	0.00	0.00	0.00
01	Meat and meat preparations	0.10	0.20	0.00	0.18	0.22	0.13	0.11	0.09
02	Dairy products and birds' eggs	0.40	0.70	0.05	0.49	0.40	0.31	0.35	0.23
03	Fish crustaceans and molluscs	0.70	1.00		0.68	0.53	0.64	0.54	0.39
04	Cereal and cereal preparations	0.50	0.60	0.07	0.81	0.77	0.61	0.47	0.50
05	Vegetables and fruits	4.20	5.10	0.50	5.28	3.80	2.99	2.91	2.61
06	Sugar and sugar preparations and nes honey	5.90	5.80	0.58	5.48	6.97	5.11	4.58	4.69
07	Coffee, tea, cocoa and spices	3.10	3.20	0.36	3.11	3.24	1.46	1.88	1.79
08	Feeding stuff for animal excluding unmilled cereals	0.00	0.00	0.00	0.07	0.07	0.06	0.17	
09	Miscellaneous edible products and preparations	1.40	1.90	0.18	2.01	1.60	1.13	1.10	0.93
11	Beverages	3.40	3.80	0.50	4.35	4.38	4.94	4.65	4.57
12	Tobacco and tobacco manufacturers	1.00	0.10	0.00	0.00	0.00	0.00	0.00	0.00
21	Hides, skins and fur skins raw	0.00	0.00	0.00	0.00	0.00	0.00	0.00	0.00
22	Oil seeds and oleaginous fruit	0.00	0.00	0.00	0.00	0.00	0.00	0.00	0.00
23	Crude rubber	0.00	0.00	0.00	0.00	0.00	0.00	0.00	0.00
24	Cork and wood	0.00	0.00	0.00	0.00	0.00	0.00	0.00	0.00
25	Pulp and waste matter	0.00	0.00	0.00	0.00	0.00	0.00	0.00	0.00
26	Textile fibres other than wool tops and their waste not manufactured into yarn	0.00	0.00	0.00	0.00	0.00	0.00	0.00	0.00
27	Crude fertilizers and crude minerals	0.30	0.30	0.00	0.35	0.28	0.37	0.23	0.11
28	Metalliferous ores and metal scrap	52.90	60.30	6.32	65.41	65.35	69.41	64.17	65.35
29	Crude animal and vegetable materials	0.10	0.10	0.00	0.09	0.09	0.08	0.06	
33	Petroleum, petroleum products	0.30	1.20	0.26	2.43	2.39	7.53	13.74	15.45

Table 1.3. Continued

Year	Section Name	2000	2001	2002	2003	2004	2005	2006	2007
34	Gas, natural and manufactured	0.00	0.00	0.00	0.00	0.00	0.00	0.00	0.00
41	Animal oils and fats	0.00	0.00	0.00	0.00	0.00	0.00	0.00	0.00
42	Fixed vegetable oils and fats	0.00	0.00	0.00	0.00	0.00	0.00	0.00	0.00
43	Animal and vegetable oils and fats, processed and waxes of animal or vegetable origin	0.00	0.00	0.00	0.00	0.00	0.00	0.00	0.00
51	Organic chemicals	3.00	3.90	0.35	3.62	4.27	2.57	2.89	1.33
52	Inorganic chemicals	1.00	0.50	0.00	0.19	0.38	0.31	0.22	0.28
53	Dyeing, tanning and colouring materials	0.10	0.10	0.00	0.12	0.11	0.09	0.07	0.08
54	Medicinal and pharmaceutical products	0.10	0.20	0.00	0.20	0.15	0.10	0.09	0.12
55	Essential oils and perfumes	0.60	0.70	0.06	0.61	0.44	0.38	0.34	0.35
56	Fertilizers, manufactured	0.00	0.00	0.00	0.00	0.00	0.00	0.00	0.00
57	Explosives and pyrotechnics	0.00	0.00	0.00	0.00	0.00	0.00	0.00	0.00
58	Artificial resins and plastic material and cellulose esters and ethers	0.00	0.00	0.00	0.07	0.00	0.00	0.00	0.00
59	Chemical materials and products N.E.S	0.20	0.20	0.00	0.14	0.10	0.08	0.06	0.14
61	Leather, leather manufacturers, N.E.S. and dressed fur skins	0.00	0.00	0.00	0.00	0.00	0.00	0.00	0.00
62	Rubber manufacturers N.E.S.	0.10	0.20	0.00	0.27	0.35	0.00	0.00	0.00
63	Cork and wood manufacturers (excluding furniture)	0.20	0.10	0.00	0.09	0.09	0.09	0.08	0.00
64	Paper, paperboard and articles of paper pulp, of paper and paperboard	0.20	0.10	0.00	0.06	0.00	0.00	0.00	0.00
65	Textile yarn, fabrics, made up fabrics N.E.S. and related products	0.00	0.00	0.00	0.00	0.00	0.00	0.00	0.00
66	Non-metallic mineral manufacturers N.E.S.	0.10	0.10	0.00	0.10	0.00	0.00	0.00	0.00
67	Iron and steel			0.00		0.00	0.00	0.00	0.00
68	Non-ferrous metals	0.10	0.10	0.00	0.07	0.06	0.00	0.00	0.00
69	Manufacturers of metals N.E.S.	0.20	0.20	0.00	0.19	0.35	0.14	0.34	0.14
71	Power generating machinery and equipment	0.50	0.10	0.00	0.15	0.07	0.00	0.00	0.00

Year	Section Name	2000	2001	2002	2003	2004	2005	2006	2007
72	Machinery specialized for particular industries	0.10	0.20	0.00	0.06	0.06	0.00	0.00	0.00
73	Metal working machinery	0.00	0.10	0.00	0.00	0.00	0.00	0.00	0.00
74	General industrial machinery and equipment N.E.S. and parts N.E.S.	0.30	0.20	0.00	0.14	0.15	0.00	0.00	0.00
75	Office machines and automatic data processing equipment	0.00	0.10	0.00	0.06	0.07	0.00	0.00	0.00
76	Telecommunications and sound recording and reproducing apparatus & equipment	0.10	0.00	0.00	0.22	0.20	0.00	0.00	0.00
77	Electrical machinery, apparatus and appliances N.E.S. and parts	0.10	0.10	0.00	0.13	0.06	0.00	0.00	0.06
78	Road vehicles (including air cushion vehicles)	0.50	0.10	0.00	0.22	0.44	0.00	0.00	0.00
79	Other transport equipment	0.20	0.30	0.00	0.51	0.66	0.00	0.00	0.00
81	Sanitary, plumbing, heating and lighting fixtures and fitting N.E.S.	0.00	0.00	0.00	0.00	0.00	0.00	0.00	0.00
82	Furniture and parts thereof	0.00	0.10	0.00	0.07	0.05	0.00	0.00	0.00
83	Travel goods, handbags and similar containers	0.00	0.00	0.00	0.00	0.00	0.00	0.00	0.00
84	Articles of apparel and clothing accessories	10.80	7.30	0.17	1.00	0.80	0.59	0.21	0.09
85	Footwear	0.00	0.10	0.00	0.00	0.00	0.00	0.00	0.00
87	Professional, scientific and controlling instruments and apparatus N.E.S.	0.10	0.10	0.00	0.00	0.06	0.00	0.00	0.00
88	Photographic equipment and supplies and optical goods N.E.S.; watches and clocks	0.00	0.00	0.00	0.00	0.00	0.00	0.00	0.00
89	Miscellaneous manufactured articles N.E.S.	0.70	0.50	0.07	0.69	0.56	0.47	0.42	0.33
99	Other N.E.S.	6.00	0.00	0.00	0.00	0.00	0.00	0.00	0.00

Source: STATIN (various issues), External Trade.

Percentage figures represent SICT contributions to total merchandise exports.

Nes: Not elsewhere stated.

N.B. 0 % means that the contribution of those items to total export could not be ascertained.

Besides metalliferous ores (e.g., bauxite and alumina) and traditional agricultural products, all other items contribute an extremely small amount to the total merchandise exports from the economy. Importantly, these are the items that are generally produced by micro and small firms (e.g., essential oils, chemicals, baked products etc.). Interestingly, they also have a growing demand on the world market. So, yes, the data is telling us that Jamaica does have something to sell to the world. Therefore, it appears that there is scope for Jamaica to improve its export performance. The salient point is that there is an opportunity for more small firms to get involved in the export trade. They indeed have something to offer to the world economy.

To determine whether or not the world will buy anything from Jamaica, data on the destination of Jamaica's exports were also analysed. Table 1.4 shows the destinations of the range of exports from the economy. The analysis shows that almost every region of the world has a taste of Jamaica's exported products. Markets as far as Lebanon, Saudi Arabia etc. purchase Jamaican products. This signals that Jamaica's exports enjoy wide acceptance across the world and therefore suggests that there is definitely scope for improved performance.

Table 1.4. Destination of Jamaica's export by region and areas of the world

Year	**1994**	**1995**	**1996**	**1997**	**1998**	**1999**	**2000**	**2001**	**2002**	**2003**	**2004**
Trading Area											
Caribbean Common Market (CARICOM) & ACS	5		9	8		8	9		9.3	9.4	10.7
European Union (EU)	23	28	26	22		23	27		27.2	27.0	37.7
European Free Trade Association (EFTA)	10	9	8	7		8	10	7	8.3	3.3	4.2
African Lome Trade Convention Countries	4	3	3	6	1	2		2	1.9	0.2	
Caribbean Lome Trade Convention Countries	5	4	4	3	4	4	4	10	4.3	4.8	4.9
Central America Common Market								1	0.1	0.2	0.1
Latin America Integration Association (LAIA)	3	2	1	1	1	1	1	1	1.1	0.5	0.8
Organisation of Petroleum Exporting Countries (OPEC)							1		0.1	0.0	0.4
Australia and New Zealand Closer Economic Relations									0.2	0.2	0.2
Economic Community of West African States (ECOWAS)	4	3	3	6	1	2	1	2	1.9	0.2	
North American Free Trade Area (NAFTA)			40	40		43	45	47	37.6	40.5	34.6
Other Countries	45	6	6	7	10	8	1		8.0	13.6	6.2

Source: STATIN (various issues), External Trade. Missing figures mean exports to those regions in that particular year were not obtained. Export figures are based on US$ value and not volume since the latter was difficult to obtain.

The data from both sets of tables above reveal that Jamaica has a wide and diversified array of merchandise exports. Also, their reach is very wide, touching almost all continents on the globe. The evidence suggests that the country has what to export and also that people are willing to buy Jamaican products. Therefore, it is not a demand problem why Jamaica is unable to improve exponentially, its export growth. It appears that the firms are poorly or inappropriately stimulated to trigger their involvement in exporting.

Further, from the data in Tables 1.3 and 1.4, one cannot reasonably claim that Jamaica's poor export performance over the last decade results from a lack of competitive advantage in the products it offers to the international market place. In fact, McIntyre, (1995) after developing a comparative advantage index to analyse the export performance of Caribbean economies, revealed that Jamaica had a comparative advantage in products such as: essential oils and perfumes. Nicholls et al., (1989) after analysing strategies for marketing non-traditional exports, listed a number of products which Jamaica has a competitive edge in (mainly because of its unique circumstances) but not exploiting those advantages in nearby US markets. Some of the products listed include for example, Blue Mountain coffee, sauces, spices, and rums, which are generally produced by the micro and small firms in the economy. Indeed, other works also argue that the country has competitive advantage in sub-sectors such as: footwear and leather goods, furniture, food process and agro-industries (e.g., see Garvey, 2000). These arguments tend to support the claim by international trade theorists (e.g., Krugman & Obstfeld, 2003), who argued that developing countries such as Jamaica, will have a comparative advantage in primary commodities (such as agricultural products, for example, sugar, bananas)and labour intensive manufactures (for example, garments).

If the poor export performance is not a demand driven problem, then clearly it must be supply driven. Ayub, (1981) concluded that the major constraint to strong exporting by Jamaican firms was a supply side problem rather than a lack of demand. In other words, people want to buy Jamaican products but it is the Jamaican firms which are unwilling or unable to supply these products to them. The issue therefore is whether or not Jamaica has anything to sell to the world, or the world wanting to buy anything from Jamaica. Instead, Jamaica's poor export performance seems to be a matter of Jamaican firms' unwillingness or inability to sell to the world. This unwillingness and/or inability to sell to the world may have been derived from a number of factors including, but not limited to the international orientation of the major decision makers in the enterprises in the Jamaican economy (Garvey, 2000). Further, because of the market imperfections in this economy, government support for these small firms to initiate export is critical.

INCENTIVE REGIME AND TRADE SUPPORT

Small firms in small, developing economies will be at a disadvantage in trying to develop an export business given the characteristics of their enabling environment. The smallness of demand and the limited supply of factors of production will severely limit these firms ability to gain economies of scale in production, an important condition for exporting in a globalized competitive economy. Further, because these small markets are dominated by a few firms, there are huge barriers to entry, poor infrastructure, high cost of international transportation, the absence of clusters of firms that can constitute an industry and, inefficient government bureaucracy, the markets in these economies are not competitive and do not foster the dynamics necessary for improved competitiveness. Therefore, for small firms to develop their export business there has to be special circumstances that enable exporting. This is why there is a strong need for support services and incentives in these small, developing economies. However, it must be noted that incentive and trade support will not work unless there is strong leadership at the firm level to spot opportunities in the international market and take advantage of them.

Incentives are critical, especially for small firms from small, developing economies. They will help to offset disincentives and distortions (e.g., macro economic and social instability, inadequate infrastructure, inefficient bureaucracy etc.) that arise from features of the economic and social environment in which they operate. Evidence suggests that properly managed export incentives are effective in contributing to sustained economic development (e.g., see Seringhauss & Rosson, 1991; Kotabe & Czinkota, 1992). Indeed, given the socio-economic characteristics of the Jamaican economy, the need for properly managed export incentives cannot be overlooked. Incentives in Jamaica are an essential mechanism for providing comparative parity to small firms in the export business. This is necessary because of the level of disincentive and distortions in the local economy.

Structure of Export Incentives

Under the Export Industry Encouragement Act (EIEA) enacted in 1956, a number of incentives were made available to exporters. These incentives fall under two broad categories: a) income tax exemption and b) custom duties exemptions[16]. Table 1.5 outlines the incentives in the agricultural and manufacturing sectors. It provides information on the type of incentives offered to exporters and the criteria that must be met in order to obtain them.

These incentives serve as critical enablers in helping firms to overcome some of the barriers to exporting due to their limited resources. They also give them the confidence to enter foreign markets. Overtime, the Act included firms from other sectors (e.g., tourism, under the Hotel and Resorts Incentive Act, film and motion pictures, information processing) which are active in the economy[17].

Preferential Market Access

Another type of incentive that is not generally mentioned but which is prevalent in developing countries like Jamaica is *Trade Preference*. This type of incentive guarantees preferential access for products from developing countries to export markets mainly in North-America and Europe through quotas, price agreement and in some cases direct subsidies (Seyoum, 2006). Most of Jamaica's traditional agricultural exports (e.g., sugar, bananas etc.) have benefited from this system for many decades[18]. Since the 1980s, manufactured products,

---

[16] In the early years of the act, only manufacturing firms were qualified for these incentives.

[17] It is important to note that each sector has its own Act however; the provisions for income tax and duty exemption to encourage exports to third country (Non-Caricom) markets are similar.

[18] The old preferential arrangement between Jamaica and the European Union is now replaced by a new trade pack that is more WTO compatible. It is called the Economic Partnership Agreement (EPA). The agreement was initialled in December of 2007 between Caricom, the Dominican Republic and the European Union. This initialled agreement has ignited vigorous debates in the academic and public policy circles on the merits and

most notably apparel, have had similar preference in the North American market under the Caribbean Basin Initiative (CBI).

Table 1.5. Export incentives available in Jamaica

Sectors	Incentives offered	Requirements	Concessions
Manufa-cturing	Export Industry Encouragement Act (EIEA)	Full-Exporter- Designed to encourage export manufacturing to hard currency (Non-Caricom) markets. All production must be exported	Concessions of income tax for 10 years (the income tax rebate is given according to the percentage of export profits to total profits.
		Partial Exporter- Producers must export a threshold of 5 percent of their production to Non-Caricom markets	Concession on income tax and exemption from import duties on raw material and machinery. For new exporters, the rebate is calculated based on the percentage export intensity, while for existing exporters it is calculated based on incremental export sales over a base year
	Jamaica Export Free Zone Act	All transactions by the Free Zone company must be conducted in U.S. currency. Firms outside the Free Zone complex are allowed to benefit under the single entity free zone incentive. To get this status, a company must: a) be registered according to the provisions of the companies act b) export at least 85 percentage of its production c) receive an approval from the BOJ	Duty relief on raw material in perpetuity
	Moratorium on Duties	Granted to companies which do not qualify under existing incentives legislation and have the potential to contribute significantly to foreign exchange earnings, employment etc.	Ministry of Finance can grant relief from import duties for up to three years

demerits of the trade pack for the small, developing economies of the Caribbean region. These debates are beyond the scope of this book. For an update on these debates visit the CRNM website at www.crnm.org

Table 1.5. Continued

Sectors	Incentives offered	Requirements	Concessions
	Modernization of Industry (MOI)	The investor must provide relevant support or raw material to export manufacturers or be involved in export trade or plan to enter the export market	Relief from General Consumption Tax (GCT) on capital goods
	Accelerated Depreciation/ Special Capital Allowance	Qualified businesses must be certified by the ministry of Industry. For data processing/system development business, at least 20 percent of its gross income must be derived from exports	A certified business is allowed to deduct 50 percent of the full cost of any new machinery in the year of purchase and a further 50 percent in the following year
Agriculture	Approved Farmer Status	Farmer must grow certain crops but most agricultural products qualify Companies involved in hatching eggs also qualify for relief	Income tax relief and duty concessions for up to ten years and is renewable

Source: Personal interviews with Staff at JAMPRO now Jamaica Trade and Invest (JTI). These incentives are for the two sectors looked at in this study. They relate to those which assist firms that are exporting from the local economy.

The post-Uruguay round of the GATT negotiations in 1994 which gave birth to the WTO had serious implications for the incentive regime structure in developing economies and in Jamaica in particular. The conclusions derived from the Uruguay round of negotiations suggest that a number of the export incentives which are offered to Jamaican firms are not WTO compliant. As such, the entire incentive system has come under close scrutiny. For example, concession on income tax for full exporters under the EIEA has to be phased out because it is non-compliant with the WTO regulations governing subsidies and countervailing duties[19].

However, the strongest impact of the post-Uruguay negotiations is on the system of trade preference. Preferential market access for sugar and bananas has come under severe threats due to developments in Europe, North America and large developing countries such as Brazil. The European Union for example, decided to cut the price it pays for sugar from countries such as Jamaica by 37 percent, starting 2007. This move will make Jamaican sugar uncompetitive in the European market which is its major export market. This could mean a total devastation of the country's sugar industry if immediate actions are not taken to improve its competitiveness[20]. What these developments reveal however, is that in the long run,

[19] At the time of collecting data for this project, lawyers and trade consultants were busy restructuring the country's incentive system to make it WTO compliant.

[20] Merely privatizing the industry will not ensure its survival. There are structural problems such as education level of the workers, land terrain on which sugar is cultivated etc. These problems will have to be tackled head-on

eventually all trade preferences and other incentives which are not WTO compliant will be phased out. The implication is that Jamaican firms will have to develop internal competencies to drive innovation and improve their international competitiveness.

This inevitable end to the system of trade preference and WTO non-compliant incentives, has forced private and public sector policy makers to join forces to develop strong trade support networks for existing and potential exporters. The aim of these networks is to help firms to overcome the major barriers to exporting and therefore become motivated to carry out the activity.

Trade Support Network

Cognisant of the changes in the structure of world trade and the increasing emphasis on the export trade as the most sustainable path to economic prosperity, both public and private entities have combined resources to provide assistance to the export sector[21]. During 2004, the trade support network in Jamaica consisted of 20 members from both the public and private sectors. These members were involved in the provision of services in the areas of: capacity and competency development, market access and development, transaction issues and issues relating to the social and economic development as a result of exporting.

Interestingly, but by no means surprising, none of the export incentive schemes or trade support services reviewed concentrated specifically on the micro and small firm. The general tendency was to treat all firms (i.e. large and small) as the same. These incentives and trade support schemes are a clear sign of the "one-size-fits all" approach to export assistance. However, this is not always very effective in dealing with the issues micro and small firms face in their export development efforts. Small firms generally lament the ineffectiveness of incentive schemes in promoting export growth in the economy. The general argument is that small firms are normally the last to be recognised when export assistance is given. Further, there is the feeling that some of the criteria used for providing export assistance are too arbitrary; most organisations are subject to bureaucratic delays and inefficiencies and some assistance are not relevant to the needs of the small firm. This lack of specific focus however, is generally blamed on the absence of reliable data from these small businesses, therefore making it difficult to develop a comprehensive policy framework geared towards providing relevant export assistance.

Despite the lack of reliable data, a more concerted effort can be made to provide situation specific assistance to these smaller firms. The most common form of assistance given to these firms is financial aid. In 2004, the major government support to the small business sector was in the form of credit facilities. These facilities provided loans to small firms through agencies such as: Export/Import Bank (EX-IM Bank), Jamaica Exporters' Association (JEA), Development Bank of Jamaica (DBJ), Trafalgar Development Bank (TDB), Self Start Fund

---

with effective strategies such as rationalization of the work force, improve mechanization, improved planting techniques etc.

[21] During the data collection phase for this book, interviews were held with export policy makers from major institutions which provide incentives and assistance to firms to help them to become exporters. From these interviews, it was revealed that the main objective of these networks is to develop internationally competitive enterprises through the provision of relevant support services for both existing and potential exporters.

and the Micro Investment Development Agency (MIDA). The total loan to this sector was J$1008 million in 2004.

Besides financing, firms also received some form of technical support. The JTI through the Private Sectors Development Project (PSDP) financed by the European Union provided technical assistance for small firms to improve their competitiveness and to access export markets. The Jamaica Exporters' Association also provided market information services and assistance in dealing with export documentation, cash flow projections and inventory control. A number of projects are also being undertaken in the areas of cluster development, intellectual property protection, standards and marks etc. which will help micro and small firms to improve their export competitiveness[22].

CHAPTER SUMMARY AND CONCLUSION

This chapter provided a profile on the export development and performance of the Jamaican economy. The aim was to show how the enabling environment impacts on export activities in firms and more specifically the micro and small firm. The chapter began with a historical overview of the patterns of industrial development in the economy. This review revealed that the major policy which formed the bedrock of the country's industrial development was one designed under the umbrella of import substitution and dependence on external economies. It involved policy makers inviting firms from abroad to produce domestically, those commodities that are normally imported, with little or no focus on the export market. As the world economy underwent radical changes in the post world war era, the country's development policy shifted to a more outward oriented approach, where exporting was put at the centre of the development model. The chapter therefore moved to analyse the country's export performance over the last half century to better understand its poor economic and export performance to date.

It is almost conclusive from the data that; after the early 1950s and 1960s when the country had its golden years in terms of export performance (due mainly to favourable developments in the international trading arena), export performance has been unimpressive since. The fall in commodity prices on the world market coupled with the short sightedness of Jamaican entrepreneurs to take advantage of other export products for which demand was rising on the world market and, socio-economic inefficiencies are factors that contributed to this poor performance. The weak enabling environment also played a role in the poor export growth of the economy. This led the chapter to review the incentive schemes and support networks that are available in the economy.

The review revealed that the present incentive system is untenable in light of developments in the WTO. Most importantly, the data showed that there will be an inevitable end to preferential treatment from external economies given to exports from Jamaica and other developing economies. The implication for firms is that they will have to improve their international competitiveness and be innovative in their product offerings or else, they too

[22] Despite the credit facilities and the technical support programmes, the small firm sector continues to face serious challenges in its quest to become internationally competitive. There is still low access to credit facilities due mainly to the perceived risk from small businesses also, the challenge of weak business and management skills in this sector are obstacles to over come. Because of the weak business and management skills, there is a need to provide more technical and institutional support to this sector in order to woo these firms into exporting.

will fail to exist much longer. Since all firms are now obliged to participate in the global market (whether they go international or remain domestic), it is important that managers understand that it is internal competencies that will drive competitiveness, not external assistance or preferential treatment.

There is no doubt that Jamaica's current export performance is unimpressive. The country produces and sells products that have a growing demand in the export market. Further, it is in close proximity to one of the largest export markets in the world, the United States. Despite these positives, it does not take the opportunity to exploit such lucrative market (Nicholls et al., 1989). Additionally, the country has a large number of micro and small firms that are not exporting and need to be engaged in the export trade. A number of them are in a state of export readiness but need to be stimulated to get engaged in the activity. Understanding the factors that stimulate those firms that are exporting will provide some lessons to export policymarkers as to how they can stimulate other similar firms to initiate exporting. To motivate this understanding however, it will require a model that takes into account the idiosyncrasies of the small firm and more so those from small, developing economies. The export development model presented in the subsequent chapter provides this insight.

Chapter 2

THE EXPORT DEVELOPMENT MODEL

INTRODUCTION

Globalization has forced many small and micro firms to internationalize their operations. This has obliged public policymakers and managers to develop an in-depth understanding of how these firms become international. Without an understanding of this process, public policy makers will not be able to design effective policies that will improve the enabling environment so that more firms can go international. Further, managers in these firms are unable to effectively identify export opportunities, assess the risks involved in exporting and thus reap the success of doing business internationally. It is important however that managers and policymakers have effective explanatory frameworks to guide their understanding of the international operations[23] of these firms. Importantly, for firms in small, developing economies, the frameworks from larger developed economies may not be useful in explaining their international involvement. Although these firms face similar challenges like all other firms when operating internationally, they also face additional challenges such as having a small home market, inadequate infrastructure, unstable macro-economic environment etc. Therefore, new models and ways of thinking about these small firms' international involvement are needed to explain their international activities.

The decision to go international will involve a lot of variables both internal and external to the firm. In essence, the decision to export from the small firm is a complex one. No single factor can explain why some small firms go international while similar others remain local, although they face the same industry conditions and operate in the same market. To capture the complexity involved in making the decision to enter export markets, the export development model presented in this chapter illustrates how both the factors in the external environment and the firm's capabilities (absorptive capacity) interact to determine the final decision of whether or not the firm enters into exporting. The development of this model draws on a number of theoretical frameworks in the areas of strategy, international business and economics to explain the international activities of the micro and small firms from small, developing economies. This model can be used by public policymakers to develop profiles of

---

[23] In this book, the international operation of the firms is used here to refer to exporting. The book focuses only on outward international operations which in the case of micro and small firms, narrows down to exporting.

firms that have a strong proclivity towards exporting. Managers in micro and small firms can also use this model to help them to better understand what capacities they must cultivate in their organisations in order to make it export ready.

BACKGROUND TO THE MODEL

Most of the theoretical frameworks that address the reason(s) some small firms export while similar others do not, draw on the acquisition of knowledge and organisational learning- stage theory of internationalization[24] as the basis for explaining the firm's international involvement. Several other theoretical frameworks such as the ***eclectic paradigm*** (Dunning, 1988) and the ***product life cycle*** (Vernon, 1966) have also been used. However, these frameworks have their genesis in explaining the international involvement of large and multinational firms. Large and multinational firms due to their abundance of resources face different challenges from small, resource poor firms when making the decision to internationalize.

In fact, the same frameworks that are used to provide explanations regarding the international behaviour of large firms are not always appropriate for small firms (Rialp & Rialp, 2001; Axxin & Matthyssen, 2001; Rialp et al., 2005). Besides the standard analysis of internal and external factors that impact international activities (e.g., see Adams & Hall, 1993; Zou et al., 2003; Madsen & Servias, 1997), these frameworks need to incorporate the role of inter-organisational linkages and networks as important drivers of international business for small and micro firms[25]. Indeed, managing relations such as the set of collaborative networks that the firm has, personal relations of the founder etc. are found to be the essence of improved competitiveness for the small and micro firms (Etemad, 2004). Therefore, any model of small firm's export behaviour must take these factors into consideration[26].

Although previous theoretical models have added much to our knowledge of firms' international behaviour, they have not provided a good understanding of the international operation of micro and small firms, especially those from developing economies. Most of these frameworks do not take into account the role of the entrepreneur(s) and the resource stock of the small firm; two critical variables in any explanation as to why micro and small firms decide to engage in international operations (Moen & Servias, 2002; Knight, & Cavusgil, 1996; Westhead et al., 2001). The resources and capabilities gathered by the entrepreneur have a critical impact on the ability of the small firm to enter export markets (Westhead et al., 2001; Ibrahim, 2004; Bloodgood et al., 1996; Autio et al., 1997; Vatne, 1995). The majority of previous theoretical contributions focus more on factors external to the firm and do not consider the internal environment of the firm in trying to explain its

---

[24] Examples of these studies include: Coviello & McAuley, 1999; Johanson & Vahlne, 1977, 1990; Bilkey & Tesar, 1977; Czinkota, 1982; Andersson et al., 2004; Moen & Servias, 2002.

[25] This argument is well developed in published works of Hinttu et al., 2004; Fadahunsi, 1999; Caviello & Munro, 1995; Ellis, 2000; Etemad, 2004.

[26] It is suggested by some researchers (e.g. Welch, 2004) that some of the older models of the firm's internationalization behaviour (e.g. the Uppsala model) appear to have inter-organisational linkages and networking embedded in their explanation of the firm's internationalization behaviour.

internationalization behaviour (e.g., Bilkey & Tesar, 1977; Cavusgil, 1984a; Zou et al., 2003 etc).

The model presented in this chapter tries to remedy this shortfall by including the capacity of the firm as one of the variables that impact the decision to export. The extant literature argues that the background, competencies, motivations and attitude of the entrepreneur as well as the characteristics of the firm and the firm's external environment all influence the decision to export abroad[27]. Therefore, it is critical, in addition to previous theoretical work that this model also focuses on the absorptive capacity of the firm which can influence its decision to engage in exporting. In determining absorptive capacity, the resource-based theory becomes a useful tool for providing explanations on the small firms' international involvement[28]. In fact, Rialp et al., (2005) in their review of studies on early internationalizing firms proposed an exploratory theoretical model of the firm's internationalization using the resource-based theory as the underlying theoretical framework. They also posited that such an approach seems to offer a better explanation of the foreign market entry decision process than other rival approaches (ibid. p 162). Other researchers have also concurred that the resource–based theory can be a valid framework for shedding light on the international activities of new ventures which are by their nature small and have limited resources (Young et al., 2003; McDougal et al., 1994).

Resources in the Micro and Small Firms

The resource-based view of the firm focuses on the stock of available factors owned or controlled by the firm (Penrose, 1959; Barney, 1991; Amit & Schoemaker, 1993). According to many scholars in the strategy literature, these resources include the background characteristics and aspirations of the entrepreneur e.g., human capital resources, physical assets, and organisational assets etc. (Chatterjee & Wernerfelt, 1991). These resources will determine the firm's absorptive capacity which is important for making the decision to invest in exporting (Tseng et al., 2003). For example, research shows that firms tend to enter markets where resource requirements match their resource stock and capabilities (Andersen & Kheam, 1998).

The environmental conditions in small, developing countries make the resource-based theory a useful tool for analysing why some small firms export while others do not. It is indubitable that the success of international activity for any firm is predicated on having a strong enabling environment at home (Etemad, 2004; Deng, 2008). In developing economies, the supply of the factors of production (e.g., qualified graduate) is very limited. This will impact negatively on the absorptive capacity of the firms from these environments that are seeking to operate internationally. Further, the limited amount of resources that are available will have to be put to the most efficient use to ensure that allocative and productive efficiencies are achieved. This book proposes the use of the resource-based theory as one of the theoretical lens for developing the export model. It will therefore provide to managers

[27] See, for example; Bijmolt & Zwart, 1994; Leonidou et al., 1998; Dudley, 1989; Eshghi, 1992; Madsen & Servias, 1997.

[28] See for example; Dhanaraj & Beamish, 2003; Zou et al., 2003; Westhead et al., 2001; Westhead et al., 2004; Barney, 1991 for the development of this point. Some of these studies also used the resource-based theory as their theoretical framework in trying to understand the firm's international behaviour.

and export policymakers, an indication of the resources that are more amenable to improving the firm's absorptive capacity and getting it to enter into exporting.

The resources in the firm will also play a critical role in mediating how the firm responds to factors in the environment (stimuli- e.g., unsolicited order from foreign customer, government export assistance etc.) which help them to identify export opportunities abroad. This is very important as without opportunity identification, exporting would not be possible in the first place. Therefore, having an understanding of the firm's resources will provide better and richer explanations of how micro and small firms determine their international operations, specifically the decision to export part of their production abroad. The core assumptions underlying the resource-based theory will be discussed in chapter 4 of the book.

Other Theoretical Views

Besides the resource-based theory, the development of the export model presented in this book drew on other theoretical lens such as Process Theory of Internationalization (Johanson & Vahlne1, 1977) and Network Theory (Johnason& Vahlne, 2003; Hinttu et al., 2004) to provide an explanation of the international behaviour of small enterprises in developing economies[29]. The rich literature in the field Entrepreneurship[30](e.g.,Amit & Schoemaker, 1993) ; Internationalization[31](e.g., Zou et al., 2003); and Strategy (e.g., Barney, 1991) were drawn upon to build the model. Much richer and theoretically robust explanations are likely to come from the use of multiple theories when trying to understand small firms' international operations (Rialp et al., 2005; Bell et al., 2004; Etemad & Wright, 1999, Lado et al., 2006). This approach to building the model will answer calls in the field of international entrepreneurship for a cross fertilization of literature to better understand the complex issues involved in the small firm's internationalization process (Coviello & Jones, 2004).

The Model

The model presented in Figure 2.1 was derived from insights gained from a pilot study of eight small firms in the manufacturing and agricultural sectors in Jamaica and a review of the extant literature on export behaviour of the firm, internationalization and international entrepreneurship.

The pilot interviews and literature review pointed to the fact that the decision to initiate exporting in the micro and small firm is multi-faceted and no single factor or theory can explain the process (see also Etemad & Wright, 1999; Etemad, 2004 for a similar conclusion). The process is an interaction of a number of factors both internal and external to the firm. As such, this new model basically argues that to initiate, develop and further sustain exporting in the micro and small firm, there are stimuli (latent or manifest) both internal and external to

[29] A review of these theoretical frameworks is beyond the scope of this book. However, for an update on the literature on these theories see Rialp et al., 2005, Jones et al., 2004, Anderson, 1993.

[30] See, for example, Fillis, 2002; Ellis & Pecotich, 2001; Covin & Slevin.1991; Jones & Coviello, 2005; Coviello & Jones, 2004; Rosa, 2003; Rosa, 1993; Rosa & McAlpine, 1991; Schumpeter, 1961 etc.

the firm which trigger this decision. These stimuli alone cannot result in the firm becoming an exporter. The absorptive capacity of the firm (its resources) is critical in activating these stimuli to enable the firm to enter into exporting. These activating forces are normally referred to as background factors (Leonidou, 1995a) or capabilities (Deng, 2008). They are generally derived from the characteristics of the entrepreneur (e.g., educational background, international experience) or the characteristics of the firm (e.g., firm size). It is this interaction between absorptive capacity (resources) and stimuli that form the basis of the explanatory model presented in this chapter.

The logic of the model follows that of Cavusgil et al., (1979) export development model which argues that the decision to enter export markets can be captured as stimuli, organism, response model. The stimuli (S) are considered to be driving forces in helping managers effectively spot export opportunities. The organism (O) refers to those resources which form the firm's absorptive capacity and allow it to respond positively or negatively to the stimuli. The response (R) is whether or not the firm enters into exporting or remains focused on its domestic market. Following this interpretation, the proposed model in Figure 2.1 is therefore referred to as the SOR model of micro and small firms export behaviour.

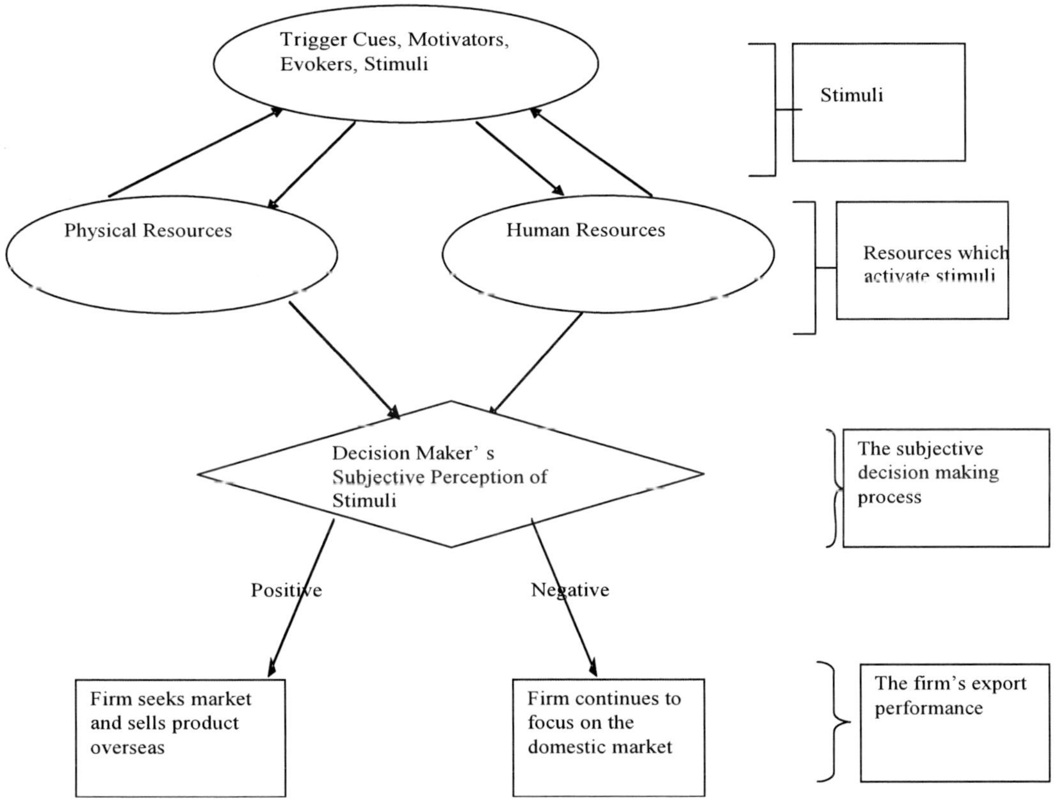

Figure 2.1. The SOR model of small and micro firms export behaviour[32].

[31] See, for example, Johanson & Vahlne, 1977, 1990; Wiedersheim- Paul et al., 1978; Bilkey & Tesar, 1977; Lee & Brasch, 1978; Simmonds & Smith, 1968 etc.

[32] The double arrows in the diagram reflect the notion that export initiation is a dynamic and interactive process. The characteristics of the firm, the entrepreneur and the environment all play a significant role in influencing

The diagrammatic representation of the model captures the central thesis of this book. The interpretation of the diagram is that; the firm's export initiation is a function of a number of factors. Firstly, factors internal or external to the firm (stimuli) influence the decision to export. Then, the absorptive capacity of the firm (referred to in some places as background factors, resources etc.) activate these stimuli and allow the firm to produce a response of whether or not to enter the export business. Critical to note in this model is that stimuli by themselves cannot result in the firm becoming an exporter. These stimuli have to be brought to the attention of the entrepreneur who then, based on his/her subjective perception[33], will produce a response. Importantly, if the entrepreneur's interpretation of the stimuli is negative, the firm will not enter the export business and thus remains focused on its domestic market. On the other hand, if the interpretation is positive, the firm will make the decision to enter the export business.

At the heart of this model is the assumption that it is the entrepreneur who makes the final decision regarding export sales. This individual can either reject or accept export stimuli based on how s/he views the organisation's goal or mission. If exporting does not fit into the overall mission of the organisation, then irrespective of how strong the stimuli are, they will be rejected. By recognising the role of the entrepreneur in these small enterprises, this book has moved beyond the narrow focus of the *Internationalization and Export Behaviour* literature to incorporate the broader literature of *International Entrepreneurship*. This latter literature focuses heavily on the role of the entrepreneur in decision making in the firm, therefore distinguishing small firms' export behaviour from larger and multinational firms export behaviour where decisions are made by a board of directors and not any single individual. In addition, the model will answer calls from a number of recent researchers who request a closer look at the characteristics of the entrepreneur in trying to understand the internationalization process of the small firm (Ibrahim, 2004).

Variables Relevant to the Validation of the Model

Once research involves testing and verification, it ought to involve some form of measurement. Measurement becomes critical in research because it provides a link between the conceptual and the empirical levels of a concept. In developing measurements, there must be an effective conceptual definition of what is to be measured and a rule as to how to assign numbers to the observable properties in that concept. The quality of information gained from the field will be contingent on the type of measurement that was used. Simply put, bad measurement will produce bad results.

To validate the SOR model developed in this chapter, a number of variables were derived from the field interviews and coded for further analysis. In arriving at the most effective measures for model validation, the conceptual definition of what is to be studied was first determined. This was followed by the application of operational property to those

the decision to enter into exporting. It is this dynamism in the model which distinguishes it from most of the other models which take a linear view of the export initiation process (e.g. Bilkey, 1978, Bilkey & Tesar, 1977, Johanson & Vahlne, 1977 etc.).

33 These perceptions are formed based on the entrepreneur's background (e.g. level of education, previous job experience, travel experience etc.), and also the firm's absorptive capacity (capabilities) to engage in international business.

definitions[34]. These operational properties are in keeping with previous work on the subject. As such, it helps to improve the reliability of the study. Table 2.1 summarizes these key variables and their operational measurements. The previous literatures which informed these measurements are also listed in the table.

Table 2.1. Operationalization of research variables

Concepts	**Operational measure**	**Previous studies**
***Dependent Variable*:** Export Performance	Dummy variable 1= exporter 0 = non-exporter	Obben & Magagula, 2003, Rodriguez & Rodriguez, 2005, Cavusgil & Nevin, 1981, Yaprak,1985,Caughey & Chetty, 1994, Burton & Schlegelmilch, 1987
Independent Variables: Firm Size	Number of employees	Pope, 2002, Mehran & Moini,1999, Obben & Magagula, 2003, Bilkey, 1982
Firm Age	Number of years that elapsed since firm was legally established	Keng & Jiuan, 1989, Das, 1994, Daniels & Guyburo, 1976, Brouthers & Nakos, 2005
Standardized Product	Dummy variable 1= no changes made to the product for export 0= changes made to the product before export	Christensen et al., 1987, Tybjee, 1994, Vernon,1966, Tookey, 1964, Madsen & Servias, 1997, Diamantopoulos & Inglis, 1988, Brouthers & Nakos, 2005
Product Quality	Firm's quality accreditation 1= firm has quality accreditation 0= otherwise	Miesenbock, 1988, Mittelstaedt et al., 2003, Hatten, 1997
Age of Entrepreneur	Years of business experience	Obben & Magagula, 2003, Ross, 1989
Foreign Experience	Dummy variable 1= worked or lived abroad for > 1 year 0= otherwise	Aaby & Slater, 1989, Daniels & Guyburo, 1976, Williams & Chaston, 2004
Foreign language Proficiency	Dummy variable 1= speak foreign language 0= do not speak foreign language	Obben & Magagula, 2003, Daniels & Guyburo 1976, Williams & Chaston, 2004

[34] The full details of the coding process for the variables and the operational definition is beyond this book. For a detailed account of the research method, the author can be contacted to provide such information. For a book of this nature, not all readers will be interested in such detail.

Table 2.1. Continued

Concepts	Operational measure	Previous studies
Education level	Last school which the entrepreneur attended 1= Primary 2= Secondary 3=Vocational Training College 4= University 5= Other	Obben & Magagula, 2003, Keng & Jiuan, 1989, Manolova et al., 2002, Brouthers & Nakos, 2005
Previous job experience	Dummy variable 1 = have worked in a senior position in a company that does exporting before starting own business 0= Otherwise	Yaprak, 1985, Aaby & Slater 1989, Philp, 1998 Westhead et al., 2001
The Firm's Technology	The firm's spending on R&D as a portion of sales	Moen, 1999, Burton & Schlegmilch, 1987, Tybjee, 1994, Rodriguez & Rodriguez, 2005
Stimuli	Likert scale	Leonidou, 1998, 1995a, Katsikeas & Piercy, 1993, Moen, 1999

Following the tradition of previous research in this area, the stimuli are measured on a Likert scale. These measures are generally ordinal in nature. The scale ranges from 1–5 with 5 being the most important and 1 being the least important. A value of 5 however does not signify that a stimulus is 5 times more important than if a value of 1 is given. It only implies that the stimulus is more important than if it had received a value of 1. This reflects the ordinal nature of the scale.

The variables identified in Table 2.1 are at the heart of this book. They are used to test different aspects of the model in trying to explain why some small firms export while others do not. The remainder of the book revolves around the use of these variables in different chapters to provide an explanation for the small firms' export behaviour.

The Evolution of the Book

The research that led to the writing of this book progressed in three non-mutually exclusive stages. The first is labelled the ground work phase. In this stage of the project, a comprehensive review of the literature was done. This aided in putting a focus to the research topic and also operationalized it in an appropriate manner for it to be researchable. Other activities in this stage included a pilot study to determine the feasibility of the proposed topic, designing of the research instrument, arranging contacts for interviews, among other things. After these activities, a book proposal was then completed which sets the stage for phase two of the work to begin.

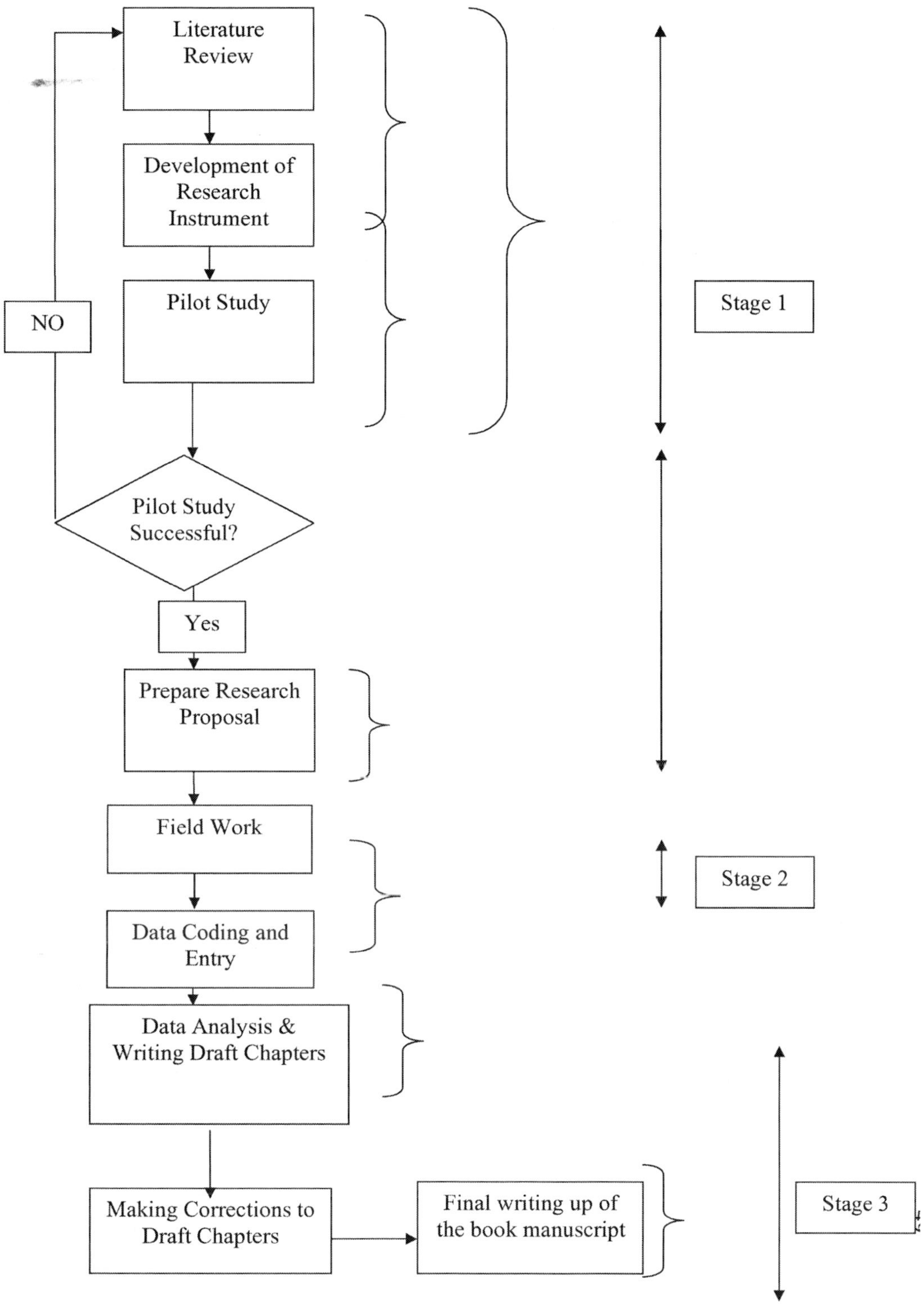

Figure 2.2. The evolution of the book.

Phase two of the work is labelled *The Field Operation*. This stage involved primary data collection, collection of literature from the study context including secondary data from records and periodicals. At this stage, data coding and entry into computer software packages for analysis also took place. It must be noted that during this phase, the review of the literature continued.

The final stage of the work (documentation) could be regarded as most rigorous. It involved critical engagement with the data. Activities included data analysis, writing draft chapters, making correction to draft chapters, and putting the final manuscript together. There was a lot of critical thinking and analysis in order to make the contribution of the work very clear. Figure 2.2 depicts the evolutionary sequence of the book.

This chapter presents a detailed account of the model developed by the author to explain the export behaviour of Jamaican micro and small firms. Due to the unique circumstances under which these firms operate (they are domiciled in a small, developing economy); a new model had to be derived to explain their export behaviour. It would be inappropriate to merely replicate models from larger and developed economies where the enabling business environment is much stronger. To this end, insights from a cross fertilization of theoretical perspectives (e.g., stage theory, resource-based view theory, network theory etc) were used to develop a stimuli, organism and response model (SOR model) to explain the export behaviour of the small firms from this geographical location.

The main thrust of the model is that export initiation is a function of stimuli both internal and external to the firm. However, the mere presence of stimuli will not result in the firm becoming an exporter. The firm will have to possess the absorptive capacity which included the entrepreneur(s) positive perception of exporting in order to provide a positive response. The role of the entrepreneur as the major decision in these small firms is a very important consideration which the model takes into account. A positive response from the entrepreneur means that the firm will enter exporting as a line of business while a negative response signals that the firm will remain focused on its domestic market. This model is useful for export policymarkers interested in stimulating micro and small firms to enter exporting as it can provide profiles of firms that have a high chance of becoming an exporter. Further, entrepreneurs in the small and micro firm can use the model to determine what capacity they need to develop in their firms in order to increase their chance of entering the export business. Testing of this model forms the basis for the remainder of the chapters in this book.

Chapter 3

EXPORT STIMULI

INTRODUCTION

Small firms generally do not start exporting until something triggers that decision. The huge literature on the export behaviour of the firm[35] tends to agree that trigger cues or stimuli are the driving force behind the export initiation decision. Indeed, early researchers on the subject (e.g., Bilkey, & Tesar, 1977; Bilkey, 1978; Joynt, 1982; Miesenbock, 1988 etc.) arrived at a consensus that factors in the external environment (e.g., unsolicited order from abroad) are the most important element in motivating the small firm to export. These factors are generally referred to as "trigger cues", "evokers" "motivators" or "stimuli" (Leonidou, 1998, 1995a, Wiedersheim-Paul et al., 1978; Garvey, 2000). Additionally, others argue that without stimuli, there would be no export response at all (Thomas & Araujo, 1985). Stimuli it appears; are at the heart of the decision to initiate exporting. Surely, in the small firm, exporting is normally seen as a difficult task, which involves huge risks and a lot of resources[36]. Therefore, small firms, with limited resources, cannot engage in such activity until it is sure that some benefits will result[37].

The aim of this chapter is to identify those stimuli (whether internal or external to the firm) that trigger the decision to initiate exporting. This will provide export policy makers and managers in the small firm with insights regarding which stimuli are important and need to be present in the firm's internal and external environment in order to motivate export initiation. Among other things, the chapter will provide a theoretical overview of export stimuli and then provide empirical results to show which stimuli are most relevant in the Jamaican

---

[35] Some of the literature in this area include: Andersson et al., 2004, Tookey, 1964, Simmonds & Smith, 1968, Bilkey, 1978, Miesenbock, 1988, Leonidou & Katsikeas, 1996, Aaby & Slater, 1989, Madsen & Servias, 1997, Wiedershiem-Paul et al., 1978, Burpitt & Rondinelli, 2000, Katsikeas & Morgan, 1994, Cavusgil & Zou, 1994, Seringhaus & Rosson, 1990, Whitey, 1980, Simposn & Kujawa, 1974, Westhead et al., 2001, Söberdom, 2002, Masurel, 2001, Majocchi & Zucchella, 2003, Gumede, 2004 etc.

[36] To appreciate the task involved in exporting and especially the challenges smaller firms are confronted with, see Deschampsneufs, (1984) book on Export for the Small Business. The book shows how to identify the customer, the market and sell the product. It also discusses how small firms should ensure they are paid for their products. Overall, the book deals with exporting in a practical and concise way.

[37] Some of the benefits to be derived from exporting are: improved competitiveness for the firm, increased profitability, spreading of business risk, a sense of job satisfaction and prestige for workers in the firm.

context. The insights gained from the empirical evidence on Jamaican firms can be extended to other similar small, developing economies like Jamaica.

Which Stimuli Are Important?

Although there seems to be a general consensus in the literature that the decision to initiate exporting results from an interplay of stimuli internal and/or external to the firm (Wiedersheim-Paul et al., 1978; Aaby & Slater, 1989), what remains unclear is the relative importance of the vast number of stimuli which impact the process. For example, some studies conclude that the most important stimulus in this process is the need to achieve growth and extra profit (e.g., see Simpson & Kujawa, 1974; Cavusgil, 1984a etc.), others argue that it is the receipt of unsolicited order from overseas customers (e.g., see Tesar & Tarleton, 1982; Bilkey & Tesar, 1977; Simmonds & Smith, 1968 etc.). Still, there are those who argue that the social network of the entrepreneur (i.e. friends, family, college colleagues etc.) is the most important stimulus inducing the export decision (e.g., see Ellis, 2000; Ellis & Pecotich, 2001, etc.).

This apparent controversy has no doubt left a gap in our understanding as to whether export initiation in the firm arises from a systematic investigation of opportunities in the foreign market or is it a result of unplanned fortuitous circumstances. A clear understanding of the relative importance of the stimuli which trigger the decision to initiate exporting can provide an answer to this critical question (Kaynak & Stevenson, 1982). Importance is a critical issue because a large number of firms are given assistance by governments to initiate exporting; however, the majority remains poorly motivated (Demick & O'Rielly, 2000). This is precisely because the relative importance of the various stimuli impacting the export initiation decision is not known; therefore, the incorrect stimulus is given. An understanding of the relative importance of these stimuli will result in more appropriate assistance being given to firms to motivate them to initiate exporting.

The extant literature lists a plethora of stimuli which are generally seen as inducing the decision to initiate exporting. However, the ability to generalize the findings outside of the study context seems to be lacking (see Albaum et al., 1989; Lee & Brasch, 1978; Jaffe et al., 1988; Lashley, 2003 for a similar conclusion). The literature argues correctly that firms in different geographical locations will provide a different export response to the same stimuli (Leonidou 1998, 1995a; Siringhaus & Rosson, 1990). Therefore, it is important that geographical-based studies be done in order to verify which stimuli are most important in a particular context. Moreover, having done these geographical-based studies, it will provide insights into which stimuli can be generalized across geographical context and thus better aid in the replication of policies for export stimulation (Das, 1994; Wortzel & Wortzel, 1981; Dominquez & Sequeira, 1993). Critically, it will give insights to export behaviour theorists who are trying to develop a general theory to explain export stimulation in small and micro firms (Fillis, 2001; Tesar & Tarleton, 1982). Actually, the current theories will provide some insights into which stimuli are relevant for the export initiation process.

THE THEORETICAL LITERATURE ON EXPORT STIMULI

This section of the chapter presents theoretical justifications for categorizing triggers to export initiation as stimuli. The discussion focuses on a number of theoretical frameworks that have been put forward to explain the export behaviour of the firm. The aim here is to justify theoretically, the items identified as stimuli in the subsequent section.

Export Behaviour Theories

Export behaviour theories use behavioural variables (e.g., age of the entrepreneur, educational background of the entrepreneur etc.) to explain why some small firms choose to export while similar others remain focused on their domestic market. Behavioural frameworks differ from the conventional macro-economic theories which generally explain exporting in that they focus on the individual firm's competencies rather than the country's resource endowments (Ganier, 1982). Behavioural theories try to understand why and how firms get involved in international business, with some since the 1970s focusing specifically on the small and medium-sized enterprises (see, for example, Leonidou & Katsikeas, 1996 for a review of these works). These behavioural theories generally focus on firm, managerial and environmental factors that influence the decision to initiate exporting. Those theories which focus specifically on export stimuli which induce export initiation decision will be of central importance in this chapter.

The Pre-export Behaviour Model

In an attempt to understand why some firms export while others remained focused on their domestic market, even though they face similar market conditions, Wiedershiem-Paul et al., (1978) developed a fairly comprehensive conceptual model of the firm's pre-export behaviour. In that model, they take into account the firm's enabling environment, the characteristics of the decision maker (the entrepreneur) and the characteristics of the firm. The central argument of this model is that; the firm is exposed to various kinds of stimuli (e.g., saturated domestic market, excess production capacity, unique products, unsolicited order from overseas customers among others) that will induce the decision to enter export markets. The firm will however respond to these stimuli based on: a) the characteristics of the firm (e.g., its vision, its size, its age etc.); b) the quality of its external environment (e.g., availability of information on export market, competitors etc.), and c) the characteristics of the decision maker (age, education, travel experience etc.). If the decision maker perceives the stimuli in a positive way, then, s/he will make the decision to enter into exporting. A negative response to the stimuli will see the firm remaining focused on its domestic market. Given a positive response, the firm will start collecting information about export markets and *ceteris paribus*, it will start selling overseas. In essence, the model posits that it is stimuli which induce the decision then, the decision maker, based on his/her perception of the benefits of the induced action (exporting), will respond negatively or positively to these stimuli.

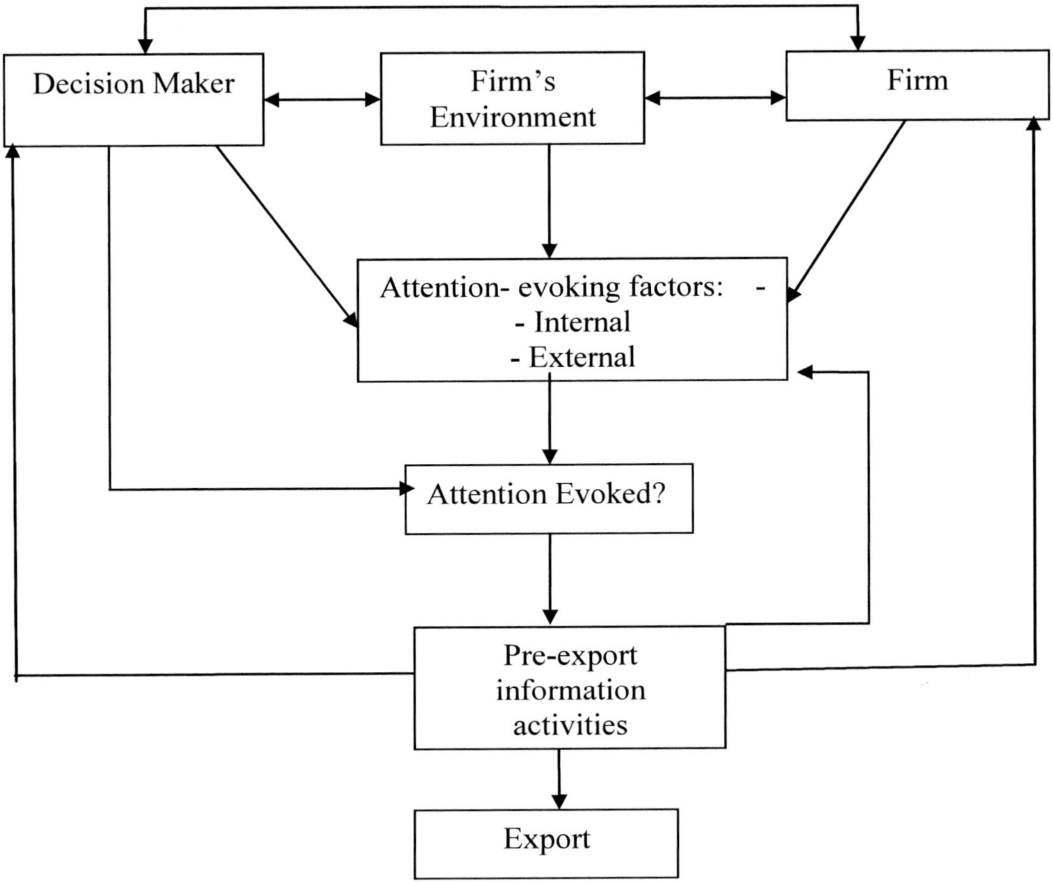

Source: Wiedersheim- Paul et al., (1978), "Pre-Export Activity: The First Step in Internationalization", Journal of International Business Studies, 9, 1, pp 47-58.

Figure 3.1. Pre-export behaviour model of the firm.

However, it is note worthy that the decision maker's perception is shaped by his/her personal characteristics (e.g., age, education, professional experience etc.), the objectives of the firm (e.g., growth or employment satisfaction) and also the environment within which s/he operates. This dynamic interrelationship is captured in the diagram above.

The diagrammatic schematization shows clearly that the decision maker is influenced by his environment, but simultaneously, creates an environment based on his actions and the firm's activities. In other words, the decision maker's characteristics (e.g., age, international experience etc.) helps him/her to interpret stimuli while at the same time, these profiles allow him/her to develop unique capabilities in the firm (e.g., high quality products) so that the firm can attract stimuli. These stimuli, it is argued, are at the heart of any explanation as to why the firm makes a decision to enter the export market (Cavusgil et al., 1979). The model asserts that they are meaningless until they are brought to the attention of the decision maker. In essence, the entrepreneur is at the core of the decision making process for export initiation in the micro and small firm.

This pre-export behaviour model demonstrates that stimuli can be categorized into two conceptually meaningful groups: a) internal and b) external. Internal stimuli focus on those factors that are derived from the firm's own processes and operations (e.g., management urge for growth, excess production capacity, possession of a unique product etc.). External stimuli are those factors that are independent of the firm's operations or process (e.g., government export assistance, unsolicited order from foreign customers, saturated domestic market etc.). Although this typology is quite general, it serves as a useful framework for bringing some order to the multiplicity of factors which induce export initiation decision in the firm. It may not lead to any robust theoretical insights; however, it can provide policy makers with a framework that can be used to identify the source of the stimuli and thus better aid in the type of assistance given to firms to stimulate exporting[38].

To gain further insights into the sources of export stimuli, other researchers have refined the typology into more focused conceptually meaningful groups. For example, Albaum et al., (1989) have extended the categorization to include categories such as proactive and reactive. Where, the latter refers to stimuli which do not involve active steps to solicit an export order, the former refers to stimuli which are derived from the firm's active pursuit for export opportunities. The new typology by Albaum et al., (1989) categorized stimuli as internal proactive/reactive and external proactive/reactive. Theoretically, this categorization appears to better aid in determining whether or not the decision to initiate exporting is a systematic planned decision or is a mere response to fortuitous order.

The value of the pre-export behaviour model in helping us to understand the nature of export stimuli lies in its dynamic relationship with firm and environmental variables. This relationship among the possible factors that trigger exporting is helpful in identifying stimuli (internal and external) that will induce the decision to initiate exporting in the firm. Further, it provides support for the hypothesis that the pre-export activities are very essential in stimulating decisions to enter export markets.

In their conclusion, the developers of the model stress the importance of pre-export activities in export initiation decisions. The nature of this activity will determine whether or not the firm continues with its quest for selling overseas (Welch & Wiedersheim-Paul, 1980). For example, a bad experience in trying to gather export data may turn the firm away from considering exporting in the future, while a good experience will provide encouragement to fully implement the decision. Indeed, researchers show that the quality of the pre-export preparation is critical in determining whether or not the firm continues to export after an initial order. However, it must be noted that pre-export activities require a lot of time and resources. This is particularly important for small, resource poor firms to bear in mind.

The Innovation Diffusion Model

Exporting, like many other activities, is seen by some researchers as an adoption of change or innovation (e.g., Simmonds & Smith, 1968; Samiee et al., 1993 etc.). Drawing on the innovation diffusion literature (Rogers, 1962), export behaviour researchers argue that the findings can be applied to explain why some firms export and others do not. They see a parallel between exporting and innovation. Exporting is innovative in the sense that it represents a break away from the normal course of events in the firm (Aharoni, 1966; Samiee et al., 1993; Simmonds & Smith, 1968). Within the narrow confines of the firm's internal

---

[38] See, Williams (2008) for an application of this categorization in determining the source of export stimuli. This table style was adopted from Leonidou (1998).

environment, the first export order is seen as innovative because, exporting is not a normal activity for the firm therefore, it represents something new[39].

Early studies looking at the firm's export behaviour tried to understand whether the decision to export was initiated by internally perceived problems or needs or whether it grew out of an unplanned reaction to information about the process (Lee & Brasch, 1978). This investigation, it is believed, will help to determine whether the first export order is derived from an innovation or not. Critical to this understanding are triggers (stimuli) that induced the decision to get that first order. Understanding these stimuli will provide better insights into the nature of the innovation.

In their U.S. study of Nebraska's small exporting firms, Lee & Brasch, (1978) found that export initiation was more of an innovation rather than a mere problem solving activity. It was stimulated by the decision makers' need for growth, risk averseness and drive to be innovative. Simmonds & Smith, (1968) in their study of exporting firms in the U.K. found that the characteristics associated with innovators from other fields were similar to those of export decision makers. Some of these characteristics are: extensive travel experience, some previous experience regarding the particular task, aggressiveness, competitiveness and, motivated by rewards from the innovation. Importantly, these characteristics are also seen as hallmarks of an entrepreneur (Beaver, 2002; Covin & Slevin, 1991). In the small firm, the key decision maker and the entrepreneur are one and the same; the reasoning therefore is; if the entrepreneur possesses these attributes, the chance of producing innovative decisions is also higher.

The innovation diffusion literature shows a strong link between the innovator's cosmopolitan ties and innovation (Rogers, 1962). Individuals with strong cosmopolitan ties are more likely to transfer experience from other environments, thus allowing a breakaway from traditional behaviour. This breakaway within the confines of the firm is seen as innovative. Cosmopolitan ties, as argued in the export behaviour literature; is shaped by ones social network (Coviello & Munro, 1997; Wiedersheim-Paul et al., 1978). Social networks are critical stimuli for inducing innovation; for example, the decision to enter export markets (Ellis, 2000). In fact, from the early studies done on British small exporting firms, Simmonds & Smith, (1968) found that the innovation (export initiation) was driven by forces outside the firm rather than from within. They found that in most cases, the first export order was a result of unsolicited order from overseas customers or the push from parent companies. This finding supports the critical role of stimuli in inducing the decision to enter export markets.

Clearly, the innovation diffusion model shows that stimuli (mainly external ones) are at the heart of the innovation (first export order) and therefore have to be analysed in an effort to understand why some firms choose to export while others remain focused on their domestic market.

The Stage Hierarchy Model

Another school of thought that has emerged in the literature on the export behaviour of the firm is the stage hierarchy school. Basically, this perspective argues that the firm's export involvement takes place in a gradual rather than a radical manner. The firm moves from a

[39] In the broader interpretation of the concept of innovation i.e. something happening for the first time, exporting would not be seen as an innovation, because the firm is not the first to adopt the concept and it is not a new practice given that many other firms have been doing it.

situation where there is little or no interest in exporting to a position where there is a high level of commitment to the process when it starts gaining a significant portion of its revenue from the export market (Johanson & Vahlne, 1977, 1990; Bilkey & Tesar, 1977; Czinkota, 1982; Reid, 1981). This argument found general consensus among export behaviour researchers of the 1970s and 1980s. However, this consensus was absent in the 1990s given the rise in "born-globals" and "international new ventures" due mainly to changes in technology and the integration of world markets[40].

Bilkey & Tesar, (1977) in looking at the export behaviour of the small firm argued that the export development process of the firm tends to progress in stages. They also found that stimuli which impact the movement from one stage to another tend to differ by stages. It is those stimuli that are identified by the stage theorists that are of importance in this chapter.

Reid, (1981) has identified a number of these stimuli which impact the decision to enter foreign markets. He offers a hierarchical schematization of the firm's involvement in the export market from the first export order to full engagement. His model consists of five stages, starting with a mere awareness of exporting to fully accepting exporting as a business function. At each stage, there are specific stimuli which induce the decision to enter exporting. Table 3.1 captures this hierarchical process of the firm's entry into exporting.

The model captures the interaction between the firm and the decision maker (entrepreneur) in an attempt to understand the decision to initiate exporting. It captures the various stimuli which induce the adoption stages and then progressing from having a mere intention to fully accepting the process as normal business activity.

The model shows that export adoption cannot be done uni-dimensionally. It states that the decision maker's attitude towards and preferences for foreign market and export entry together with his/her perception and expectations of the results from such entry are major determinants of the firms export behaviour. This re-emphasizes our need to study stimuli as a first step to understanding why some firms export while similar others do not. Indeed, the model shows that, the export decision is a complex phenomenon and therefore, no single variable alone can explain it. This model provides some strong insights from the stage hierarchy perspective, of the stimuli which are important in driving the export initiation decision. More recent models (e.g., Mehran & Moini, 1999) which focus on stage theory were advanced; however, they do not pay much attention to the role of stimuli.

The value of stage models in shedding light on stimuli which induce the decision to enter export markets lies in their assumptions. These assumptions are basically that: a) firms move incrementally to enter export markets and b) firms choose to export first to countries that are close psychically[41] and then move to more distant markets. In this regard, firm size becomes an important predictor of international involvement. Firms that are larger (assuming they have equivalent resources to match their size) will feel more confident in taking on operations in an uncertain environment since they can do the necessary research and gather information (Katsikeas & Piercy, 1993). The assumptions reveal that factors which deal with geographical closeness, religion, language, culture etc. are central in stimulating the decision to enter export markets. Because of the high level of uncertainty associated with operations in foreign

[40] For early studies on this new phenomena of born globals and international new ventures see for example Knight & Cavusgil, 1996; Knight & Cavusgil, 2004; Lie et al., 2004; Lamb & Liesch, 2002; Autio, 2005; Oviatt & McDougal, 1994; Madsen & Servias, 1997 etc

[41] This concept of psychic distance refers to all those factors (legal, cultural, economic etc,) that makes one country differs from another. For a good explanation of the concept, see Johanson and Vahlne, 1977.

markets, one would expect that stimuli associated with psychic distance will indeed be critical in determining whether a firm exports or not[42].

Table 3.1. Export behaviour as an adoption of innovation process

	Stage1 export awareness	**Stage2 export intention**	**Stage3 export trial**	**Stage4 export evaluation**	**Stage5 export acceptance**
Export Adoption Stages	Problem or opportunity recognition, arousal of need	Motivation, attitude, beliefs and expectancy about export contribution	Personal experience from limited exporting	Results from engaging in exporting	Adoption of exporting/ rejection of exporting
Decision makers variables involved	Past experience export related or not, type level and amount of foreign information exposed to, associated individual characteristics, unsolicited foreign order	Expectation from entry into foreign market, foreign market orientation, export orientation, underlying attitude towards foreign involvement	Sought foreign orders through search of foreign markets	Profitability, sales stability	Export expansion activity shown by continued export growth as: 1) increased export as a percentage of sales; 2) continued entry into new markets; 3) continued absolute export growth; 4) continued introduction of new products into export markets
Firm variables involved	Past firm performance, reputation and visibility	Managerial goals and existing firm resources	Unsolicited foreign orders, existence of available managerial and financial resources	Results from engaging in export behaviour	

Source: Reid, S.D (1981), "The Decision Maker and Export Entry and Expansion", Journal of International Business Studies, 8, 1, pp 101-112.

42 The present day reality of information flow through the internet has reduced the level of uncertainties that would arise from psychic distance.

Born Globals

With the advances in information and communications technology, and the integration of world markets driven mainly by economic liberalization, researchers have observed that firms do not always internationalize in an incremental manner but do so radically. Indeed, many firms have internationalized early in their evolution. These firms that have internationalized at their founding are referred to as "Born Globals". Some even operate in the export market before they start operation locally. The observation of these firms' export behaviour has led to the emergence of a new school of scholarly enquiry. This field of scholarly enquiry is called international entrepreneurship[43]. The major thesis of this school of thought is that stimuli which triggers early export behaviour are contingent on the entrepreneur's international orientation and also the new business environment presented by globalization. Factors such as travel abroad, colleagues/friends who live in other countries, previous work partners from other countries among other things, induce the decision to export from the firm's evolution. Indeed, this scholarly field of enquiry has pointed to a number of stimuli that may stimulate exporting in the firm, especially in the early years. A number of these stimuli are incorporated in the empirical analysis in this chapter.

THE EMPIRICAL LITERATURE ON EXPORT STIMULI

The theoretical models presented in the previous section support the argument that exporting in the firm is a complex and multi-faceted process. There is no one factor that can solely explain why some firms are involved in exporting while similar others do not (Reid, 1981). As a result, most of the models adopt a dynamic approach in trying to understand this behaviour. They are dynamic in the sense that the outcome of one process is the input into another (Lee & Brasch, 1978). These models it appears, interpret export initiation as a stimuli, organism, response process similar to Cavusgil et al., (1979) and the SOR model in chapter 2 of this book. The importance of the model is that they identify stimuli that are relevant to the process.

Although there is an extensive literature on export stimuli, only a limited number of studies have done a comprehensive analysis of the plethora of stimuli that exists and, assess their relative importance in the decision to initiate exporting (Leonidou, 1995a). The more recent studies of the 1990s (e.g., Leonidou, 1998; Katsikeas, 1996 etc.) have moved away from the tradition of looking at only a few stimuli and instead, take into account all the factors from previous studies and analyse their relative importance on the export initiation decision. However, due to the multiplicity of factors involved, schematization typologies have been used to bring some order to the multiplicity of factors that exist. The Albaum et al., (1989) typology described earlier have been used extensively in this area. Because of the comprehensive nature of this typology, it can be used to compare results from a large number of previous empirical works. To get a comparative understanding of the work that has been done before on export stimuli, Tables 3.2a to 3.2g provide a comprehensive list of previous empirical studies and their results on the relative importance of stimuli on the decision to enter export markets. Importantly, all the stimuli listed have their basis in the theoretical discussion looked at earlier.

Table 3.2a. Rank order of export stimuli from past research

Research Study	Simpson & Kujawa (1974)	Pavord & Bogart (1975) A	Rabino (1980)	Brooks & Rosson (1982)	Johnston & Czinkota (1982)
Export Stimuli					
Internal /Proactive Stimuli					
Achievement of economies of scale		6			
Special managerial interest/urge, aspiration		3			4
Products with unique qualities					2
Possession of special competitive advantages					1,3, 7
Potential for extra profit/ sales	2	7	1	6	
Need to achieve corporate growth				6	
Internal/Reactive stimuli					
Offsetting sale of seasonal product					
Utilization of idle operating capacity	4	5	6	1	
Stagnation/ Decline in domestic profit/sales		4		7	
Reducing dependence/ risk on domestic business		2	3		
External /Proactive stimuli					
Encouragement by external agents/organisation					
Identification of attractive foreign opportunities		8		4	
Exclusive information on foreign markets				4	
Government export assistance/ incentives			4		5
Contacts after participating in trade fair/ mission	5				
External/Reactive Stimuli					
Initiation of exports by domestic competitors	3		7	9	
Competitive pressure in the domestic market				3	6
Favourable foreign exchange rates				8	
Saturation/ shrinkage in the domestic market	5	1	2	7	
Receipt of unsolicited order	1			2	

[43] Pioneers in this field include Oviatt & McDougall, 1994, Cavusgil & Knight, 1996 and Rennie, 1993

Table 3.2b. Rank order of export stimuli from past research

Research Study	**Joynt (1982)**	**Ogram (1982)**	**Tesar & Tarleton (1982a)***	**Tesar & Tarleton (1982 b)****	**Kaynak & Kothori (1984a)*****
Export Stimuli					
Internal /Proactive Stimuli					
Achievement of economies of scale	4				
Special managerial interest/urge, aspiration			11	8	
Products with unique qualities			1	1	
Possession of special competitive advantages			2,3,4,6,8	2,3,4,7	
Potential for extra profit/ sales		1			
Need to achieve corporate growth					
Internal/Reactive stimuli					
Offsetting sale of seasonal product					
Utilization of idle operating capacity	**2**		**10**	**5**	**3**
Stagnation/ Decline in domestic profit/sales			10	3	
Reducing dependence/ risk on domestic business					
External /Proactive stimuli					
Encouragement by external agents/organisation	7				
Identification of attractive foreign opportunities					1
Exclusive information on foreign markets			5	6	
Government export assistance/ incentives	6				
Contacts after participating in trade fair/ mission					
External/Reactive Stimuli					
Initiation of exports by domestic competitors	9				
Competitive pressure in the domestic market	3		7	9	
Favourable foreign exchange rates					
Saturation/ shrinkage in the domestic market			7	8	4
Receipt of unsolicited order	1	2	1	1	2

Table 3.2c. Rank order of export stimuli from past research

Research Study	Kaynak & Kothori (1984b)****	Karafaki-oglu (1986)	Kaynak et al, (1987)	Jaffe et al (1988)	Leonidou (1988) A
Export Stimuli					
Internal /Proactive Stimuli					
Achievement of economies of scale					
Special managerial interest/urge, aspiration					
Products with unique qualities	1	7			
Possession of special competitive advantages		7		2,3	
Potential for extra profit/ sales	4			1,4	2,5
Need to achieve corporate growth		6			3
Internal/Reactive stimuli					
Offsetting sale of seasonal product					
Utilization of idle operating capacity	2		3		6
Stagnation/ Decline in domestic profit/sales			6		8
Reducing dependence/ risk on domestic business					
External /Proactive stimuli					
Encouragement by external agents/organisation			7		
Identification of attractive foreign opportunities			4		4
Exclusive information on foreign markets					7
Government export assistance/ incentives		4			
Contacts after participating in trade fair/ mission					
External /Reactive Stimuli					
Initiation of exports by domestic competitors					12
Competitive pressure in the domestic market			5		9
Favourable foreign exchange rates					
Saturation/ shrinkage in the domestic market	5-6	1	2		1
Receipt of unsolicited order		2	1		10

Table 3.2d. Rank Order of export stimuli from past research

Research Study	**Albaum et al., (1989)**	**Ghauri & Kumar (1989)**	**Koh (1989) A**	**Kothari (1989 a)*******	**Kothari (1989 b)*******
Export Stimuli					
Internal /Proactive Stimuli					
Achievement of economies of scale					
Special managerial interest/urge, aspiration	4		4	5	9
Products with unique qualities	5		1	1	3
Possession of special competitive advantages	8		3_6		7
Potential for extra profit/ sales	2				
Need to achieve corporate growth	1				
Internal/Reactive stimuli					
Offsetting sale of seasonal product	9				
Utilization of idle operating capacity	6	2	9	2	1
Stagnation/ Decline in domestic profit/sales			8		
Reducing dependence/ risk on domestic business	3		7		
External /Proactive stimuli					
Encouragement by external agents/organisation	10	6			
Identification of attractive foreign opportunities					
Exclusive information on foreign markets			13		
Government export assistance/ incentives			15	8	
Contacts after participating in trade fair/ mission		5			
External/Reactive Stimuli					
Initiation of exports by domestic competitors		4			
Competitive pressure in the domestic market	7		5		
Favourable foreign exchange rates					
Saturation/ shrinkage in the domestic market	4-8	3	10	6	2,4
Receipt of unsolicited order	4	1			

Table 3.2e. Rank order of export stimuli from past research

Research Study	**Diammant et al., (1990) A**	**Kaynak (1990 a)********	**Kaynak (1990 b)********	**Sullivan & Bauer (1990) A**	**Weaver & Pak (1990) A**
Export Stimuli					
Internal /Proactive Stimuli					
Achievement of economies of scale				1	
Special managerial interest/urge, aspiration	3			9,15	
Products with unique qualities					
Possession of special competitive advantages				13	
Potential for extra profit/ sales					
Need to achieve corporate growth	1			2	6
Internal/Reactive stimuli					
Offsetting sale of seasonal product	3	4	6	3	4
Utilization of idle operating capacity		1	1	3	
Stagnation/ Decline in domestic profit/sales		5	4	17	3
Reducing dependence/ risk on domestic business				8,12	
External/Proactive stimuli					
Encouragement by external agents/organisation				28,29	5,10
Identification of attractive foreign opportunities					
Exclusive information on foreign markets				11	1
Government export assistance/ incentives				30	
Contacts after participating in trade fair/ mission		7-8	6-7		
External/Reactive Stimuli					
Initiation of exports by domestic competitors		7		23	11
Competitive pressure in the domestic market	3	7	6	21,26	
Favourable foreign exchange rates					7
Saturation/ shrinkage in the domestic market	3	6	5	5	9
Receipt of unsolicited order	2	2	2	24	12

Table 3.2f. Rank order of export stimuli from past research

Research Study	Baker & Kaynak (1992 a)*******	Baker & Kaynak (1992b)*******	Ifju & Bush (1993)	Katsikeas & Piercy (1993)	Leonidou (1995a)
Export Stimuli					
Internal /Proactive Stimuli					
Achievement of economies of scale			16	8	2
Special managerial interest/urge, aspiration			6-9	3	9
Products with unique qualities				9	3
Possession of special competitive advantages					11
Potential for extra profit/ sales			1		1
Need to achieve corporate growth	8	7	4	1	2
Internal/Reactive stimuli					
Offsetting sale of seasonal product					9
Utilization of idle operating capacity	6	5	12	6	16
Stagnation/ Decline in domestic profit/sales			3	17	11
Reducing dependence/ risk on domestic business	2	2		2	4
External/ Proactive stimuli					
Encouragement by external agents/organisation	7	8	2,7,13	16	12
Identification of attractive foreign opportunities	1	1			8
Exclusive information on foreign markets				7	
Government export assistance/ incentives			8-10	15	7
Contacts after participating in trade fair/ mission					14
External /Reactive Stimuli					
Initiation of exports by domestic competitors			18		15
Competitive pressure in the domestic market				13	5
Favourable foreign exchange rates				5	
Saturation/ shrinkage in the domestic market			5	14	10
Receipt of unsolicited order	4	6	15	6	13

Table 3.2g. Rank order of export stimuli from past research

Research Study	**Katsikeas (1996)**	**Ramsameshan & Soutar (1996) A**	**Leonoidu 1998**	**Fillis 2002**
Export Stimuli				
Internal/Proactive Stimuli				
Achievement of economies of scale	11		5	
Special managerial interest/urge, aspiration	1		3	6,16
Products with unique qualities	5		8	
Possession of special competitive advantages			6	
Potential for extra profit/ sales	4	2	1	11
Need to achieve corporate growth	4	1	2	
Internal/Reactive stimuli				
Offsetting sale of seasonal product			13	
Utilization of idle operating capacity	8		11	13
Stagnation/ Decline in domestic profit/sales	4	3	11	14
Reducing dependence/ risk on domestic business	4		7	5
External/Proactive stimuli				
Encouragement by external agents/organisation			18	15
Identification of attractive foreign opportunities			4	10,17
Exclusive information on foreign markets			8	8
Government export assistance/ incentives	6,7		16	11
Contacts after participating in trade fair/ mission			10	1
External/Reactive Stimuli				
Initiation of exports by domestic competitors			17	
Competitive pressure in the domestic market	11	4	14	
Favourable foreign exchange rates	9		12	
Saturation/ shrinkage in the domestic market	12	3	9	9
Receipt of unsolicited order	2		15	4,2

This table was adapted from Williams, D.A. (2008). Export Stimulation of Micro and Small Locally-Owned Firms from Emerging Environments: New Evidence. *Journal of International Entrepreneurship 6; pp 101-122.*

Wisconsin Study **; Virginia Study ***; Nova Scotia Study ****;Texas Study ***** 1997/1998 study respectively; Atlantic/Prairre regions study respectively******; Initiating/Ongoing Stimuli respectively*******. **A**= studies taken from Leonidou (1998).

The stimuli in the tables are ranked based on the firm's response to a large array of variables that may induce the decision to enter export markets. The stimulus that received the highest number of response is ranked as the most important and is given a value of 1. Higher numbers means that the stimulus in question has a lower level of importance on the decision to initiate exporting in the firm. So, the highest number in any single study implies that the individual stimulus has the least impact on the decision to initiate exporting. In some studies, the mean is used as the criterion for ranking (e.g., Leonidou, 1998) while in others, percentage response (e.g., Johnston & Czinkota, 1982) is used. Still, others used the number of responses received (e.g., Brooks & Rosson, 1982).

An important observation is that one stimulus may have three different rankings. This results from the use of more than one item to operationalize that particular stimulus. For example, in table 3.2a, the stimulus "possession of special competitive advantage" has three rankings 1, 3, 7. This is due to three different items (marketing advantage (7), profit advantage (1), technological advantage (3) that were used to measure it.

The empirical literature in the tables above, though comprehensive in terms of the range of stimuli covered is very limited in geographical focus. That is, the majority of studies were conducted in developed countries in North-America and Europe while only a few were carried out in developing countries (e.g., Leonidou, 1995a, Leonidou, 1998). This observation supports the call for more empirical studies to be carried out in the developing world; especially small, developing economies in an effort to better understand the role of stimuli in the export initiation process. Indeed, context specific studies are very important as the importance of stimuli may vary based on location. For example, studies done in the U.S. show that economic factors tend to have a high influence on the export initiation decision (e.g., see Rabino 1980; Johnston & Czinkota 1982 etc.), while in European studies, unsolicited orders tend to have the strongest influence on the decision (e.g., see Tesar & Tarleton, 1982).

The empirical literature lends strong support to the argument that it is very difficult to identify any single factor as solely responsible for export initiation in the firm. Indeed, it appears almost impossible to pin down any one reason for the decision to invest abroad Aharoni, (1966). The interpretation of the theoretical and empirical literature is that; although a large number of stimuli impact the decision to enter export markets, there seems to be a consensus that stimuli external to the firm are most important in driving the decision[44]. In this regard, the most commonly cited external stimulus is unsolicited orders from overseas customers (Leonidou, 1995a).

Analysing export stimuli in this chapter will help to determine whether or not the decision to enter export market results from a systematic investigation into export opportunities or is merely unplanned and a reaction to unsolicited orders. This investigation is important to understand the broader issue of why some firms export while similar others, facing similar market conditions do not.

[44] For example, see, Simmonds & Smith, 1968; Simpson & Kujawa, 1974; Tesar & Tarleton, 1982; Ghauri & Kumar, 1989; Leonidou 1995a etc for this conclusion.

The Investigation Process

As a first step to understanding why some small firms export while similar others remain focused on their domestic market, this chapter provides an empirical analysis of a comprehensive list of export stimuli that the theoretical and empirical literatures argue as being important to firms making the decision to enter into exporting. Specifically, analysing these stimuli will shed some light on one of the questions that this book intends to investigate that is; whether or not the export initiation decision results from a systematic investigation of export opportunities or is a mere unplanned response to some stimuli. Other researchers have suggested that investigation of export stimuli will help to answer this question (e.g., see Kaynak & Stevenson, 1982).

Hitherto this study, very few studies empirically investigated the full range of stimuli in the context of a small, developing country. Indeed, after a comprehensive review of studies in this area, Leonidou 1998, 1995a called for more studies on export stimuli to be carried out in the developing world. The aim is to provide a better understanding of the extent to which individual stimuli can be generalized outside of their study context. Inherent in most of the previous empirical studies is the assumption that stimuli can be generalized across study context. However, it is argued, and correctly, that this is not the most prudent approach to building a general theory on the subject (Fillis, 2001; Leonidou 1995a). Practically also, this approach is not the best for policy makers who design export promotion programmes to stimulate firms in their economy to enter exporting. The fundamental reason is that, firms' response to stimuli varies with time frame, geographical context and also industrial coverage (Leonidou, 1998).

Further, to understand whether or not the decision is proactive or reactive, analysing the source of the stimuli can provide this insight. In this regard, the typology developed by Albaum et al., (1989) will provide a good starting point. This framework is very comprehensive and it allows for results from other context to be compared without much problems.

In this study, a list of stimuli derived from a review of the extant literature and the pilot study interviews were tested to determine whether or not the export initiation decision is planned or unplanned. The literature review and interviews produced twenty possible stimuli for examination. These stimuli are grounded in the theoretical models and empirical literature which analyse the firm's export behaviour and presented in an earlier discussion in the chapter.

Given the large number of stimuli identified, to prevent having too many factors that are specific but lack parsimony theoretically, it is advised that they should be organised into conceptually meaningful groups. To do this, the multivariate statistical technique of factor analysis is highly recommended by statisticians and other researchers in the field (e.g., see Hair et al., 1998, Leonidou, 1998). In other words, rather than having twenty stimuli to analyse individually, factor analysis would group together stimuli that have similar characteristics and therefore produces smaller groups that are parsimonious and still has meaning. This would make it more meaningful to analyse the plethora of stimuli that impact export initiation decision.

The data gathered for this research is ideal for factor analysis. However, the sample size inhibits such an analysis from taking place. Statisticians advise that a sample size of no less than 50 observations should be the minimum criterion for attempting factor analysis (e.g., see Hair et al., 1998). Theoretically, they have posited that the number of observations should be four times the number of variables under investigation in order for factor analysis to produce robust results. Following these recommendations, the minimum sample size that would be required for factor analysis to produce meaningful results in this study is responses from eighty (80) firms. The sample for this research does not meet any of these criteria; therefore, factor analysis cannot be used to help us to determine the relative importance of stimuli in this geographical context.

Instead of using factor analysis, the descriptive statistic of the sample mean ($\overline{X}$) is used to provide insights into the issue under investigation. Although this technique lacks the sophistication of factor analysis, it is very straightforward and still produces very robust results. Importantly, it is heavily used in the existing literature for carrying out similar analysis to that of this chapter[45].The mean will be used as the criterion for ranking stimuli to determine their relative impact on the decision to initiate exporting in the firm. Further, the typology developed by Albaum et al., (1989) will be used to provide insights into the source of the export stimuli. The application of this technique follows the tradition in this stream of literature when trying to provide useful insights into relative importance of export stimuli in inducing firms to initiate exporting. Further, it will also ensure that the results obtained are comparable with other findings in the extant literature from other geographical jurisdiction.

The Relative Importance of Stimuli in the Jamaican Context

This section of the chapter reports the results obtained from the analyses of the lists of export stimuli derived from the Jamaican environment. Where appropriate, qualitative evidence will be added to these results in order to facilitate the quantitative findings (see Coviello et al., 1998 for a similar approach). Importantly, the results are placed in the context of the earlier theoretical and empirical discussion.

Stimuli Inducing Initial Exports

Table 3.3 lists, in order of importance, stimuli that induce Jamaican micro and small firms to enter exporting. Theoretically, it is argued that these stimuli are at the heart of the decision to enter into exporting. Without them, there would be no export response in the first place (Cavusgil et al., 1979). Besides, the SOR model presented in chapter 2 of the book sees these as very critical for export initiation in the micro and small firm. However, not all stimuli have the same impact in inducing this decision. The final decision narrows down to one or a few stimuli (Miesenbock, 1988). The relative importance of these stimuli in the Jamaican context is shown in the table on the following page.

[45] For an example of some of the studies that use this technique, see, Harris, 1997; Albaum et al, 1989; Leonidou, 1998; Johnston & Czinkota, 1982; Simpson & Kujawa, 1974; Brooks & Rosson, 1982 etc.

Globally, the profit motive is the most important stimulus which induces the decision to initiate exporting in Jamaican micro and small firms. The next most important stimulus is the need to achieve growth for the business and the identification of attractive foreign markets. Importantly, these triggers have been cited quite frequently in the extant literature as being very critical in influencing the decision to initiate exporting in the firm (see Leonidou 1998; Cavusgil, 1984a; Tesar & Tarleton, 1982 etc.).

Table 3.3. Rank order of export stimuli

Rank	Stimuli	Mean score $\overline{X}$
1	Potential for extra profit and sales	4.64
2	Need to achieve growth for the business	4.32
2	Identification of attractive foreign market opportunities	4.32
3	Special managerial urge/ interest	4.02
4	Firm possesses unique product	3.80
5	Firm possesses unique competitive advantage	3.77
5	Unsolicited order from foreign customers	3.77
6	Encouragement by external agency/ organisation	3.36
7	Unsolicited order from overseas agent	3.25
7	Reduce dependence on domestic business	3.25
8	Utilize excess capacity	3.16
9	Unsolicited order from domestic partner with overseas business	3.11
10	Competitive pressure in the domestic market	3.09
1	Saturated domestic market	3.02
12	Contact after participating in trade fair	3.00
13	Unsolicited order from social groups overseas	2.66
14	Decline in domestic sales/ profit	2.64
15	Off setting sales of seasonal product	2.55
16	Competitor began exporting	2.20
17	Government assistance/ incentive	2.09

Ranks are used as a proxy for level of importance. Lower numbers in the rank column imply higher level of importance while the highest number implies least importance.

Following closely behind the profit motive is managerial urge/interest. Again, this finding is strongly supported in the extant literature (Reid, 1981; Leonidou, 1998). Behind managerial urge/interest is the fourth ranking stimulus; the firm's possession of a unique product. Completing the top five most important stimuli is the possession of unique competitive advantage and unsolicited order from foreign customers. These seven stimuli are ranked as the top five most important reasons inducing the decision to enter into exporting. They have mean score ranging from $\overline{x} = 4.64$ to $\overline{x} = 3.77$.

Table 3.4. Most important reason for export initiation

Reasons (Stimuli)	**Percentage of Firms**
Need to achieve growth for the business	34.1
Potential for extra sales and profit	18.2
Identification of attractive foreign market	11.4
Contacts after participating in trade fair	6.8
Encouragement by external agency	6.8
Competitive pressure in domestic market	4.5
Reducing dependence on domestic business	4.5
Saturated domestic market	4.5
Utilize excess capacity	2.3
Government assistance	2.3
Decline in domestic sales/ profit	2.3
Firm possess unique product	2.3
Total	**100**

Table 3.5. Source of export stimuli

Export stimuli and their category	**Rank**	**Mean $\overline{X}$**
Internal Proactive Stimuli		**4.11**
Potential for extra sales/ profit	1	4.64
Need to achieve growth for the business	2	4.32
Special managerial urge/ interest	3	4.02
Possession of unique product	4	3.80
Possession of unique competitive advantage	5	3.77
Internal Reactive Stimuli		**2.9**
Reduce dependence on domestic stimuli	7	3.25
Utilize excess capacity	8	3.16
Decline in domestic sales/ profit	14	2.64
Offsetting sales of seasonal product	15	2.55
External Proactive Stimuli		**3.20**
Identification of attractive foreign market	2	4.32
Encouragement by external agency/organisation	6	3.36
Contact after participating in trade fair	12	3.00
Government assistance/ incentive	17	2.09
External Reactive Stimuli		**3.01**
Unsolicited order from foreign customers	5	3.77
Unsolicited order from overseas agent	7	3.25
Competitive pressure in the overseas market	10	3.09
Unsolicited order from domestic partner with business overseas	9	3.11
Saturated domestic market	11	3.02
Unsolicited order from social group overseas	13	2.66
Competitor began exporting	16	2.20

Ranks are used as a proxy for level of importance. Lower numbers in the rank column imply higher level of importance while the highest number implies least importance.

The eight other stimuli have a medium impact on the decision to enter into exporting. They have mean scores concentrated in the range of ($\bar{x}$ = 3.36 to $\bar{x}$ = 3.00). These concentrated mean values imply a relatively uniform but modest stimulating impact on the export market entry decision. The stimuli falling into this range are: encouragement by external agency/organisation, unsolicited order from overseas agents, reducing dependence on domestic business, utilization of excess capacity, unsolicited order from domestic partner with business overseas, competitive pressure in the domestic market, saturated domestic market and, contact after participating in trade fair.

The remaining stimuli have a relatively low impact on the decision to initiate exporting. Their mean values are concentrated in the range of ($\bar{x}$ = 2.66 – $\bar{x}$ = 2.09). The stimuli in this category are: decline in domestic profit/sales, off setting sales of seasonal product, unsolicited order from social groups residing overseas, competitor began exporting, and government assistance/incentives. The result that stood out most in this category is the relatively low impact of government assistance/incentives. This result however, finds support in the literature (e.g., see Leonidou, 1998; Samiee et al., 1993). Further insights into this finding will be discussed in the next section.

Because the decision to initiate exporting narrows down to one or a few stimuli (Miesenbock, 1988), further analysis of the data was done to determine the most important reason for starting exports in the firm. Table 3.4 highlights this result.

The above result indicates that the need to achieve growth is the single most important stimulus inducing the decision to enter into exporting. This is a very interesting observation given the size and sometimes informal operations of these enterprises. It is indeed an important observation that will be discussed in the next section.

A further analysis to determine the source of the export stimuli was also carried out. This was important in order to determine whether the decision to initiate exporting results from a systematic investigation into export opportunities or is a mere unplanned response to some stimuli such as an unsolicited order. The typology developed by Albaum et al., (1989) along with the statistical mean was used to provide some insight into this investigation. Table 3.5 highlights the results from this analysis.

The mean score for each category in the above typology was used as an indicator from which to draw inference about the source of the stimuli. Each of the four categories has a number of stimuli assigned to it. Each stimulus has a mean score and its equivalent ranking taken from Table 3.3. The mean score of all the stimuli in each category is summed to derive an overall mean for the category (bold numbers in the table)[46]. The mean for the category is used to provide inference regarding the overall impact of the category on the decision to initiate exporting in the firm. The category with the highest mean score implies that it has the most important impact on the decision to initiate exporting.

From this analysis, the typology *Internal/Proactive* appears to have the highest impact. In other words, it appears that small firms' decision to enter exporting is induced by the internal dynamics in the firm rather than external factors. That is, export market entry decision is systematic and planned rather than a mere response to an unsolicited order. This result is consistent with findings from previous studies (e.g., see Leonidou, 1998, Brooks & Rosson,

[46] The formula for calculating this means is $(\sum yi)/n$ where y_i is the mean for each stimulus and n is the number of stimuli in the category.

1982; Johnston & Czinkota, 1982 etc.). Further, the literature specific to exporting from larger firms in Jamaica points to a similar conclusion (e.g., Ross, 1989, Garvey, 2000). Ross, (1989) argued that it is the internal dynamics of the firm such as age of manager and product uniqueness that are the sources of export initiation. Garvey, (2000) also argued that it is the mind set of the decision maker that determines whether or not the firm exports. Indeed, this typology, although not rigorously tested with sophisticated statistical techniques, has provided very critical insights regarding the source of the export stimuli. The results will go a far way in shedding light on the issue at the heart of this chapter (whether or not the export initiation decision is planned or a mere response to an unsolicited order).

Discussion of Analytical Results

The above results, while generally reflecting findings from other geographical context reported in the extant literature, still have elements that are specific to the geographical context in which this study was done. The aim of this discussion is to provide some insights into these differences.

Government incentive/assistance had a relatively low impact in influencing the decision to initiate exporting in the micro and small firms in Jamaica. This however, seems to be consistent with results from other empirical studies in other geographical jurisdiction (e.g., Leniodou, 1998). In fact, probing a selected sample of micro and small firms through open ended interviews shed more light on this finding. The entrepreneurs in these firms generally lament that government assistance is not tailored towards the needs of their firms. They argue that government programmes generally apply the "one-size-fits- all" approach and that their firms' specific needs are not met. For example, some entrepreneurs argue that they require assistance in areas such as quality control and labelling of products. However, the government assistance they receive is mainly in the form of loans. Moreover, the loans are not sufficient to acquire the services of professionals to help in these areas. As a result, they render government assistance as ineffective in trying to stimulate exporting. Unsurprisingly, organisations such as the SBAJ, JEA and other private umbrella groups of which these firms have membership, appear to provide more effective assistance. This explains their high ranking among stimuli inducing export initiation compared to government assistance. Government programmes may need to copy the methodology used by these organisations in order to improve the effectiveness of their assistance to the micro and small firm sector.

Many previous empirical studies argue that unsolicited order is the most important stimulus which induces the decision to initiate exporting[47]. This study has found otherwise. Fortuitous order did not score highly as a stimulus impacting the export initiation decision. It appears that this minimal impact results from the limited resources which these firms possess and also the relative poor enabling business environment in which these firms operate. The micro and small firms in the Jamaican economy do not have sufficient resources to promote their products abroad; as such foreign customers are unaware of their offerings. Further, because the business environment is not very attractive (e.g., high cost of production, poor infrastructure to get goods to foreign customers on time etc.) foreign customers will not

[47] For example, see, Simmonds & Smith, 1968; Simpson & Kujawa, 1974; Wiedersheim-Paul et al., 1978; Tesar & Tarleton, 1982; Ghauri & Kumar, 1989 etc.

generally look to Jamaican small firms to supply them with goods and services. These factors may help to explain the relatively poor impact of unsolicited order in motivating Jamaican small firm to initiate exporting.

The need for government assistance to improve the role of unsolicited order is critical (Nicholls et al., 1989). Government programmes can provide assistance in the form of promotion on the international market for those products made by these small firms. This will give foreign customers more awareness of their (small firms) product offerings and can lead to an unsolicited order in the future. With the country's push toward an export led development policy, the government needs to play a stronger role in stimulating small firms to enter the export market. It will have to make the enabling environment more attractive so that these firms can get the unsolicited order to help stimulate their export business.

Excess production capacity had a moderate impact in this study. Due to their limited resources, small firms operating in small, developing countries suffer from limited and sub-standard production. As such, they usually do not have excess capacity for exports. Indeed, most entrepreneurs in these firms lament that one of the most significant problems they face is the ability to expand production. Many of them are desirous of more space to be able to operate at their full potential. An inhibitor to increased production in these firms also, is the lack of highly qualified workers. It appears that the qualified workers tend to work for multinationals or larger firms where the salary and benefits are far superior to those in the smaller firms. This limited supply of human capital again speaks to the need for improvement in the enabling business environment in which these firms operate if they are to seriously engage in the export trade.

Saturated domestic market is not very influential in inducing exports from Jamaican small firms. The Jamaican market by any measure (geography, economic etc) is very small (Ocompo, 2002). This finding however seems to contradict the notion that these firms export in order to grow their business. Why would they want to export when there are enough opportunities to grow in the domestic market? A deeper analysis however, shows that even though the domestic market is not saturated exporting becomes important for competitiveness reasons. The major tenet of the international business literature is that increased presence in foreign markets will increase the firm's performance (Contractor et al., 2003). Exporting will increase the firm's international competitiveness (World Bank, 2000, Deschampsneufs, 1984) and also enhance its competitive position locally. Therefore, although the domestic market is not saturated, firms may still engage in exporting.

The need for growth as the most important stimulus driving export initiation in the small firms in Jamaica is understandable. The entrepreneurs in these firms recognise that if they are to compete effectively in an increasingly global market place, then it is imperative that they will have to become larger. Micro and small firms, especially the ones that are engaged in activities that require economies of scale to compete, have no choice but to increase in size. Size is an important pre-requisite for scale (Bernal, 2006). Indeed, these firms will have to find strategies that will contribute to their growth. Engagement with the export market is definitely one such avenue.

An important pre-requisite for growth is the need for the firms to be entrepreneurial in their outlook and focus. The firms in this study seem to recognise this. For example, the internal/proactive forces which are seen as the most significant factor in inducing exporting gives support to the entrepreneurial nature of these firms. The fact that growth and the identification of attractive foreign markets are also highly rated in this study is another evidence of the entrepreneurial nature of these small firms. Studies both in the developing world (e.g., Garvey, 2000, Leonidou, 1998 etc.) and the developed world (e.g., Cavusgil, 1984a etc.) conclude that the profit motive has the highest impact in inducing the decision to enter exporting. Entrepreneurship is about seeking and exploiting opportunities (Covin & Slevin, 1991). If these firms recognise this, and if exporting can achieve this aim, then they will get engaged in the activity.

Indeed, the operation of micro and small firms in regional trading blocks (e.g., Caricom) is also important for their growth prospects. These economic arrangements provide a bigger market for small firms to better achieve economies of scale in production and thus better enable them to compete in main stream markets in larger, developed economies (Lantaneau, 2000). Thus, regional economic arrangements such as the CSM is important for Jamaican small firms as it will provide extensive opportunities for entrepreneurs in these firms to improve their profitability and competitiveness through increased exporting. It is for the entrepreneurs in these firms to see these opportunities and take advantage of them. Surely, it will require a rethinking of production and operational strategies in these firms as currently, a number of the output supplied by Jamaican small firms are uncompetitive internationally. This however does not mean that Jamaican small firms should not embrace an arrangement such as the CSM. It just means that they will have to work harder in order to achieve the benefits to be derived.

CONCLUSION

This chapter systematically analysed whether micro and small firms' decision to enter exporting results from a systematic investigation into export opportunities or if it is unplanned and a mere response to an unsolicited order. This analysis is important as it highlights those stimuli in the SOR model that are relevant for export initiation in Jamaican small firms.

Due to the small sample size of exporters, the statistical mean, a descriptive statistic, was used instead of the more powerful factor analysis to rank stimuli based on their relative impact on the decision to initiate exporting. This is in essence, a replication of previous empirical work in a new geographical context. Its major contribution however, is that it considers a comprehensive list of stimuli compared to most other studies of the 1980s and early 1990s (e.g., Joynt, 1982; Bilkey &Tesar, 1977; Czinkota & Tesar, 1982 etc.) which looked at only a few stimuli and from firms in developed economies.

The analyses reveal that micro and small firms from the study population are proactive in making the decision to initiate exporting and do not merely respond to stimuli from the external environment. Indeed, this implies a form of systematic planning and rational export behaviour (Lee & Brasch, 1978). Importantly, it stresses the fact that the very simplistic notion that unsolicited order is the most important stimuli inducing the decision to initiate exporting should be rejected. The results show that no single stimulus can solely explain the decision to enter export markets, a finding which strongly supports the theoretical position of export behaviour theories. Indeed, a number of stimuli were found to impact heavily on the decision to enter exporting. However, the most important of all is the need to achieve growth for the firm.

Economic stimuli generally have the highest impact on the decision to initiate exporting. This however should not be interpreted as diminishing the role of social factors in explaining small firms' export initiation. Stimuli such as unsolicited order, personal contact and so on had a moderate to low impact. This is significant for export policy makers who are trying to stimulate more small firms to export. For, if the wrong stimuli are given then firms can become poorly or incorrectly motivated (Kotabe & Czinkota, 1992).

The findings in this chapter provide us with a better understanding of the nature of the export initiation decision. Importantly, it provides critical insights into the triggers that are relevant for export initiation in small firms from small, developing economies. In essence, it gives us some indication of the elements that are important for the stimuli aspect of the SOR model. This understanding is critical in the investigation of why some firms export while similar others remain focused on their domestic market. However, as the SOR model argues, stimuli alone cannot result in a firm becoming an exporter. They are necessary but not sufficient to get the firm to initiate exporting. A sufficient condition is that the firm must possess the requisite absorptive capacity (resources) in order to take advantage of any export opportunities that present themselves. Therefore, to better understand how the SOR model works, it is important to understand what resources and capabilities are more amenable to exporting in the small firm.

Chapter 4

ABSORPTIVE CAPACITY AND EXPORT PROPENSITY

INTRODUCTION

Resources will play an important role in determining whether or not firms respond to export stimuli positively or negatively. The stock of resources which the firm possess will determine its competitive advantage both in the local and international market (Rodriguez & Rodriguez, 2005). These resources are generally categorized as physical or human resources and are seen as relevant to the firm's export propensity[48]. Without them, stimuli would have no real impact on the decision to export. For, if a stimulus is present (e.g., unsolicited order from foreign customer) but the firm does not have the absorptive capacity to fill the export order, then it will not respond positively to that stimulus. However, as with stimuli, not all resources in the firm will be amenable to exporting. Indeed, it is not always the amount of resources but the type of resources available to the firm that determine its export performance (Wolf & Pett, 2000; Pla-Barber & Alrgre, 2007). The aim of this chapter is to identify those resources that are more amenable to getting the firm to initiate exporting after stimuli trigger the decision. This understanding is very important for decisionmakers at the firm level and also export policymakers who are interested in stimulating micro and small firms to export because, it will provide a profile of firms that have a high proclivity towards exporting. These profiles can be used to select firms for export assistance. Further, managers in small firms know what resources they will need to mobilize in order to motivate their firms to export.

This chapter will examine the resources that are responsible for enhancing the firm's ability to enter export markets. In essence, it will provide some answers to the second research question posed in the introduction to this book. Among other things, the chapter will provide an analytical discussion on the resource-based view theory which forms the conceptual framework for analysing the research question. Following this discussion, the chapter will look at the theoretical link between the resources and the firms export propensity, then, there will be a description of the analytical tool that is used to provide insights into the

---

[48] Export propensity refers to the probability of the firm becoming an exporter or not. This construct is heavily used when determining the export performance of the firm. See for example, Bonaccorsi, 1992; Phillip, 1998; Obben and Magagula, 2003)

research question. The subsequent sections will present the results from the analysis, a discussion of the findings and some conclusions.

THE RESOURCE-BASED VIEW THEORY

The mere existence of export stimuli will not result in the firm becoming an exporter. The firm must have a stock of resources that will allow it to respond positively to these stimuli. For, it is these resources that will ultimately determine whether or not it will have the capacity to fill an export order and sustain its export business in the long run. However, for the small firm, the majority of these resources are embodied in the owner/entrepreneur (Bloodgood et al., 1996). Therefore, any attempt to analyse resources in the small firm will have to start with an analysis of the entrepreneur's capabilities.

It is unsurprising therefore that the literature argues that a sufficient condition for export market entry is that export stimuli must be brought to the attention of the entrepreneur in the firm [49]. The entrepreneur, based on his/her interpretation of the firm's capacity to fill an export order, will either respond negatively or positively to the export stimuli. This interpretation however, is shaped by a number of factors including but not limited to the resource stock of the firm and the domestic environment in which the firm operates[50]. The discussion on the resource-based view theory will focus specifically on those resources in the small firm that are relevant in activating stimuli and getting the firm to enter export markets.

Several theories from the field of international business, economics and strategy have tried to explain why firms engage in international activities[51]. However, these theories fail to provide a robust explanation for this phenomenon, especially in the context of the micro and small firm. The major weakness in these explanations is that they do not take into account, the aspirations of the entrepreneur and the resource stock (both quality and quantity) of the micro and small firm (Westhead et al., 2001; Ibrahim, 2004). For example, the product life cycle theory argues that firms enter international markets so as to protect their existing markets of mature products (Vernon, 1966); network theory suggests that firms enter international markets by developing mutually supportive interactions with other firms or through the owner's social network (Johnson & Vahlne, 2003; Ellis, 2000); stage theory asserts that firms gradually enter international markets as they gain knowledge and experience about the international arena (Johnson & Vahlne, 1977, 1990).

However, the majority of the theoretical explanations do not consider explicitly, the resource needs of these firms that are relevant for initial internationalization. The stage model implied this in its explanation. It argues that with increased knowledge and experience, the firm will expand internationally. Because this knowledge and experience are embodied within the individual(s) who operate these firms, they can be classified as relevant resources for international market operation (Bloodgood et al., 1996). However, other size-related

[49] See, for example, Aaby & Slater, 1989; Miesenbock, 1988; Simpson & Kujawa, 1974; Wiedersheim-Paul et al. 1978; Leonidou et al. 1998; Bijmolt & Zwart, 1994.

[50] See, for example, Westhead et al., 2001; Bijmolt & Zwart, 1994; Christensen, 1979; Vatne, 1995; Westhead et al., 2004 for a full explanation on this point.

[51] Some of these theoretical frameworks include Product Life Cycle: Vernon, 1966, Stage Theory of Internationalization: Johanson & Vahlne, 1977, Bilkey & Tesar, 1977, Reid, 1981, 1983, Czinkota, 1982, Cavusgil, 1982, Network Theory: Coviello & McAulley, 1999, Coviello & Munro, 1997 etc.

resources such as marketing capabilities have been ignored. Further, the theory does not recognise that some firms start international operations from inception and in some cases even go international before operating domestically (Madsen & Servias, 1997). This has implications for the quality and type of resources in these firms. These resources will play a critical role in moderating how stimuli contribute to the decision to initiate exporting.

The firm can be conceptualized as a collection of productive resources (Penrose, 1980). Resources are generally conceptualized as the assets, capabilities, processes, routines and knowledge possessed by the venture (Barney, 1991). In other words, resources refer to the stock of available factors owned or controlled by the venture (Amit & Schoemaker, 1993).

Owing to the many definitions of the construct (resource), various classifications exist. For example, Chatterjee & Wernerfelt, (1991) show a body of work that classifies resources into three categories: physical, intangible and financial. Barney, (1991) categorized resources into three types: human capital, physical capital and organisational capital. Still, Amit and Schoemaker, (1993) classified resources as: know-how, financial or physical assets and human capital. However, going back to Penrose (1959) seminal contribution to the theory of the growth of the firm, she classified resources as human and physical resources. From the rich literature on the resource-based theory, it appears that there is full consensus on these categories (Anderssen & Kheam, 1998).

Building on the resource-based view of venture internationalization (e.g., Westhead et al., 2001; Bloodgood et al., 1996; Rialp et al., 2005) this study will analyse those physical and human resources which are considered relevant to increased competitive advantage and thus give the firm greater confidence to enter foreign markets. Moreover, these resources are easily identifiable and embody the characteristics of the entrepreneur who is very crucial in the firm's decision to enter export markets (Westhead et al., 2001; Ibrahim, 2004). Indeed, Aaby & Slater (1989, p.16) after reviewing 55 studies looking at the firm's export behaviour concluded that: "it appears as if it is the managements' commitment, perception and attitude towards export problems and incentives that are good predictors of export success". In a similar vein, Wiedersheim-Paul et al., (1978) argued that if the stimuli are not brought to the attention of the decision maker(s) in the firm then, exporting will not be initiated. Miesenbock, (1988) in a comprehensive literature review of studies looking at the firm's export behaviour also shared the view that it is the persuasion of the decision maker that will determine whether or not the firm exports and not the presence of a stimulus per se.

These resources are critical in determining what actions the firm can take (Covin & Slevin, 1991; Tseng et al, 2004) regarding domestic or international operations. Researchers (e.g., Bloodgood et al., 1996) argue that new ventures ability to enter foreign markets is directly related to their resource stock. For example, firms with a high percentage of technical and scientific employees may possess a greater ability to export than those with less of those employees. With a large number of scientific and technical workers, the firm will have a greater chance at innovation, a critical resource for competitive advantage in the market place (Pla-Barber & Alegre, 2007). This competitive advantage will better prepare the firm to respond positively to export stimuli and thus allow it to enter export markets.

The resource-based theory asserts that the type, magnitude and nature of a firm's resources are important determinants of its profitability (Amit & Schoemaker, 993). Researchers argue that firms which possess a combination of resources that are valuable will have a greater proclivity towards internationalization (Bloodgood et al., 1996). The quality of the resources which the firm possess, not so much the quantity, will have a huge impact on its decision to go abroad. International activity is critical as firms see it as one of the strategies by which to gain potential profit opportunities outside their home market (Contractor et al., 2003). Resources no doubt will play an important role in this endeavour.

Although there are paradoxes[52] in the resource-based view literature, this theory is utilized in this chapter because of its ability to provide a clear link with the firm's export behaviour and its domestic environment. The majority of the resources that firms, especially smaller firms will mobilize; normally come from their domestic environment. If the domestic environment is not sophisticated enough to provide the valuable resources that the firm needs for its international operation, the theory will be able to pick this up. In the case of small, developing economies where the domestic environment is so critical for the firm's entry into international operation, there is no doubt that the resource-based theory provides a useful analytical lens for looking at the relationship between resources and the firms export propensity.

Importantly, the resource-based theory will provide insights into the differences in export behaviour of small firms from developed and developing environments, where the former has a larger stock and higher quality of resources which can influence the firms internal resource stock (Vatne, 1995) and better push it towards international market operations. Further, the variables associated with the resource-based view are relatively easy to collect. This is critical for a study that is done in small, developing economies where data availability is a significant challenge (Kaynak, 1978; Tindigarukayo, 2001).

Like stimuli, not all resources will have the same level of importance in getting the firm to respond positively to circumstances that trigger exporting. Although some efforts have been made in trying to understand the effects of resources on export performance, the results remain contradictory and thus warrant further research. The impact of these resources on the firm's export decision for firms in small, developing economies definitely needs further clarification. The discussion below will summarize the previous work in the area and provide some insights into the theoretical relationship between those resources and the export performance for firms in small, developing economies.

The Relationship between Resources and Export Propensity

In this section, the link between the propensity to export and the human and physical resources of the firm are discussed. After reviewing the extant literature, theoretical relationships (hypotheses) that will provide deeper insights into the problem are formulated. These relationships will provide insights into those resources that are more amenable to getting the small firm to respond positively to export stimuli and enter export markets.

[52] The paradoxes identified do not undermine the importance of the resource-based theory as one the most powerful theoretical contribution to understanding firm strategy. The weaknesses identified in the resource-based theory are generally present in all forms of theorizing in the social sciences. The epistemological value of the arguments is definitely worth looking at; however, they are not strong enough to discount the use of this

Physical Resources

Physical resources consist of tangible things (Penrose, 1980; Williamson, 1975; Chan, 2005). These include the physical plant, technology, land and natural resources, raw material, unsold stock of finished products etc. According to the logic of the resource-based theory of venture internationalization, these resources are critical in helping the firm to gain a competitive advantage (especially if they are valuable and non-substitutable) thus giving it more confidence to enter foreign markets (Bloodgood et al., 1996).

Physical resources are normally characterized by fixed capacity. Therefore, if excess capacity exists, to gain improved profitability, these firms will have to seek new markets. These new markets are generally overseas. Moreover, the type, magnitude and quality of these resources will determine if the firm can access these new markets overseas. Firms will enter new markets where the resource requirements match their resources and capacity (Andersen & Kheam, 1998). The physical resources that can provide this capacity are discussed below.

The Firm's Technology

Technology in general and Research and Development (R&D) more specifically is regarded as an important physical resource that will influence the firm's decision to enter export markets (Cavusgil & Nevin, 1981; Tybjee, 1994; Tseng et al., 2004; Rodriguez & Rodriguez, 2005). The firm's investment in R&D reflects a commitment to innovation. Researchers from the innovation diffusion school of thought argue that investments in R&D show a favourable attitude by firms toward exporting (e.g., Lee & Brasch, 1978; Samiee et al., 1993; Simmonds & Smith, 1968). With increased research and development, the firm will have more unique products to offer thus increasing its competitive advantage and its chance of survival in the export market (Rodriguez & Rodriguez, 2005; Pla-Baber & Alegre, 2007).

Innovation through research and development also leads to firms possessing unique products. With unique product offerings, firms are more likely to react positively to export stimuli because there is the perception that they will have a competitive advantage in the export market (Moen, 1999; Cavusgil & Nevin, 1981; Burton & Schlegelmilch, 1987; Rodriguez & Rodriguez, 2005). Small firms, due to their limited size, cannot compete in international markets on the basis of price. Because of the lack of resources that can provide technological economies of scales (Penrose, 1980) they will be less competitive compared to larger firms which are offering similar products at a lower price. Unique product offering therefore, is an opportunity for small firms to develop a niche market (Rialp et al., 2005). This will give them a competitive advantage in the international market place (Dimitratos & Liokas, 2004).

The relationship between the firm's technology and export propensity has received some attention in the literature[53]. However, there is still some contradiction regarding its impact on

theory. For persons interested in the scientific enquiry into knowledge development and theorizing, the Lado et al., (2006) article makes an important read.

[53] For some of the studies that have analysed this relationship see, Kumar & Siddharthan, 1994; Tseng et al., 2004; Andersson et al., 2004; Cavusgil & Nevin, 1981; Aaby & Slater, 1989; Miesenbock, 1988; Christensen et al. 1987; Tybjee, 1994; Dhanaraj & Beamish, 2003; Rodriguez & Rodriguez, 2005 etc.

export propensity and intensity[54]. In relation to export propensity, some researchers find a positive relationship (e.g., Tseng et al., 2004; Andersson et al., 2004 etc.), while others find no statistically significant relationship (e.g., Tybjee, 1994; Rodriguez & Rodriguez, 2005 etc.). However, the results are even more contradictory as it relates to export intensity. For example, Reid (1986) found that technology will encourage the firm into early exporting but, in terms of its impact on future success (e.g., increased export revenue) there was no strong relationship discovered. Tybjee, (1994) found that R&D has a positive influence on export intensity. The results from this study show that firms in industries with high R&D spending reported a higher proportion of their sales from international markets. In a similar vein, Rodriguez & Rodriguez, (2005) found R&D spending to be significant with regard to export intensity.

The effect of R&D on the firm's export performance cannot be divorced from its industry structure. The nature of the industry will impact the strategies and performance of any firm (Barney, 1991; Rodriguez & Rodriguez, 2005). Firms in industries that are technology driven are more likely to innovate and thus export (Tybjee, 1994). This is because of the competitive advantage to be gained from developing unique and customized products with the new technology. A large number of empirical studies show that firms in high technology industries are more likely to be exporters (e.g., Bell et al., 2004; Crick & Jones, 2004; Tybjee, 1994 etc.).

It is critical to point out that the sectors studied in this research are non-high technology sectors (manufacturing and agriculture) therefore; the role of technology in this context may not be as significant as in other geographical context where industry sectors are heavily technology-based and more internationalized. The level of R&D spending in these sectors is very low. Thus, few firms will have the sophisticated technology necessary to develop unique competences and therefore feel confident enough to enter into foreign markets.

Investment in R&D does not automatically translate into increased capacity to help the firm gain access to foreign markets. The investment may not result in product innovations, and process innovations that could give the firm a competitive advantage. The competitive advantage from this investment will be derived from what is achieved (e.g., reduction in production costs) from using the technology. The mere investment will not provide technological economies of scale which is what firms need to be better able to access foreign markets. From the logic of the resource-based theory, it appears that a higher stock of technological resource will lead to greater competitive advantage (Barney, 1991), which will give the firm greater incentive to enter foreign markets. This logic has guided our theoretical expectation regarding the relationship between technology and the firm's export propensity. This relationship is summarized as:

> $H_{4.1}$: *Small firms with higher spending on Research and Development will positively respond to export stimuli and make the decision to enter export markets.*

---

[54] Export intensity refers to the export sales as a percent of total sales for the company. It does not look at whether or not the firm exports.

The Firm's Product

The firm's product is an important physical resource that will determine its competitive advantage and by extension its ability to enter foreign markets. The nature of the product takes into account the degree of standardization, quality, uniqueness, usage:- consumer or industrial etc. (Cavusgil & Nevin, 1981; Christensen et al. 1987; Aaby & Slater, 1989, Wiedershiem- Paul et al. 1978, Leonidou & Katsikeas, 1996). Since unique product is assumed to be a function of the firm's technology and the study is confined to consumer goods, this discussion will focus on the two other critical dimensions of the product which are relevant for improved competitive advantage and also the firm's ability to enter export markets. These are: a) Degree of standardization and b) Product quality.

The literature argues that firms which possess products that are not adaptable to conditions in the export market to be sold there, are more likely to be engaged in exporting (Christensen et al., 1987; Vernon, 1966; Tookey, 1964). That is, firms which have products that can be sold both in the domestic market and the international market without much variation will get involved in exporting easier than those firms which have to make significant changes before the product can be sold overseas. Tookey, (1964) in a study of hosiery firms in the Leicester area in Britain found that a large number of firms did not export because they failed to adapt their products to the demands of the export market. Importantly, adaptation of a product to the conditions in an export market is important to small, resource poor firms mainly because of the costs involved. The fixed costs involved in having two separate production lines can be quite exorbitant for small firms. Therefore, they try to produce a product which can be sold locally and with possible minor adjustments (e.g., adding contents to labels) can also be sold in the export market. This cost may be trivial for firms in the service sector, but for firms in the merchandise trade sector, it can be exorbitant.

An interpretation of the literature which looks at the relationship between the firm's product and its export propensity seems to suggest that firms which do not have to adapt their products to the conditions in the export market are stronger candidates for export market entry than those that have to (Balabanis et al., 2004; Tookey, 1964; Contractor et al., 2003). However, for increased export revenue, the literature is strongly biased towards adaptation of the product to the demands of the export market (Christensen et al., 1987; Tybjee, 1994; Rodriguez & Rodriguez, 2005). It is important to note that the adaptation or standardization of the firm's product is a function of other features of the product and also the line of business in which the firm operates. For example, products such as toilet tissue can be sold in almost all markets without any adaptation to specific market conditions. However, certain garments (e.g., winter coats) cannot be sold in tropical countries without modifications. Therefore, firms producing these coats would have to make substantial alterations before selling in an export market in a country with a tropical climate.

In relation to the product quality, the literature is biased towards a positive relationship with export propensity (e.g., see Christensen et al. 1987; Burton & Schelegelmilch, 1987; Daniels & Guyboro, 1976; Aaby & Slater, 1989). In a Brazilian study, Christensen et al., (1987) found that product quality is the strongest discriminator between exporting and non-exporting firms. Daniels & Guyboro, (1976) also found product quality to be a strong discriminator between exporters and non-exporters in Peruvian firms. Other researchers such as Joynt, (1982) found product quality to be the most important competency among Norwegian exporters. None of these studies however, provided a theoretical rationale as to why product quality is such an important resource for export market entry decisions.

If traditional strategic analysis theories are anything to go by, one would expect that quality represents a resource which the firm can leverage to gain a competitive advantage in the market place (Barney, 1991; Porter, 1990). The possession of a resource that can lead to a competitive advantage will provide firms with more confidence to operate in international markets. Firms will therefore want to exploit this advantage by selling both locally and overseas, especially where home market is small. Following the logic therefore of the resource-based theory, quality and standardized products are invaluable resources that will give small firms a competitive advantage in the market place. Therefore, the expected relationship with export propensity is captured as follows:

$H_{4.2}$: Small firms selling products that do not have to be adapted to the export market will react positively to export stimuli and make the decision to enter into exporting

$H_{4.3}$: Small firms with products that are of a high quality will react positively to export stimuli and make the decision to enter into exporting.

Human Resources

Human resources, according to Penrose, (1980) are embodied in the employees of the firm. Some scholars refer to this type of resource as human capital (e.g., Becker, 1964). Human capital refers to the accumulation of personal attributes (e.g., knowledge, personality, experience etc.) that will allow human beings to function (Pena, 2002). According to Becker, (1964) the most seminal work on this concept, sees human capital as knowledge embodied in people. This knowledge is an important resource for running the operations of the firm (Cooper et al., 1994; Rosa, 2003). For micro and small firms, the human capital resource is normally embodied in the entrepreneur. Westhead et al., (2001) see the entrepreneur as the provider of tangible and intangible resources to the firm. They argue that these resources are the properties of individuals who have accrued them through education and experience[55].

The number of literature reviews (e.g., Aaby & Slater, 1989; Cheety & Hamilton, 1993; Leonidou et al., 1998 etc.) on managerial characteristics and the decision to enter export markets, leaves no doubt that some progress has been made on the subject. This critical mass of work gained momentum because the owner/entrepreneur in the small firm is regarded as the most important variable in making the final decision to initiate exporting in the firm (Miesenbock, 1988; Leonidou & Katsikeas, 1996; Ibrahim, 2004). Despite this extensive literature, Leonidou et al., (1998) concluded that the research stream is in its exploratory stage of development and lacks a well defined theoretical framework. Moreover, the findings from the empirical work are generally contradictory. Leonidou et al., (1998) after reviewing 46 studies on managerial characteristics and their impact on the firm's export behaviour, argue that it is one of the most widely studied areas in research on export behaviour of the firm but has the least conclusive results.

The experience, skills and competencies which entrepreneurs possess are generally regarded as critical human capital resources influencing decision making in the firm (Storey,

[55] Penrose, (1980) did not confine her definition of human resource to just those of the owner of the firm but to every employee, because this study focuses on the small firm where the owner is the most important decision maker. The human resources that are looked at here will be focused on those of the owner of the small firm.

1994; Mathur, 1999; Manolova et al., 2002). In this section, those critical measurable and easily identifiable resources which entrepreneurs gather through education and experience will be analysed in order to link human resources and export propensity.

Entrepreneur's Age

In the small firm, decision making is normally concentrated in the hands of one or a few individuals. This individual is normally the owner of the firm. In the entrepreneurship literature, s/he is referred to as the entrepreneur[56]. The knowledge which this individual brings to the firm is seen as a valuable resource which can lead to the firm gaining a competitive advantage in the market place (Barney, 1991; Andersen & Kheam, 1998). Researchers consider the age of the entrepreneur as a reflection of life and learning (e.g., Westhead et al., 2001). Therefore, in the context of the resource-based theory, it is seen as a proxy for the level of knowledge the entrepreneur brings to the firm. From a resource-based view, the older the entrepreneur the higher will be the stock of knowledge and as such, the more valuable is his/her age to the firm. Because age is a proxy for knowledge, then older age signal higher knowledge set, which will lead to a greater competitive advantage for the firm.

It can be argued that older entrepreneurs, who have been operating in business for a long time, will have a better understanding of operational issues, obstacles, and general business know-how. This experience will give them enough confidence to take on business in foreign markets where business practices are different and uncertainties are high. Although the export market is different in many respects compared to the domestic market, the ability to overcome problems in the domestic market will serve as a re-enforcement for taking on more complex problems. Younger entrepreneurs, who have not had such experience, would possibly be overwhelmed by obstacles in the export business and thus shy away from such activity.

Age can also be a reflection of life long personal networks. Social networks can be viewed as a valuable resource that will give the firm a competitive advantage in the market place (Ellis, 2000). Older entrepreneurs, because of their length of time in business, would build up essential contacts and networks. These contacts and networks will help the firm to get orders that it would otherwise not have gotten in the export market[57]. For younger entrepreneurs who are just entering the business arena, they may not have these contacts and networks thus making them less likely to get orders from the export market. Actually, the role of networks (social and business) in helping small businesses to access international market is well appreciated by researchers on the subject[58].

In light of the above arguments which are grounded in the resource-based view logic, it is not surprising that the empirical literature argues that there is a positive relationship between export propensity and the entrepreneur's age (e.g., Usric & Czinkota, 1989). Other studies however, have found that exporting firms do have younger managers than non-exporting firms (e.g., Dichtl et al., 1990; Jaffe et al., 1988). The argument they proffer is that physical energy is also a valuable resource in the firm. Besides knowledge acquisition, age can also be a reflection of the store of physical energy which the entrepreneurs possess (Storey, 1994). In

[56] See, for example, Beaver, 2002; Coviello & Jones, 2004; Covin & Slevin, 1991; Rosa, 1993; Rosa & McAlpine, 1991 for this classification.

[57] See, Dana & Wright, 2004; Johanson & Vahlne, 1990; Coviello & McAulley, 1999; Coviello & Munro, 1997, Westhead, 1995 for further development of this point.

[58] Some of these include Dana & Wright, 2004; Buckle & Ghauri, 1999; Caviello & Munro, 1997; Coviello & McAulley, 1999; Johanson & Vahlne, 2003; Coviello & Jones, 2004 etc.

fact, this can become a critical resource in determining the firm's competitive advantage in foreign markets. Exporting takes a lot of time and energy; it requires regular travel to foreign countries, constant negotiation with distributors and overseas customers. Therefore, it will require a lot of physical energy to take on such onerous tasks. The reasoning is that younger entrepreneurs will more than likely have a higher store of energy than older ones. As such, they will be better able to take on extensive travel, longer work hours and, the cut and thrust of international negotiations among other strenuous tasks. These advantages to be derived from age, the resource-based theory of venture internationalization argues, can help the firm to gain competitive advantage, thus better positioning it to enter foreign markets.

However, theorists of the network persuasion believe that network is much more important than physical energy in selling abroad. Moreover, network theory suggests that with a wider social and business network, the firms' ability to sell their products abroad will be greatly improved (Coviello & McAulley, 1999; Coviello & Munro, 1997) without the hassle of intense negotiations. Given that small firms are generally constrained by limited resources, any opportunity that reduces the need for the use of extra resources to compete internationally will definitely lead to a greater competitive advantage for these firms. If age therefore is a proxy for networks, then one would expect that firms with older entrepreneurs should have a greater proclivity towards exporting. Based on this logic, the expected theoretical relationship is captured as follows:

$H_{4.4}$: Firms with older decision maker/entrepreneur will react positively to export stimuli and make the decision to enter the export market

Educational Background

Entrepreneurs acquire invaluable resources for their firm through their educational experience (Cooper et al., 1994). Researchers contend that entrepreneurs with higher levels of formal education are more likely to have a broader international outlook and thus being better able to evaluate the benefits from international business (Obben & Magagula, 2003; Leonidou et al., 1998). It is generally acknowledged that education enhances the knowledge and capabilities of an individual therefore, providing greater analytical power to deal with complex issues in the international business arena (Cooper et al., 1994; Becker, 1964; Mathur, 1999). Therefore, education becomes an invaluable asset which is important for the firm's competitive advantage.

Despite the perceived theoretical significance of education in creating a competitive advantage for the firm, the empirical evidence remains contradictory. Some studies found education to be a strong discriminator between exporters and non-exporters (e.g., Daniels & Guyboro, 1976; Simpson & Kujawa, 1974; Dichtl et al., 1990). Other studies found no statistically significant difference between exporters and non-exporters based on the entrepreneur's educational background (e.g., Obben & Magagula, 2003).

Indeed, the non-statistical significance of the education variable in some studies should not be seen as a lack of importance of education in creating a competitive advantage for the firm. What it may imply is that for modelling purposes, education is a redundant variable. Education will pass on the requisite skills to build the networks and contacts in the export market, win negotiations, raise finance etc. which are all critical in improving the firm's competitiveness and enhancing its ability to enter export markets. These are the factors that are most important in the export decision making process,and not merely having a formal education (Cooper et al., 1994). The possession of high academic qualifications will not automatically lead to the success of a firm (Storey, 1994). It is how and what this qualification is used for (e.g., problem solving, motivation etc.) which is important. Therefore, it is not just having a formal education that is important for exporting; it is the benefits derived from having this education (self confidence, motivation, analytical skill etc.) that really matters.

In this study, education is considered a critical resource because it affords entrepreneurs a higher analytical power and a more open-minded approach to global issues. With a higher level of educational achievement, one is expected to be more open-minded and therefore more accepting of new ideas, for example, finding new markets to achieve higher profitability. Highly educated entrepreneurs are also likely to be more interested in international affairs thus, being in a better position to spot opportunities in the international market. Education will also enhance an individual's negotiation skills, increase his/her personal and business networks, and improve his/her ability to raise finance for business operation. With all these benefits accruing from having a higher level of formal education, it is expected that education as a human resource will play a critical role in shaping how small firms respond to export stimuli and make the decision to enter foreign markets. The expectation is that the relationship should be positive. Thus, the relationship is summarized as follows:

$H_{4.5}$: Small firms with entrepreneurs that are highly educated will react positively to export stimuli and make the decision to enter into exporting.

Previous Job Experience

The previous professional experience of the entrepreneur can provide the firm with detailed knowledge of the business environment in which it operates (Westhead et al., 2001). This knowledge can allow the firm to develop more appropriate niche markets in order to gain greater competitive advantage in the market place. This competitive advantage will give the firm greater confidence to take on operation in international markets. It is demonstrated empirically that entrepreneurs who have had previous export experience are more likely to engage their firms in exporting (Leonidou et al., 1998). This argument rests on the assumption that the experience gained in the previous job will enhance entrepreneurs' business and personal networks, and also their experience in international business (Bloodgood et al., 1996). Because of these benefits, it is argued that this resource increases the odds of the firm becoming an exporter (Reid, 1981).

Following the logic of the internationalization process theory, it can be argued that previous professional experience (especially from the same industry) will reduce psychic distance, thus enabling the firm to take advantage of international business opportunities. From past job experience, the entrepreneur would have learnt about foreign markets' culture and business practices and therefore being better able to take on operations there.

Moreover, it is argued that previous experience (those specifically related to exporting) will provide entrepreneurs with a working knowledge of the export market. It will give them an idea of the possibilities and practicality of exporting (Westhead, 1995). This will enable them to feel more comfortable operating in these markets compared to someone who has never operated there before. This confidence may also allow them to be more aggressive in seeking market opportunities. The entrepreneur will be in a better position to evaluate the feasibility of foreign market opportunities since s/he has an idea of the obstacles that will be faced.

The argument advanced in this book as to why the entrepreneur's previous job experience is an important human resource lies in its ability to improve the firm's business and social networks. Also, this experience may lead to a reduction of psychic distance through the acquisition of knowledge and experience[59]. Entrepreneurs who have operated in the export market before would have met potential customers and distributors. They may have formed business relationships or even personal friendship over this time. These relationships can serve as an avenue through which the firm can get information about export markets and also as a means of getting its products into these markets. As argued before, these types of networks are an important mechanism for small firms to sell a portion of their sales abroad.

This appears to be one of the few variables that has received full consensus regarding its impact on export propensity in the extant literature. Almost all studies argue that this resource has a positive effect on the firm's export propensity (e.g., see Dichtl et al., 1990; Usric & Czinkota, 1989; Leonidou et al., 1998). As a result, the expected theoretical relationship is summarized as follows:

> $H_{4.6}$: *Small firms with entrepreneurs who have had previous work experience in an exporting firm or the export sector will respond positively to export stimuli and make the decision to enter into exporting.*

Foreign Language Proficiency

The entrepreneur's competency in a foreign language can provide the firm with a competitive advantage in dealing with customers in international markets. According to the resource–based view of venture internationalization, firms which possess such a valuable resource will have a greater proclivity towards internationalization (see Bloodgood et al., 1996). Empirically, language proficiency has also received a lot of attention in the extant literature. Leonidou et al., (1998) in a review of 46 studies on managerial characteristics and the firm's export performance found that over 50 percent of those studies accounted for this variable in their empirical analysis. The majority of studies conclude that firms with entrepreneurs who have a good command of a foreign language are more likely to enter export markets (e.g., Lautanen, 2000; Obben & Magagula, 2003; Dichtl et al., 1990; Karafakioglu, 1986). However, there are other studies which found no relationship between the entrepreneur's language competency and export propensity (e.g., Daniels & Guyboro, 1976; Ursic & Czinkota, 1989). Like Daniels and Guyboro, (1976); Obben & Magagula, (2003) also found that when decision makers are monolingual i.e. speak only their native language, there is often a negative relationship with export propensity.

The literature argues that proficiency in a foreign language distinguishes between those firms that export and those that do not. This however can be very context specific based on the geographical location to which the firm exports. In the context of the Jamaican market, the majority of exports go to the United States, where English is also the native language. In this case, foreign language proficiency may not be an important resource for these firms to

---

[59] Indeed, it must be appreciated that psychic distance may not be an important variable today as it was in the early 1970s due mainly to the rapid evolution in information and communication technologies. For an update on the importance of psychic distance in international market operations see Brewer, (2007)

have. However, in an increasingly liberalized trading environment where non-English speaking markets are becoming very important, Jamaican entrepreneurs will have to improve their proficiency in other languages besides English. Indeed, with the new EPA between Cariforum and the EU, a large part of the EU market does not speak English. If Jamaican firms want to take advantage of the new market opportunities from this trade agreement, then entrepreneurs' foreign language competence will have to be improved.

Foreign language competency is an important resource to the firm, especially relating to the export function, because of the benefits to be derived from its possession. Having competency in a foreign language will facilitate effective planning and control of business operations in the export market. It will also assist in understanding foreign business practices; improve communication and interaction with foreign customers and help to establish social and business contacts. With these specific advantages to be derived from the possession of this resource, given the reduction in trade barriers in the international trading environment, there is expected to be an increase in the number of firms with multi-lingual entrepreneurs taking on exporting.

If the logic of the process theory of internationalization is to be followed, one would expect that competency in a foreign language will reduce the psychic distance to that country. With reduced psychic distance, entrepreneurs will exude greater confidence in carrying out business in these markets (O'Grady & Lane. 1996; Johanson & Vahlne, 1977). Thus, the expected theoretical relationship is captured as follows:

> *$H_{4.7}$: Small firms with entrepreneurs who are proficient in a foreign language will respond positively to export stimuli and make the decision to enter into exporting*

Foreign Travel Experience

The most important point from the stage theory of internationalization is that; the more international experience a firm has, the better it is able to expand abroad. Indeed, from the resource-based theory of venture internationalization, international experience is seen as a valuable asset from which the firm can gain a competitive advantage thus better enabling it to enter foreign markets. Bloodgood et al., (1996) argue that some of the international experience in the firm is located within individuals who form these firms (entrepreneurs), thus they may capitalize on this experience and expand internationally.

Having lived, worked or studied abroad will provide entrepreneurs with some amount of international experience. They will have a better knowledge of foreign cultures, business practices, laws and regulations in those societies. This knowledge will better prepare them to take on business in foreign markets which are more complex and different from their domestic market. It will also help to reduce the psychic distance to these markets. If stage theory has any validity then, we expect that with reduced psychic distance, more firms with entrepreneurs who have a high level of foreign travel experience will enter export markets. International experience is also critical for network building, another valuable resource in improving the competitive advantage of the firm. Foreign travel will allow entrepreneurs to meet prospective customers, identify business opportunities and eventually generate foreign sales for the firm's products.

This variable has received extensive empirical attention in the literature with the results biased towards a positive relationship with export propensity (e.g., see Williams & Chaston, 2004; Keng & Jiaun, 1989; Dichtl et al., 1990; Obben & Magagula, 2003). If the logic from both the network theory and stage theory are anything to go by, then it is expected that there should be a positive relationship between this resource and the firm's export propensity. This relationship is formally captured as:

> *$H_{4.8}$: Small firms with entrepreneurs who have a high level of foreign travel experience will respond positively to export stimuli and make the decision to enter into exporting*

Control Variables

Because the stock of resources in a firm and by extension export performance may be affected by other factors such as industry, geographical environment, size of the firm, age of the firm and so on, other important variables are also included in the model to control for these effects. The control variables used here, which are hypothesized to affect the firm's export performance are: firm size and firm age. These variables were chosen because of the ease with which data can be found on them. Indeed, when making the decision as to what variables should be used in a model, it always comes down to a decision of what is theoretically sound and empirically feasible. In this case, size and age are both theoretically sound and empirically feasible. Further, these variables are used in several other studies as controls for other factors that may affect the firm's export propensity (see, for example, Bloodgood et al., 1996; Westhead et al., 2001; Rodriguez & Rodriguez, 2005 etc.).

Firm Size

According to the resource-based theory, larger firms due to their number of employees, will have access to more resources (e.g., human capital such as qualified managers, financial resources etc.) than smaller firms. Because exporting demands a large amount of resources, small firms will find it difficult to mobilize the necessary resources for such activity. Large firms are said to have more resources (e.g., financial, technology, human capital etc.) than smaller firms thus are more successful in the export market (Aaby & Slater, 1989; Katsikeas & Piercy, 1993; Philp, 1998). The firm size is seen as a useful surrogate measure of the firm's resource stock (Bonaccorsi, 1992).

Despite these claims about the stock of resources and the firm's ability to operate internationally, the empirical evidence remains contradictory. Researchers argue that for all the attention given to this variable, there seems to be very little agreement regarding its impact on either export propensity or export success (Aaby & Slater, 1989). Indeed, this variable has received quite a lot of attention in the literature on the firm's export behaviour[60]. Most studies however argue that there is a positive relationship (e.g., see Miesenbock, 1988), while other studies have even suggested a minimum size for exporting. For example, Mittelstaedt et al., 2003 recommended that the minimum size should be 20 employees. Below

[60] A large number of studies have analysed the relationship between this variable and the firm's export behaviour over the last 30 years. Some of these studies include Calof, 1993, 1994; Daniels & Guyboro, 1976; Andersson et al., 2004; Mittelstaedt et al., 2003; Hall & Tú, 2004; Hall et al., 2005; Yaprak, 1985; Keng & Jiuan, 1989; Pope, 2002; Bilkey & Tesar, 1977; Leonidou & Katsikeas, 1996; Miesenbock, 1988; Burton & Schlegelmilch, 1987; Reid, 1981; Czinkota & Johnson, 1983; Cavusgil & Nevin, 1981; Whitey, 1980; Bonaccorsi, 1992; Cavusgil, 1984a, 1984b etc.

this number, they argued that exporting becomes infeasible. Because size reflects the productive capacity of the firm, then below a critical minimum, the firm will not have sufficient capacity to initiate exporting. Bilkey, (1978) also discovered that beyond a certain point, exporting is positively correlated with firm size, but below a minimum point there is no correlation. Also, there are firms with fewer than this number that are engaged in exporting. For example, firms with less than five employees are observed operating in the export market (e.g., see Bilkey & Tesar, 1977; Philp, 1998; Calof, 1993; Moen & Servias, 2002 etc.). This seems to support the point that size may not be a barrier to exporting.

However, the empirical relationship between firm size and export performance is not always consistent. For example, Hall & Tú, (2004) looked at the impact of size on both measures of export performance (propensity and intensity) and found different results. For export intensity, they found a negative relationship with size, while for export propensity there was a positive relationship with size. Pla-Barber & Alegre, (2007) also found that size was not important for export propensity for science-based firms. Further, some researchers found no relationship with size and export intensity (e.g., Czinkota & Johnson, 1983; Cavusgil, 1984b etc.). Czinkota & Johnson, (1983) concluded that size did not substantially differentiate between managers' attitudes and the firm's experiences in exporting. However, the methodological soundness of this study comes up for serious scrutiny (Christensen et al., 1987, Keng & Jiuan, 1989).

From a more critical look at the size and export propensity debate, Hall & Tú (2004) argue that it is the fixed cost associated with entry which makes size an important variable in the decision to export. This is even more important for industry sectors such as manufacturing and agriculture which require economies of scale to compete. Economies of scale is a function of the firm's resources and the sector within which it operates. Achieving scale will lead to a reduction in the unit cost of output therefore, allowing firms to sell products at a more competitive price. Small firms, due to their limited resource stock, will not be able to gain the same level of economies of scale as large firms. It is therefore reasoned that the larger the firm, the greater the prospects for economies of scale thus, the more confidence it will have to enter foreign markets.

The high fixed cost involved with exporting is important because small firms which are resource poor are more vulnerable to sunk costs. To elucidate, fixed cost associated with search for market, negotiation, certification (e.g., ISO 9000 or HACCP), can be exorbitant. Small firms which are resource poor will not be able to afford these costs, as such; it may dissuade them from responding positively to export stimuli. However, with the recent developments in the network literature, it can be argued that small firms can collaborate to overcome the fixed cost problem. If the firm has a competitive product, it can find partners in the export market that can help it to gain access. Some small firms may also network with larger firms which are resource rich and have already borne the fixed cost involved in exporting (see, Coviello & McAulley, 1999; Beamish, 1987; Bonacorssi, 1992; Lipparini & Lorenzo, 1999 for further development of this point). In addition, the government can help firms to writedown a lot of these fixed costs by setting up agencies that help with issues such as certification, market search, and negotiation.

Because the industries looked at in this study are ones that require economies of scale to compete internationally, it is reasoned that size will be important for exporting. Thus the expected theoretical relationship is captured as follows:

$H_{4.9}$: The larger the firm, the more likely it will respond positively to export stimuli and make the decision to enter into exporting

Firm Age

The resource-based view predicts that older firms will have considerably more resources than younger firms. This premise is based on the assumption that firms acquire resources over time (Autio, 2005). Because older firms will have a larger stock of resources than younger firms, the resource-based view of venture internationalization argues that they will be better able to build an international base (Bloodgood et al., 1996).

Further, the process theory of internationalization posits that firms progress in a stepwise manner when moving from their domestic market to international markets (e.g., see Johanson & Wiedersheim-Paul, 1975; Johanson & Vahlne, 1977, 1990; Czinkota, 1982; Cavusgil 1980 etc.). Underlying this gradual process is the assumption that firms will need to develop their knowledge of the foreign market before allocating huge amounts of resources there. In other words, managerial learning is a critical resource for firms which intend to export. Jovanovic, (1982) perceived firm age as a reflection of learning. Learning according to the postulates of the process theory is a critical resource that will enable firms to enter export markets. International markets are very diverse and business practices are different from those of home markets. To operate effectively in these markets, theorists of the incremental stage orientation argue that firms will have to develop skills relating to the foreign market (e.g., language), understand the culture in these markets, and develop confidence in overseas operation before large volumes of resources are committed. This knowledge and experience occur over time. As soon as the firm grows older, it will gather more knowledge of how overseas markets operate. The knowledge which firms acquire over time will help them to overcome the "liability of foreignness" (Hymer, 1976) and "liability of newness" (Stinchcombe, 1965), which are factors that prevent younger firms from surviving in the international markets (Welch & Weidersheim-Paul, 1980; Rhee, 2002).

However, the rise in born globals and international new ventures (see, Knight & Cavusgil, 1996, Oviatt & McDougall, 1994 for explanation of these concepts) have led to serious questions about the accuracy of the assumptions of the stage model, especially the argument that firms acquire resources over time and thus will gradually enter international markets[61]. Firms both in high technology sector and manufacturing sector are observed going international even before they start operating in their domestic market (Crick, 2004). This evidence further bemused the proponents of stage theory who argue that age is a reflection of experience, know-how, and alleviates the liability of foreignness and newness. Researchers have observed that younger firms are internationalizing at an even faster rate than older ones (e.g., Knight & Cavusgil, 2004).

Although there are sound theoretical and empirical evidences to support the born global thesis the contention in the empirical literature as to the impact of the firm's age on export performance continues (e.g., see Moen & Servias, 2002). For example, the literature in organisation theory provides arguments to suggest that younger firms are more interested in exporting than older ones (Rhee, 2002; Autio et al., 2000). This school of thought points to

[61] Examples of some of the studies that raise these questions are, Moen & Servias, 2002; Knight & Cavusgil, 2004; Caviello & Munro, 1997; Johanson & Vahlne, 1990; Oviatt & McDougall, 1994; Knight & Cavusgil, 1996; Li et al., 2004.

structural inertia as a result of age. It posits that structural inertia in a firm increases with the age of the firm. This therefore results in older firms being slower in responding to change compared to younger firms. Since exporting calls for important changes to be made in the firm's operational activities, older firms may respond slower than younger ones.

A recent Swedish study by Andersson et al., (2004) shows that the firm's age is not a significant factor in determining the level of internationalization. Keng & Jiuan, (1989) found that there is no statistically significant difference between younger and older firms' interest in exporting. They conclude that this finding does not give support to the contention that younger firms are more interested in exporting than older ones. Other researchers (e .g. Daniels & Guyboro, 1976; Brouthers & Nakos, 2005 etc.), found a positive relationship between exporting and firm size. Daniels & Guyboro, (1976) found evidence that older firms are more likely to become exporters. Peruvian firms serve their local market first then gradually move to the export market. Also, Brouthers & Nakos, (2005), although they did not measure export performance as export propensity, showed that older firms are more likely to be more successful in the export market. The interpretation is that they are more likely to become exporters.

Moreover, the argument about resource accumulation and age fits well the prediction of the resource-based view theory. Indeed, it appears that the firms in the sample for this study do acquire resources over time given their age distribution. Because export initiation requires a large amount of resources, we expect older firms to have more resources upon which to build an international basis. Therefore older firms should have a greater propensity to export than younger ones especially those in sectors that require economies of scale. Thus, the expected theoretical relationship is captured as:

$H_{4.10}$: Older firms are more likely to respond positively to export stimuli and make the decision to enter into exporting.

The resources identified above represent those elements in the firm's international environment that are critical for it to generate the necessary absorptive capacity i.e. the ability and skills necessary for operations in the domestic and international market. Testing the theoretical relationship identified above will provide some insights into which combination of resources in the firm is most amenable to getting it to be involved in exporting[62]. Table 4.1 summarizes the empirical results of previous work on export propensity and variables which reflect the firm's absorptive capacity (resource stock).

[62] It is important to note that for this study, the focus is on export propensity (whether the firm exports or not) in the firm's export development process. Therefore, the resources identified will help to identify why some firms decide to respond positively to export stimuli while similar others do not.

Table 4.1. Summary of the relationship between the firm's resources and export propensity

Variables[63]	*EDU*	*SDP*	*EA*	*EFL*	*EFT*	*EPEE*	*NEC*	*YCS*	*PQ*	*TS*
Previous Research										
Burton& Schlegelmilch 1987				+			+		+	+
Cavusgil & Naor 1987*							+			
Daniel & Guyburo, 1976	+	+	-	-			+	+	+	
Ganier 1982		+			+		+			
Handwerkskammer 1981*							+			
Hirsch 1971*							+			
Kaynak 1985*							+			
Mc Guiness & Little 1981 a, b*							+			
McConnel 1979							+			+
Reid 1982							+			
Müller & Köglmayr 1986*							+			
Tookey 1964		+					+			
Yaprak 1985							+			
Walters 1985*							+			
Bonaccorsi 1992							+			
Kirpalani & Mac Intosh 1980						+		-		+
Calof 1993, 1994							+ -			
Stenging & Mc Dougall 1975*						+				
Usric & Czinkota 1984*								+		
Ogram 1982										+
Ong & Pearson 1982*	+									
Welch & Wiedersheim 1980								-		
Topritzhofel & Moses 1979*						+				
Fenwick & Amine 1979*						+				
Musangu 1985*						+				
Seranghaus 1987/88*						+				

63 See the full name of these variables below on page 90

VARIABLES[64]	*EDU*	*SDP*	*EA*	*EFL*	*EFT*	*EPEE*	*NEC*	*YCS*	*PQ*	*TS*
Kaynak & Kothari 1984							+			
Cavusgil & Nevin 1981										+
Cavusgil et al 1979		+								
Schlegmilch & Crook 1986*										+
Hall & Tú 2004							+			
Keng & Juian 1989					+			-		
Andersson et al., 2004	+						+	–		+
Tseng et al., 2004	+						+			+
Jaffe et al., 1988	-									
Usric & Czinkota 1989	+		+	-		+				
Dichtl et al., 1990	+		-		+	+				
Obben & Magagula 2003	–			+	+					
Lautanen 2000	-			+						
Christensen et al., 1987		+							+	+
Westhead et al., 2001			+			+				

* indicates studies taken from Miesenbock, (1988); + = positive relationship.

THE ANALYTICAL MODEL

To validate the theoretical relationships identified above, this chapter adopts the multivariate statistical technique of logistic regression (the logit model). Besides following the spirit of previous empirical work, there are other compelling reasons for choosing this analytical technique.

Motivation for the Logit Model

Logistic regression provides prediction of the likelihood of getting an alternative response to a dichotomous dependent variable given a number of predictor variables. In other words, it is used to provide the highest predictive accuracy of a given set of predictors (Hair et al., 1998). This chapter is interested in finding out which combination of resources is more amenable to getting small firms to respond positively to export stimuli.

To motivate the logit model, let us assume that the likelihood of the firm becoming an exporter lies within a narrow range of 0 to 1. That is, it takes a probability distribution. It therefore implies that values outside of this range are not meaningful and therefore, will not

64 See the full name of these variables below on page 90

give an accurate prediction of the firm becoming an exporter. As a result of this restriction, regression models such as ordinary least squares (OLS) or linear probability models become meaningless for carrying out this analysis (Pindyck & Rubinfeld, 1998). The error term in these models, although normally distributed, does not have equal variance. This will lead to the problem of heteroscedasticity in these models (Gujarati, 2003). The problem of heteroscedasticity will lead to parameter estimates becoming unstable and thus prevents generalization of the model beyond its sample data. Moreover, OLS can produce probabilities that are greater than one (1). Indeed, the models from the genre of qualitative choice (e.g., Probit, Logit etc.) are more powerful and will provide more accurate results for the type of analysis this chapter aims to achieve[65].

It is also important to note that the two group discriminant analysis could be used for the purposes of this chapter. However, because logistic regression produces results that are more robust against statistical violation of basic assumptions (i.e. equal variance- covariance across groups, normality of variables compared to discriminant analysis; see Ghauri & GrØnhaug, 2002; Hair et al., 1998) this study has opted for the former.

The Theoretical Form of the Logit Model

The aim of logistic regression is to achieve the highest predictive accuracy with a given set of predictors. In this chapter, the aim is to predict the likelihood of a micro and small firm becoming an exporter based on its possession of a combination of physical and human resources.

Like ordinary least square regression (OLS), the logit model has dependent and independent variables. The dependent variable in this case however, is binary and discrete i.e. it can only take a value of 0 or 1. Therefore, the model will predict the probability of the dependent variable occurring given the predictor variables. As such, rather than taking the form:

$$Y = \beta_0 + \beta_1 X_1 + \beta_2 X_2 \dots + \beta_n X_n + \varepsilon \qquad (4.1)$$

It takes the form

[65] Theoretically, using either probit or logit model produces similar results (Pindyck & Rubinfeld, 1998). However, there are practical reasons to use one over the other. Firstly, in determining which model to use, certain assumptions will have to be made regarding the Cumulative Distribution Function (CDF) which is used to transform the model so that the results of the dependent variable can yield a probability value in the range of 0 to 1. This function (CDF) takes either a normal or a logistic distribution. If we assume a normal distribution then, a probit model is the tool of choice, while if the assumption is made that the distribution (CDF) takes a logistic form then; the logit model is the tool of choice. The assumption about the population distribution should be motivated by the dataset. In the case of this research, the population is not normally distributed and so, it was prudent to adopt the assumption that CDF takes a logistic distribution. Because the logistic CDF is not in the integral form, it makes the logit model much easier to work with. Further, statisticians have stated that the theoretical justification for the probit model is limited and it involves non-linear maximum likelihood estimators (Pindyck & Rubinfeld, 1998). Indeed, Gujarati, (2003) in a note on logit versus probit models concludes that logit model is generally used in preference to probit. For these reasons, the logit model was adopted as the tool of choice for this study.

$$P_i\,(Y=1 \mid X) = 1/\ 1+e^{-z} \tag{4.2}$$

Where:
P_i = probability of the ith small firm becoming an exporter
e = base of the natural logarithm which is approximated to be 2.78
z = unobservable observations i.e. the model in 4.1 above.

However, to determine the odds of the small firm becoming an exporter, equation 4.2 will have to be transformed to obtain the odds in favour of being an exporter. To obtain this information, the transformation is done as follows:

First, the algebraic form of the model is derived by multiplying by $1+e^{-z}$ then dividing by P_i and subtracting 1. Also, recall that e^{-z} is equivalent to $1/e^{z}$. Therefore, the final outcome from this transformation will produce the model in the form:

$$e^{z} = P_i/\ 1-P_i \tag{4.3}$$

That is, the probability of the firm being an exporter divided by the chance of being a non-exporter (the odds ratio).

Taking the natural logarithm of equation (4.3) produces the model in the form:

$$Z = \ln\,(P_i\,/1-P_i) \tag{4.4}$$

However, since Z is a linear combination of the independent variables, equation 4.4 can be written as:

$$\ln\,(P_i/\ 1-P_i) = \beta_0 + \beta_1 X_1 + \beta_2 X_2 \ldots + \beta_n X_n \qquad (4.5)^{66}$$

Equation (4.5) represents the model to be estimated in this chapter. In this model, P_i is the probability of the small firm becoming an exporter while 1- P_i is the probability of it being a non-exporter[67].

Interpreting the Model Coefficients

Similar to OLS, each predictor in logistic regression has its own coefficient (e.g., β_1). Estimating the regression provides the value of these coefficients. The interpretation behind these values is similar to that of multiple regression. The only difference is that the outcome of this regression is in logarithmic form. Therefore, it is the logit of the outcome which one reports. For example, the estimator on β_2 implies that a one unit change in the predictor

---

[66] In this equation, values close to 0 show that the outcome of the dependent variable is unlikely to occur. In this case it would mean that the firm is unlikely to be an exporter. Values close to 1 means that the likelihood of the dependent variable occurring is high i.e. the firm is likely to be an exporter.

[67] Note, if P_i happens to be 0 or 1, the odds of the firm being an exporter will be 0 or infinity (∞), thus the logarithm will not be defined.

variable (X_2) will produce a (β_2) change in the likelihood of being an exporter. For a straight forward interpretation similar to that of multiple regression the antilog of the coefficients will have to be taken. This will transform the coefficient into a normal continuous variable thus giving a straight forward interpretation.

However, given that this chapter is more interested in testing relationship rather than predicting outcomes, the most important statistic will be the significance of the variables. The wald statistic in logistic regression, like the t-statistic in OLS is used to determine the statistical significance of the variables in the model. It produces evidence to test the null hypothesis that a coefficient is not significantly different from zero. It is also calculated in similar manner to the t-statistic in OLS.

It is also noteworthy to mention that the R^2 in models of qualitative choice has a similar interpretation to that of R^2 in multiple regression. However, the conventionally computed R^2 is deemed questionable as a measure of goodness of fit in the logit model (Gujarati, 2003). As such, various alternative measures of R^2 (e.g., Nagelkerke, Cox & Snell, Model R^2 or McFadden R^2) are calculated for the logistic regression. The model R^2 or the McFadden R^2 is seen by some statisticians as a better measure of goodness of fit for the logit model. Cox & Snell R^2 for example, cannot reach the maximum value of 1 and as such is not the best measure of goodness of fit (Hair et al., 1998). The model R^2 which is calculated by taking the model chi-square as a fraction of the initial log likelihood value (Field. 2000), is also referred to as the McFadden R^2 (Verbeek,2001). Alternatively, the Nagelkerke R^2 can be used as a good predictor of the goodness of fit. It has the ability to reach the maximum value of 1. These statistics are all obtained from the estimated model.

THE MODEL TO BE ESTIMATED

This chapter aims to find out which combination of resources is more amenable to getting micro and small firms to respond positively to export stimuli. Because of the elegance of the logit model and its ability to hold up to statistical violations regarding the normal distribution of the independent variables, it will be used to provide answers to this question. The model to be estimated takes the following form:

$$\ln(P_i/1-P_i)= \beta_0+\beta_1 edu_i+\beta_2 sdp_i+\beta_3 ea_i+\beta_4 efl_i+\beta_5 eft_i+\beta_6 epee_i+\beta_7 nec_i+\beta_8 ycs_i +\beta_9 pq_i+\beta_{10} ts_i+\varepsilon_i$$

Where:

EDU = entrepreneur's educational background
SPD = the degree of standardization of the firm's product
EA = the entrepreneur's age
EFL = the entrepreneur's foreign language proficiency
EFT = the entrepreneur's foreign travel experience
EPEE = the entrepreneur's previous job experience
NEC = number of employees in the firm
YCS = the age of the firm
PQ = the firm's product quality

TS = the firm's technology

ε_i = the error term normally distributed with mean 0 and variance $1/NP_i(1-P_i)$ i.e. $\varepsilon_i \approx N\{0, 1/NP_i(1-P_i)\}$

Table 4.2. Logistic regression- unrestricted model (N=92)

Independent variables	β	*Wald*	*Sig.*	*Exp(β)*
Constant	-1.74	1.32	.25	.18
EA	-.02	.31	.58	.99
EFL	-1.22	1.57	.21	.30
EFT	1.91*	4.78	.03	6.77
EPEE	1.51*	6.65	.01	4.54
EDU	-.03	.02	.89	.97
NEC	.04*	6.38	.01	1.04
SPD	1.84*	9.04	.00	6.27
PQ	1.50*	3.82	.05	4.46
YCS	-.04	.06	.80	.96
TS	-.59	1.98	.16	.55
-2LL(Initial Model)	127.37			
-2LL(Final Model)	86.13			
χ^2(df) (Final Model)	41.24 (10) **			
χ^2(df) Hosmer & Lemeshow test	11.71 (8) ***			
Nagelkerke R^2	.48			
R^2_L	.32			
% Correct Prediction	82.6			

* Variables are significant at the 0.05 level of significance.

** Statistic is significant at the 0.05 level of significance (p=0.000).

*** Test is non-significant at the 0.05 level of significance (p=.17).

R^2_L = 1- (Final model -2LL/ Initial model -2LL).

Estimating this model will give some indications of the probability of the small firm becoming an exporter, if it possesses a certain combination of human and physical resources. Importantly, the model will identify which resources in the firm's internal environment are more amenable to getting it to respond positively to export stimuli.

WHICH RESOURCES ARE RELEVANT?

The model estimated above was inspired by variables that the physical and human resources that micro and small firms possess. The aim is to determine which combination of these resources is more amenable to getting the firm to respond positively to export stimuli. Table 4.2 highlights the resources that are considered to be most relevant for export initiation decision in the small firm.

The model reveals that the most important human resources likely to enhance the small firm's ability to respond positively to export stimuli are: the entrepreneurs' previous job experience and foreign travel experience. On the other hand, the most important physical resources are: the quality of the product and the degree of standardization of the product (i.e. whether significant changes have to be made to the product before it is sold in the export market). As for the control variables, firm size is the most significant. Importantly, of all the significant physical and human resources, the most important appears to be the degree of standardization of the product. Interestingly, some of the traditional measures of human capital (e.g., education, age etc.) and physical capital (e.g., technology) are not seen as relevant for a positive response to export stimuli. This ability, from the model remains unaffected by these resources. An explanation concerning these unexpected results will follow in the discussion section.

As a test of the robustness of these results, the model was re-tested on a sample of 82 observations, dropping ten observations arbitrarily (see Hair et al., 1998 for rationale). The coefficients and their statistical significance remained virtually unaffected by this transformation[68]. These results are captured in Table 4.3.

Table 4.3. Model with reduced sample size (N=82)

Independent variable	β	*Wald*	*Sig.*	*Exp(β)*
^	-2.29	1.36	.24	.10
EA	-.01	.17	.67	.98
EFL	-1.96	2.53	.11	.14
EFT	3.10*	7.69	.00	22.19
EPPE	1.34*	3.78	.05	3.83
EDU	.06	.043	.83	1.06
NEC	.05*	6.23	.01	1.05
SPD	3.01*	13.15	.00	20.28
PQ	1.72*	3.48	.06	5.58
YCS	-.21	1.01	.31	.81
TS	-.57	1.41	.23	.56
-2LL(Initial Model)	113.67			
-2LL(Final Model)	66.23			
χ^2(df) (Final Model)	47.44 (10) **			
χ^2(df) Hosmer& Lemeshow test	8.5 (8) ***			
Nagelkerke R^2	.58			
R^2_L	.42			
% Correct Prediction	81.7			

* Variables are significant at the 0.05 and 0.1 level of significance.
** Statistic is significant at the 0.05 level of significance (p=0.000).
*** Test is non-significant at the 0.05 level of significance (p=.39).
R^2_L = 1- (Final model -2LL/ Initial model -2LL).

Table 4.4. Restricted model (N=92)

Independent Variables	β	*Wald*	*Sig.*	*Exp* (β)
Constant	-2.64	17.53	.00	.07
EFT	1.25*	3.04	.08	3.51
EPEE	1.40*	6.12	.01	4.08
NEC	.04*	6.56	.01	1.04
SPD	1.86*	10.06	.00	6.29
PQ	1.14*	3.09	.07	3.14
-2LL(Initial Model)	127.37			
-2LL(Final Model)	90.35			
χ^2(df)-(Final Model)	37.02 (5) **			
χ^2(df) Hosmer& Lemeshow Test	4.22 (8) ***			
Nagelkerke R2	.44			
R^2_L	.29			
% Correct Prediction	78.3			

* Significant variables at the 0.05 and 0.1 level of significance.
** Statistic is significant at the 0.05 level of significance (p=0.000).
*** Test is non-significant at the 0.05 level of significance (p=.84).
R^2_L = 1- (Final model -2LL/ Initial model -2LL).

Indeed, when the model was also restricted to only the statistically significant variables found in Table 4.2, only marginal changes in coefficients and their statistical significance occurred. These changes were not strong enough to result in any of the variables becoming statistically insignificant. Table 4.4 reports these results.

For a sensitivity analysis of the results, the unrestricted model was also re-run with each variable dropped alternatively. This was done to test whether or not the results are affected by the composition of the variable set. In one case when variables were dropped, an insignificant variable became significant and a significant variable became insignificant. When the variable standardized product was dropped, the variable firm technology became significant at the 10 % level. Also, when the variable technology was dropped, the variable product quality (a significant variable) became insignificant[69]. Besides these two cases, when all other variables were dropped alternatively the coefficients and their statistical significance remained virtually unaffected. There were slight changes in the values of some coefficients however, they were not strong enough to result in any of the statistically significant variables becoming insignificant or any of the statistically insignificant variables becoming significant[70].

Further, a number of diagnostic tests[71] were done to determine the overall goodness of fit for the estimated model. All the tests show that the model is indeed robust and that the

[68] There were marginal changes in the values of some coefficients but nothing strong enough to alter the results from the model with the full sample size. The table below summarizes this result.
[69] The relationship between the firm's technology and product quality is confirmed by the Pearson R correlation coefficient at 0.38 and statistically significant at the 0.05 level. The relationship between the firm's technology and standardized product although not statistically significant is confirmed at -0.13.
[70] The results from these analyses are presented in appendix 1.
[71] See appendix 1 for the full range of diagnostic tests that were carried out on the model.

variables identified as relevant in getting the firm to produce a positive response to export stimuli can be generalized outside of the study sample.

Discussion

The analysis above revealed that the combination of physical and human resources is critical for small firms to respond positively to export stimuli. Two resources relate to the physical resources category (product quality, degree of standardization) and two to the human resources category (foreign travel experience and previous job experience). One size related resource was also found to be important, the size of the firm as measured by the number of employees. Although all five resources are seen as critical for export initiation, in terms of relative importance, the degree of standardization of the firm's product appears to be the most important. These results show that of all the theoretical relationship between resources and export propensity identified, only five were supported. Table 4.5 summarizes these outcomes.

Theoretically, these results are sound. The resource-based view of venture internationalization argues that this combination of human and physical resources is critical in enhancing the firm's ability to enter export markets. These resources can provide the firm with a competitive advantage thus increasing its confidence to enter foreign markets.

Table 4.5. Outcome of hypotheses testing

Hypotheses	Outcome
H4.1	Not Supported
H4.2	Supported
H4.3	Supported
H4.4	Not Supported
H4.5	Not Supported
H4.6	Supported
H4.7	Not Supported
H4.8	Supported
H4.9	Supported
H4.10	Not Supported

N.B. Hypotheses are supported if variables are significant at the 5% or 10% level of significance.

Table 4.6. Expected and observed signs for independent variables

Variables	Theoretically expected sign	Observed sign
EDU	+	-
EA	+	-
PQ	+	+
SDP	+	+
EFL	+	-
EPEE	+	+
EFT	+	+
TS	+	-
NEC	+	+
YCS	+	-

Further, some of the variables had signs that run counter to their theoretical predictions. Table 4.6 summarizes these results.

It appears that the difference in sign results from the geographical location in which this study was done. The nature of the industry sectors, the quality of the supply of resources etc. will determine which resources are important for export initiation and therefore, the sign that each variable takes[72].

The above results can be interpreted as follows: firms which have the following resources- managers (entrepreneurs) with international experience, managers (entrepreneurs) with previous export industry experience, high quality product, a standardized product and, a large number of employees are more likely to undertake exporting. These resources will lead to a competitive advantage for the firm, and as such gives it greater incentive to enter export markets (Bloodgood, et al., (1996).

The foreign travel background and the previous export experience of the entrepreneur reveal that networking is a critical resource for the small firms' export propensity. Networks are an important asset from which the firm can gain some advantage internationally and build an international basis (e.g., Coviello & McAulley, 1999; Coviello & Munro, 1997 etc.). It will also help the small firm to overcome barriers of costs which normally prevent them from entering into export markets.

It appears also that size matters in the exporting business. The results suggest that larger firms are more likely to become exporters. In a globalizing world economy, size is definitely important for scale economies especially for firms involved in activities that require scale to compete. The clear implication here is that if Jamaican firms are to compete successfully in export markets, they will have to increase in size. This argument extends beyond Jamaica to all small, developing economies because their firms are generally very small compared to firms in the global market (Bernal, 2006). Further, with a larger number of employees, the higher will be the stock of human resources. Therefore, the greater the likelihood that the firm will have high quality resources to chose from when participating in export markets.

The quality of the firm's product is an important resource for increased competitive advantage (Zou et al., 2003; Bloodgood et al., 1993). This will no doubt help to improve the firm's level of confidence when competing internationally. This added confidence will better position the firm to respond positively to export stimuli as it will feel more comfortable to handle the uncertainties in a foreign market.

The degree of standardization of the firm's product plays a very important role in determining the type of response it produces to export stimuli. This resource is seen by other researchers as the major factor in determining whether or not small firms enter export markets (e.g., Tookey, 1964; Philp, 1998). This finding is both empirically and theoretically sound.

A standardized product it is argued; tends to have easier access to international markets and are more readily tradable than customized products (McNaughton & Brown, 2004). It will not require costly market research/information in order to sell these products in foreign markets (Vernon, 1966). This lower fixed cost will motivate small firms to respond positively to export stimuli. Indeed, Tookey, (1964) found that the majority of British hosiery firms in the Leicester area of Britain did not export even to other European markets because they

---

[72] If firms are located in industry sectors that are international by virtue of their operations, then these firms will have to become international. Further, if they are in an industry such as high technology or science-based activities, certain resources will become very important for international operation. In this case technology may be an important resource but in other activities like agriculture, it may not.

would have to adapt their products to conditions in those markets. It is the cost involved in adapting their products to the export market that prevented these firms from responding positively to the stimuli that triggered them to export to the rest of Europe. On the other hand, those firms that exported did not have to make any major adjustments to their products before selling to the export market. Clearly, small firms that are resource poor would be more inclined to sell abroad if their products that are sold in the local market are also suited for the export market without any major modifications. Indeed, standardization appears to be a major factor in determining the type of response small firms produce when export stimuli are brought to their attention.

CONCLUSION

Why do some small firms respond positively to export stimuli while similar others do not? One possible explanation based on the analysis in this chapter, is that firms differ in their resource capacity. This type of capacity is known as absorptive capacity which is derived from the quantity and quality of resources which firms possess. This chapter highlights those resources relevant to create this absorptive capacity in the micro and small firm. These are: the foreign travel experience of the entrepreneur, the previous export experience of the entrepreneur, the number of employees in the firm, the quality of the firm's product and the degree of standardization of the product. These resources are visible, easy to access and measurable. This therefore provides policy makers with a better idea of the profile that firms need to possess in order to be qualified for export assistance to stimulate exporting. Managers in these firms will also know what resources to mobilize for export initiation.

Although the model seems quite robust, there are some limitations to the analysis. Because of the small number of cases, this precluded us from more sophisticated separated analysis of industry effects and environmental characteristics of the home country. Indeed, the socio-economic conditions of the home country can impact on a firm's propensity to export. Future research can investigate these conditions. One addition for example, is to incorporate the role of government policy in the model. Also, the variables used to convey resources are very crude estimates. Therefore, one has to be very cautious in interpreting the findings of this study, especially when dealing with insignificant results. Despite these limitations, the results are robust and provide some strong insights to both policymakers and practitioners who are interested in promoting small firms to get into exporting. They also provide insights to academics interested in building a theory on the firm's export behaviour.

Both chapters 3 and 4 have provided an explanation as to why some firms export while similar others remain focused on their domestic market. However, after this decision is made to initiate exporting, the firm still has to make a further decision about where to begin its exporting activity. This decision is even more critical for small firms because of their limited resources. It is important therefore to understand the factors that motivate this decision. Chapter 5 provides some insights into this important issue.

Chapter 5

MARKET ENTRY DECISION

INTRODUCTION

It should be no surprise that firms which possess the necessary absorptive capacity for exporting, respond more positively to export stimuli. Indeed, exporting will bring tremendous benefits to the firm if done properly. After the decision is made to get involved in exporting, the next step is to determine where to start the activity. With the world as your market and with limited resources as a small enterprise, it is sometimes a difficult decision to determine which market to enter first. Generally, managers will want to start exporting to markets that they know best as this will help to reduce the high level of uncertainty associated with operating in a new market. Most entrepreneurs will know more about certain parts of the world because they have lived, studied, read about them or have seen them on television. These are some of the factors that theorists on the export behaviour of the firm cited as relevant to the decision regarding which market to enter. However, with the emergence of born globals, a lot of questions now surround the generally accepted argument that firms will enter export markets where they know best, after they have decided to initiate exporting. The fact is, a large number of factors do determine this decision in the long run. The aim of this chapter is to provide insights into the factors that are most relevant for micro and small firms when determining where to start their export operations.

The chapter will highlight the existing research on the subject and among other things; provide evidence relating to those factors that are relevant for export market entry decision in the context of small firms from Jamaica. The lessons learnt in this context can be transferred to other small firms from other geographical locations similar to Jamaica. As far as possible, the chapter will incorporate the stage model of internationalization as the primary theoretical lens that will shed light on the research question, which the chapter hopes to answer. The chapter will try to determine if the process (stage) theory of internationalization can be used to predict where micro and small firms will start their exporting after their positive response to export stimuli. Analysing the relative importance of external factors that induce the decision to enter foreign markets will provide some insights into this issue.

THE MARKET ENTRY DECISION

Most studies in the literature on market entry conflate market entry and market entry mode. In fact, Koch (2001) shows that both are party to the same decision making process. However, this chapter has separated both concepts (market entry and market entry mode). The rationale is that, if a decision is made not to enter export markets, then entry mode decision becomes irrelevant (Whitelock & Jobber, 2004). As such, it is critical to understand the market entry decision first. In this regard, it is imperative to state for the purpose of this chapter what is meant by market entry.

Market entry is defined as the preliminary screening of countries to identify prospective ones in which to introduce the company's product (Root, 1994). Entry mode on the other hand deals with the methods used to service the foreign market e.g., exporting, licensing, joint venture etc (Buckley & Ghauri, 1999; Rasheed, 2005). These definitions show a separation of market entry from entry mode as the latter comes after a suitable country is identified. This chapter is concerned with which market to enter rather than what mode is used to enter the market. The assumption here is that exporting is the entry mode of choice for the small firm (e.g., see Hatten, 1997; Autio et al., 2000; Philp, 1998 for the basis of this assumption).

It is argued in the extant literature that probably the most important decision in the internationalization process of the firm is that of market entry (Ellis, 2000). Despite this observation however, very little research exists regarding the process by which firms identify foreign markets[73]. For example, very few studies provide any systematic empirical analysis of the relative importance of the plethora of external factors which impact foreign market entry decision (Whitelock & Jobber, 2004). Moreover, most studies are focused on the large or multinational firms which are resource rich, with the aim of transferring those insights to the micro and small firm which are resource poor. Small firms it is argued, have very little slack resources to devote to international market research (Alon, 2004). As such, their approach in looking for export markets will be different from that of larger and multinational firms. Therefore, an understanding of the factors relevant for export market entry decision in these firms will require research that is focused specifically on these firms, rather than generalizing the findings from studies looking at larger and multinational firms (Whitelock & Jobber, 2004).

THE THEORETICAL FRAMEWORK

The theoretical arguments from the process models of internationalization will provide insights into understanding the processes involved in identifying where to start exporting after the decision is made to export a portion of the firm's sales abroad. This process is not as linear as some may think. For example, some firms go to international markets that are similar to their domestic market (incremental internationalization) while others are brave enough to enter markets that are less similar to home (rapid internationalization)[74].

[73] Some of the research in this area include Koch, 2001; Ellis, 2000; Aaby & Slater, 1989; Whitelock & Jobber 2004; Brouthers & Nakos, 2005

[74] For a full treatment of the concepts of rapid internationalization and incremental internationalization see Johanson & Vahlne, 1977, Rialp et al., 2005.

Understanding this process is at the heart of the research in the area of international entrepreneurship (see for example Oviatt, 2005; Rialp et al., 2005 for this point).

A number of studies try to understand the market entry decision process[75]. However, there is very little consensus as to how it actually happens. Some researchers interpret the process as rational and based on objective information gathered through systematic research (e.g., Brouthers & Nakos, 2005). Others see it as ad-hoc and defying the logic of the market (e.g., Ellis, 2000; Harris & Wheeler, 2005). Still, it appears that most of these studies lack external validity (Axin & Matthyssens, 2002; Li et al., 2004)[76].

From the extensive literature[77] on the firm's export behaviour, it appears that most scholars agree that the decision of where to start is done in a in a stepwise (incremental) manner rather than a radical one. Taking an epistemological interpretation, it seems that most researchers see entrepreneurs as boundedly rational (Andersen, 1995). That is, because of their limited capacity to understand complex issues, they take a gradual approach to grasping complex phenomena until they are understood fully.

This gradual acquisition of knowledge is central to the stage model of internationalization. Empirical studies also show that firms enter international markets gradually, and then allocate greater resources to these markets as more experience and understanding of the complex operations in these markets are gained (Johanson & Vahlne, 1977). This school of thought has gained traction since the work of Johanson & Wiedershiem- Paul, (1975). Since the mid 1970s, a number of models have been developed to capture the internationalization process of the firm, with the majority focusing on the export behaviour of the firm. There was strong consensus in the early 1970s and 1980s regarding the incremental view. However, the research of the 1990s deviated from such consensus (e.g., see Coviello & McAulley, 1999; Knight & Cavusgil, 1996; Oviatt & McDougal, 1994). The basic assumption on which the process models rest is that learning about foreign markets is what drives the firm's internationalization behaviour. Analysing these models will provide some insights to firms as to what factors are relevant to determine where to start their exporting activity.

Models of Internationalization

Internationalization process models have been labelled as either I-model or U-model (Andersen, 1993). The former identifies discrete stages of international expansion and compares them to innovation adoption (e.g., see Bilkey & Tesar, 1977; Reid, 1981; Cavusgil, 1980; Czinkota, 1982). The latter sees the international involvement of the firm in terms of a gradual and sequential expansion driven by the interplay between market commitment and market knowledge (Johanson & Wiedershiem-Paul, 1975; Johanson & Vahlne, 1977, 1990). The discussion below will focus on each categorization of the internationalization models.

[75] For example, see, Bilkey, 1978; Miesenbock, 1988; Johanson & Vahlne, 1977, 1990; Czinkota, 1982; Madsen & Servias, 1997 etc.

[76] External validity means that the findings can be generalized outside of the study sample. For a full understanding of this concept see Ghauri & GrØnhaug (2002).

[77] For excellent reviews of this literature see, Bilkey, 1978; Miesenbock, 1988; Leonidou & Katsikeas, 1996; Coviello & Jones, 2004.

U-Model of Internationalization

The U-model of internationalization refers to the gradual internationalization model developed by researchers at Uppsala in the 1970s. Early attempts to understand the stage process were carried out by Johanson & Wiedershiem-Paul, (1975). Later, Johanson & Vahlne, (1977) took the earlier work, refined it and added more theoretical substance[78]. The model by Johanson & Vahlne, (1977) became known as the model of Knowledge Development and Increasing Foreign Market Commitment. It argues that the firm's involvement in international business goes through a gradual systematic process (incremental steps) until it becomes fully committed (e.g., establishing production facilities abroad) to the foreign market. This incremental step it is argued; results from the lack of information and knowledge about foreign markets and the high level of uncertainty which results from this information handicap (Johanson & Vahlne, 1990). The model argues that with increased knowledge about foreign markets there will be increased commitment of resources, thus advancing the firm's internationalization process. Information regarding language, culture, and business procedures. help to distinguish between those firms that remain domestic and those that go international (Wiedershiem-Paul et al., 1978; Gumede, 2004). To capture this dynamic interplay of resource commitment, knowledge of the foreign market and the firm's internationalization behaviour, the Uppsala researchers proposed a model capturing the state and change nature of internationalization. Figure 5.1 illustrates this process.

The Basic Mechanism of Internationalization- State and Change Aspects

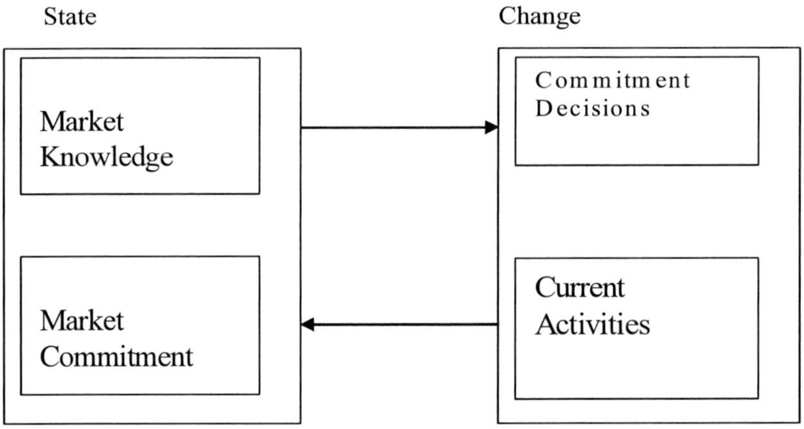

Adapted from Johanson, Jan & Vahlne, Jan- Erik.(1977), " The Internationalization Process of the Firm- A Model of Knowledge Development and Increasing Foreign Market Commitments", Journal Of International Business Studies, (pre-1986), 8,1 pp 23-32.

Figure 5.1. A schematization of the firm's internationalization process.

[78] The early model by Johanson & Wiedershiem-Paul (1975) was very descriptive and could not be used to explain observations outside of their sample. Further, there was not much link to previous knowledge from other discipline that could explain the phenomenon these researchers observed in their sample. This made their model theoretically weak.

Basically, the model argues that the present state of market knowledge and market commitment will help to determine the change phase of international involvement, that is, commitment of resources. The present state will impact the perceived opportunities and risk in international markets. It will influence future commitment decisions and the current level of international activities, which are aspects of the change phase of the internationalization process. Based on the present state of international involvement, future commitment of resources will be made to the current level of international activities, thus gradually increasing the firm's internationalization process until it becomes fully committed to the foreign market.

The commitment of resources will be made in incremental steps unless the firm has a large amount of resources and market conditions are stable and homogeneous. Firms will also avoid gradual commitment of resources if they have enough experience from other markets with similar characteristics. In other words, with increased knowledge and learning about foreign markets, there will be increased resource commitment and therefore, a greater level of international involvement by the firm. The interpretation here is that if a firm has a high stock of knowledge about foreign markets, it will not be expected to internationalize incrementally[79].

I-Model of Internationalization[80]

Since the early work at Uppsala, a number of other models have been put forward to capture the internationalization behaviour of the firm. These models see exporting as an innovation of the firm, thus they are labelled I-Models[81]. Also, some models have added more stages to the original four developed by the Uppsala researchers[82]. Others have also used three stages and, with different labels (e.g., Leonidou & Katsikeas, 1996; Mehran & Moini, 1999)[83].

The I-models, although all looking at exporting as an innovation of the firm have some peculiar differences in how they explain the process. The major differences become clear when they try to identify how the process begins. For example, Bilkey & Tesar, (1977) perceived the process as starting with firms lacking an interest in exporting then moving to become experienced exporter and moving to distant markets. On the other hand, Cavusgil, (1980), saw the firm as being interested in exporting from an early stage and making

---

[79]It must be stressed that this model was not developed to explain the internationalization behaviour of small, resource poor firms. Its applicability to explain small firms export entry is a by product of its analysis. Further, the same logic that follows internationalization (i.e. increasing foreign market involvement) is the same one that follows exporting (which in this study is a surrogate for internationalization). That is, firms will export a small amount of their sales abroad and with increased knowledge and learning about the export market; they will increase this amount gradually. This is the central assumption made by studies which use stage theory of internationalization to explain exporting.

[80] It is important to note that all the above models that explain the internationalization of the firm, are based on work from developed economies except for Wortzel and Wortzel, (1980), which looked at the process from a developing country perspective. Therefore, the implications for firms from developing countries are not clear, as the models are plagued with problems of generalizability (Fillis, 2001).

[81] For an example of these models see, Simmonds & Smith, 1968; Lee& Brasch, 1978; Moen & Servias, 2002; Samiee et al., 1993; Czinkota, 1982 etc.

[82] For the models with more than four stages see, Bilkey & Tesar, 1977; Cavusgil, 1980; Czinkota, 1982; Wortzel & Wortzel, 1980.

[83] For a content review of these models see,Leonidou & Katsikeas, 1996; Anderson, 1993.

preparations for export from inception until it becomes a committed exporter. However, a comparison with the U-model shows that Cavusgil, (1980) model concurs with those researchers on the starting point. They both see the firm as being interested in exporting from the outset.

A close analysis of the I-models reveals that there are “external push” and “internal pull” factors at play in getting the firm to determine where to start their exporting activity. Bilkey & Tesar, (1977) seemed to be suggesting that there are external push factors getting firms to determine where to export, while Cavusgil, (1980) appeared to be suggesting that there are “internal pull” factors which influence this process. This inconsistency in explaining early export behaviour however, casts doubt on the validity and reliability of the models (Anderson, 1993).

Underlying the process models is the concept of psychic distance. These models argue that because export markets are different from domestic markets, then they are psychically more distant. As a result, firms will have to gradually enter these markets in order to overcome the uncertainties involved. Indeed, if these models have any validity as a good predictor of the firm’s export behaviour then, there must be a relatively high importance placed on measures of psychic distance by firms when identifying where to start their exporting activities. That is, firms should first export to markets that are closer to home, psychically, then move their exports to more psychically distant markets as they gather sufficient information on foreign market operation.

Critique of the Models

Since the early discourse on stage models of internationalization, the world economy has evolved radically. The global economy has undergone various technological, legislative and economic changes (Axinn & Matthyssen, 2001). The reduction in transportation cost and time, the liberalization of economic space, improvements in communication technologies (reduction in information gap), have all resulted in firms internationalizing in greater numbers today, than before. As a result of these changes, it becomes salient to assess whether the process models of internationalization can provide practical guidance to firms regarding their international business behaviour. Certainly, now than ever before, firms are internationalizing in many different ways (Axin & Matthyssens, 2001), and importantly,small firms are taking a more prominent place in this new global economy (Knight & Cavusgil, 2004). Moreover, exporting is also taking on increased importance (Mertens, 2001). Small firms have become an integrated part of the international trading system and are using advanced entry modes (e.g., FDI, Joint Ventures) to enter foreign markets. This has raised questions about the ability of stage theory to practically explain their internationalization behaviour[84].

Stage models are also criticized for being too deterministic and lacking in external validity (e.g., see Axin & Matthyssens, 2001, Johanson & Vahlne, 1990). In other words, the models have an incremental process which each firm has to follow in entering foreign markets. The more serious problem however, seems to be that both types of models are very static in explaining the firm’s export behaviour. They do not show how firms move within

[84] For a critique on stage theory in this regard see, Knight & Cavusgil, 2004; Li et al., 2004; Oviatt & McDougall, 1994, 1997; Wolff & Pett, 2000.

each stage of the process; they only show movement across stages (Bilkey, 1978, Leonidou & Katsikeas, 1996). Recent work on small firms export behaviour shows that the behaviour is more dynamic than presented in the models (e.g., Cavusgil & Zou, 1994, Stlye, 1998; Johanson & Vahlne, 2003). The models were also developed within a particular environmental context therefore, their explanatory power is highly limited to the set of observed behaviour in the population or sample in that particular context. Actually, if the models should have any use in the current economic environment, they need to adopt a systems approach in explaining the firm's export behaviour rather than their existing linear approach (Johanson & Vahlne, 1990).

Further, the concept of psychic distance, a fundamental pillar of these models seems to be inadequate in explaining the rapid internationalization of the firm. Psychic distance implies that firms will enter foreign markets that are very similar to domestic markets when they first enter into exporting. As firms become more experienced in the international market the argument goes, they will then enter markets that are more distant (psychically) from their domestic market. However, in light of the new developments in the global economy (e.g., Internet, trade liberalization, e-commerce etc.) firms are observed initiatingexports to more psychically distant markets and are no longer following the gradual path described by stage theory (Moen & Servias. 2002). The rise in born globals and international new ventures show that rapid internationalization is indeed real and that the concept of psychic distance is in serious doubt, as a critical predictor of which foreign market firms will enter when they decided to start exporting.

It also appears that the concept of psychic distance is too narrowly defined. The definition uses national averages and does not take into account the idiosyncratic nature of the firm's perceived psychic distance between countries (Whitelock & Jobber, 2004). In other words, psychic distance is looked at only at the country level and not from the firm's perspective. Psychic distance is more than national culture. It has to do with issues such as language, cultural distance and structural distance such as legal and administrative differences in countries (O'Grady & Lane, 1996). The value of the psychic distance argument however, is that; it demonstrates that there is a definite link between the firm's perception of a foreign market and the decision to enter that market. Wiedersheim- Paul et al., (1978) argue that psychic distance do play a role whether negative or positive, in deciding which market to enter.

Also, most of the work on the process models used the manufacturing sector as the focus for their study[85]. However, given the increased importance of the service sector in international trade and the diverse international behaviour of firms in this sector (O'Farrel et al., 1998a); it raises questions about the generalizability of stage theory across sectors[86]. Use of the process model based on observation in the manufacturing sector to predict the internationalization behaviour of firms in the services sector can lead to erroneous conclusions. In the manufacturing sector, it is generally argued that internationalization behaviour follows the incremental path (Gankema et al., 2000). However, there is no such consensus in the service sector.

---

[85] For example, see this critique in Jones, 1999; Young et al., 2003; Bilkey, 1978; Leonidou & Katsikeas, 1996.

[86] It must be noted that, the same processes that are used to sell services (intangible products) in some cases cannot be used to sell merchandise (tangible products).

Despite the weaknesses in these models, with some refinements, they can provide a practical guide to help firms decide where to start their exporting activity once the decision to start exporting is taken. Clearly, an important area that needs to be incorporated in these models, for example, is the role of business and social networks. Networks are important for small firms' export behaviour and will play a critical role in determining where they export their goods and services once they have decided to start exporting.

The Role of Networks

Recently, researchers enquiring about export market entry have recognised that in practice, firms do not generally make market entry decision based on systematic research of objective information. Instead, they observe that firms enter foreign markets on an ad- hoc basis completely ignoring the optimization logic of the market (see, for example, Ellis, 2000; Harris & Wheeler, 2005). This occurs as some scholars argue, because of the interpersonal and business networks of which firms and entrepreneurs are a part[87]. For example, Johanson & Vahlne, (2003) argued that relationships can be used by resource poor firms to climb over country market barriers and enter their export market. Moreover, Ellis, (2000) found that knowledge of foreign market opportunities is commonly acquired via existing interpersonal links rather than systematic market research.

The traditional view of internationalization assumes that there is only one way of entering foreign markets and that is to overcome the barriers to entry. On the other hand, network models assume that there are many ways of entering foreign markets. In viewing foreign market entry as an exchange between the firm and its networks, writers of the social network persuasion view the relationship as being derived from various sources (e.g., Hinttu et al., 2004). The seller (exporter) can initiate the entry, the buyer can initiate the entry (e.g., through unsolicited order), a distributor can initiate entry etc. Also, entry can be initiated as a result of participation in trade fairs. This argument deviates from the deterministic view of normative models which argue that it is the seller who has to initiate market entry.

In the network models, foreign market entry is viewed as a function of the ongoing inter-organisational interactions between the firm and its networks. That is, foreign market opportunities are communicated to the firm through its relationship with its network partners. The network can be quite wide with firms entering into business relationship with an important customer and supplier firm, which in turn has relationships with other firms. Following this logic, all firms are a part of an unbounded business network (Johanson & Vahlne, 2003):therefore, what is most important is the strength and quality of the relationships in the network.

[87] See, for example, Ellis, 2000; Johanson & Vahlne, 2003; Hinttu et al., 2004; Ellis & Pecotich, 2001; Kingsley & Malecki, 2004; Harris & Wheeler, 2005 for a view point on this observation.

WHAT FACTORS ARE IMPORTANT FOR INITIAL MARKET ENTRY?

Koch, (2001) saw all factors which affect the firm's market entry decision as falling into three broad categories: a) Internal b) External and c) Mix between Internal and External[88]. Although Koch, (2001) conflated market entry with market entry modes, it is still noteworthy to mention those external factors that are found in that study to impact the decision as to which market to enter when starting export activities. These factors are: characteristics of the export market, market barriers, industry feasibility, popularity of the entry mode (e.g., exporting) in the particular market, market growth rate, image support requirement and global management efficiency requirements. Overall, this study reports ten (10) factors that are seen as relevant in influencing the decision regarding which export market to enter.

While Koch, (2001) conceptualization is helpful in identifying the factors that influence foreign market entry decision, it can be argued that this conceptualization is quite pedestrian. It is very general and does not give much insight (besides a general listing) into the factors that impact the decision regarding foreign market entry. Clearly, if a factor is not internal it can only be external.

In a quantitative exploratory study of industrial firms in the U.K. Whitelock & Jobber, (2004) tried to put some order to the multiplicity of external factors that impact the decision regarding which export market to enter. Using factor analysis, they analysed 33 variables derived from previous literature that are seen as important when deciding which export market to enter. The analysis revealed 10 conceptual groups in which these variables could be placed. These ten (10) groups bring some parsimony to analysing the large number of variables that impact the decision. The conceptual groups (factors) were labelled as: *geo-cultural/political similarity, developed economy, attractive market, cultural unity, common language, good market information, lack of experience marketing overseas, stable competitive environment, government attitude unsympathetic and need to follow major customers abroad*[89].

After deriving these factors, the authors went further to look at how they distinguish between the decision to enter or not to enter an export market. Using discriminant analysis, the results revealed that five of the ten factors are significant in determining entry in an export market. These are: developed economy, unsympathetic government attitude, geo-cultural/political similarity, attractive foreign market and good market information[90].

A number of other studies focusing on the firm's export behaviour have also analysed the impact of external factors on the decision regarding which export market to enter. Wiedersheim- Paul et al., (1978) looked at factors such as market opportunities, economic integration; Etgar & McConnel, (1976) considered factors such as location of the market, legal and political influences; and Yaprak, (1985) looked at factors such as tariffs and government bureaucracy. Contractor, (1984) in his empirical work on choosing between

---

[88] This chapter is concerned only with external factors that impact the decision as to where to start exporting. The assumption is that analysing the firm's absorptive capacity (see chapter 4) gives an indication of the internal factors that will determine where the firm starts exporting.

[89] Note that the factor government attitude unsympathetic implies an inverse relationship with entry decision. That is, if government attitude is unfriendly towards businesses, then, it would turn away firms from investing in that market.

[90] This study chose to use the concept of non-domestic market instead of export market. Both concepts however, are synonymous and as such do not impact the interpretation of the findings.

direct investment and licensing argued that both the environment of the host country and the industry in that country play key roles in the market entry decision. That study concluded that factors in the environment that are critical are: the country's indigenous technical capabilities, the level of economic development and government intervention and regulation. Indeed, a critical analysis of all these studies show that the variables identified can fall into the conceptual categorizations put forward by Whitelock & Jobber, (2004) or Koch, (2001).

The size, growth and demand capability of the export market are also seen as important factors that will impact the decision regarding which foreign market to enter. Terpstra & Yu, (1988) and Russow & O'Koroafu, (1996) found market size and growth to be critical in determining which export market to enter. The level of competition in the market is also seen as critical in determining entry. Goodnow & Hansz, (1972) suggested that the degree of competition from local manufacturers can have an impact on market entry. Studies on the export behaviour of the firm also found that firms move into international markets based on the movement of their competitor (Aharoni, 1966). This sort of herding effect was also observed by (Harris, 1997). It is argued that firms are obliged to follow their competitors abroad so as to maintain size and rate of growth.

Information availability is also an important variable that impacts the decision as to which export market firms enter after the decision is made to start exporting[91]. Erramilli, (1991) contended that firms will enter markets about which they have information compared to those which they have little or none. The latter markets are perceived as high with uncertainty and risk due to the lack of information. Information it is argued, is critical in the firm's decision to enter export markets because it prevents the firm from missing out on markets with great potential (Alon, 2004). Because of the critical role of information in driving the decision regarding which foreign market to enter, it is recommended that firms seek their own information rather than relying solely on information published by government bodies or other organisations (Leonidou et al., 2002; Williams & Chaston, 2004). Samiee et al., (1993) found that successful exporters rated personal and experiential information sources more highly than objective information that is, information from government bodies, multilateral institutions and so on.

Factors that capture the psychic distance concept are also seen as very important for firms when making the decision as to where to start exporting. For example, Coviello & McAulley, (1999) concluded that very rarely is there a discussion about export market entry without reference to stage theory. The concept is at the heart of stage models. It refers to the sum of the factors preventing the flow of information to and from the market. Examples of factors that capture this concept include: differences in language, education, business practices, culture and industrial development. Firms will generally enter export markets that are seen as similar on these items before they go to more distant markets. Inherent in this argument is the assumption that similar markets are easier to manage than more distant ones (O'Grady & Lane, 1996).

Researchers in the early 1970s and 1980s concurred that firms enter markets that are culturally similar first then move to ones that are more distant (e.g., see Bilkey & Tesar, 1977; Welch & Loustarinen, 1988). However, the 1990s saw a departure from this view. The

[91] See, for example, Johanson & Vahlne, 1990; Wiedersheim- Paul et al., 1978; Welch & Wiedershiem-Paul, 1980; Lamb & Liesch, 2002; Darling & Postnikoff, 1985; Demers, 2001 on the critical role of information in market entry decision.

international entrepreneurship literature strongly argues that firms do not necessarily enter markets that are psychically close before they enter more distant ones[92]. Indeed, this literature finds support for its thesis by analysing firms in high technology industries. These firms actually entered more distant markets on their first foray in international business before they entered psychically close markets. The criticism that this behaviour is only observed in high technology firms from developed countries was also refuted by evidence in the manufacturing sector and also other sectors from smaller countries which had rapid internationalization (e.g., see Crick, 2004; Madsen & Servias, 1997).

Summarily, the theoretical discussion and the empirical literature have provided some useful insights into the variables that are relevant for making the decision as to where to start exporting once the decision is made to carry out the activity. These factors will be tested in the Jamaican context to see which ones are relevant when micro and small firms in that geographical location decide where to start their exporting activity. Further, because it appears that almost all the variables identified can be classified under the themes developed by Whitelock & Jobber, (2004), their framework will serve as a good starting point for analysing the relative importance of various external factors that may impact the decision in the Jamaican context.

ASSESSING THE RELEVANT FACTORS IN THE JAMAICAN CONTEXT

After a careful review of the theoretical and empirical literature and a pilot study with small business owners in Jamaica, 17 external variables were identified as relevant in making the decision as to where to start exporting after the decision is made to get involved in the activity. This chapter aims to analyse the relative importance of these variables in order to determine whether the traditional framework of stage model is useful in predicting where micro and small firms in Jamaica should start their exporting activity.

To determine relative importance, the descriptive statistic of the mean is used. The mean is a straight forward calculation. It does not have the elegance of the more powerful multivariate technique of factor analysis however, it produces very robust results. Moreover, it is a very common technique in studies of this nature (e.g., see Leonidou, 1998, 1995a). The variables were rated on a Likert scale of 1-5 where 1 represents the least important and 5 represents the most important. The mean score is used to rank variables where ranks are proxies for level of importance in influencing market entry decision. The highest mean score gets a rank of 1 implying greatest influence while the lowest mean score gets the highest rank implying lowest influence. This type of ranking will give some idea to managers, researchers and policy makers as to the variables that are most relevant to small firms when choosing where to start their exporting activity.

To bring parsimony to the large number of variables which impact market entry decision, the chapter adopted a similar approach used by Leonidou, (2004) when analysing barriers in the exporting process. A suitable framework that can accommodate all variables was selected and used to reduce the large number of variables into conceptually meaningful groups. In this case, the framework developed by Whitelock & Jobber, (2004) was deemed most appropriate

---

[92] See for example Kinght & Cavusgil, 2004, 1996; Ellis, 2000; Oviatt & McDougall, 1994, 1997; Caviello & Munro, 1997 for a rebuttal to the psychic distance argument.

and is used to bring parsimony to the large number of variables identified. These variables were loaded along with their mean score onto the conceptual groups in the framework. The overall mean score for each conceptual group (factor) was then calculated in order to derive which factor most influences the decision. The factor with the highest mean score implies that it has the greatest influence on the decision regarding where to start exporting.

To further buttress the quantitative findings, a descriptive mini-case study is presented at the end of the chapter to provide a clear empirical illustration of the issues at the heart of this chapter. The case goes beyond market entry decision and look at other issues such as barriers hindering the firm's export development in the export market and also the future directions of the firm. Indeed, this mix of qualitative and quantitative analysis is common among small business researchers (Dimitratos, 2002).

THE MOST IMPORTANT FACTORS IN THE JAMAICAN CONTEXT

The extant theoretical and empirical literature shows a number of variables that influence the decision regarding where firms start their exporting activity. However, a comprehensive systematic empirical testing of the relative importance of these factors is very rare (Whitelock & Jobber, 2004) and, especially as they relate to the micro and small firms. This analysis is very useful as it will help to determine the effectiveness of one of the most cited frameworks (the stage models) when predicting where firms start their export activity. Table 5.1 highlights, in the context of Jamaica, those variables[93] that are relevant in the decision making process as to where micro and small firms start their exporting activity.

There are over 10 variables[94] which have mean scores above the mid point (3) on the Likert scale. This suggests that a relatively high degree of importance is being attached to these variables in making the decision regarding which export market to enter. The top five variables *(strong demand for product, freely convertible currency, growing market for the product, good transportation system, country industrialized)* found to be most important in this study are also considered in the extant literature to have the highest impact regarding which market to enter. However, because there are so many individual variables, in order to gain greater insights into their impact on the decision, they have to be organized into conceptually meaningful groups.

To gain parsimony from this comprehensive list of specific variables, the Whitelock & Jobber, (2004) framework was used. Each variable is attached to the conceptual group which Whitelock & Jobber, (2004) identified as most appropriate. The scores for all the variables under each group are added and then divided by the number of variables to provide the overall mean score for the factor. This is a very crude way of calculating the mean. However, for the purposes of this chapter, this technique appears to be sufficient (see for example

[93] Note that the variables looked at in this analysis are all external to the firm. At best, chapters 3 and 4 would have highlighted some internal variables that would be significant in this regard; therefore, they do not have to be repeated here. What we do not know however, are those external variables that impact on the decision. This is why this chapter focuses on them.

[94] We are using the concept of variables here, loosely. Because there are so many individual items that impact the decision but lack parsimony, we will have to group them into conceptually meaningful groups, to make sense of their impact. It is these groups that we will refer to as factors, as such each item that makes up the group is referred to as a variable.

Leonidou, 1995a for a similar conclusion). Table 5.2 summarizes the results from this analysis.

The analysis shows that the factors labelled attractive market and developed economy are the most significant in influencing the decision regarding where firms start their exporting activity. Geo-cultural/political similarity came third while, stable competitive environment and cultural unity are fourth and fifth respectively. In their analysis, Whitelock & Jobber, (2004) found that the factor labelled *developed economy* was most important in influencing the decision regarding which export market to enter. In this research, the factor labelled *attractive market* is most important in influencing which export market to enter[95].

Importantly, it appears that measures of psychic distance have very little impact on the decision as to where to start exporting. The factors labelled cultural unity and geo-cultural/political similarity received a low ranking among all the factors that influence the decision. These results seem to be suggesting that stage model is a weak predictor of export market entry for micro and small firms in Jamaica. The discussion below will try to shed some light on this observation.

Table 5.1. External variables that influence which export market small firms enter

Rank	Factors	Mean Score $\overline{X}$
1	Strong demand for product	4.07
2	Freely convertible currency	4.02
3	Growing market for the product	3.91
4	Good transportation system	3.59
5	Country Industrialized	3.36
6	No tariffs or quota	3.27
7	Similar culture	3.20
8	Population concentrated in easily identifiable area	3.11
9	High political stability	3.07
10	Geographically close to home	3.02
11	Competition in the market very low	2.93
12	Similar language	2.89
13	Similar system of government	2.75
14	Knew market personally	2.66
15	Pure chance	2.48
16	Population comes from one ethnic background	1.61
17	One major religion	1.32

Ranks are used as a proxy for level of importance. Lower numbers in the rank column imply higher importance while the highest implies the least importance.

95 Note that Whitelock and Jobber (2004) work was done on firms from a developed economy while this work is done on firms from a developing economy. This suggests that the nature of the enabling environment in the domestic economy may be a significant factor in determining where firms export their goods and service.

Table 5.2. External factors that influence market entry decision

Factor categorization	Mean score $\overline{X}$
Geo-cultural/ Political Similarity	**2.98**
Similar system of government	2.75
Similar culture	3.20
No tariffs or quota	3.27
Knew market personally	2.66
Geographically close to home	3.02
Developed Economy	**3.39**
Good transportation system	3.59
Country industrialized	3.36
Currency freely convertible	4.02
Similar language	2.89
High political stability	3.07
Attractive Market	**3.48**
Strong demand for product	4.07
Growing market	3.91
Pure chance	2.48
Cultural Unity	**2.01**
Population from one ethnic background	1.61
One major religion	1.32
Population concentrated in easily identifiable areas	3.11
Stable Competitive Environment	**2.93**
Competition in the market very low	2.93

Table 5.3. Country of initial exports

Country	Percentage	Number
U.S.A.	18.2	8
Europe (mainly U.K.)	9.1	4
Canada	2.3	1
Rest of the World	2.3	13
Other Caribbean	29.5	1
Exporting to more than one country	38.6	17
Total	**100**	**44**

DISCUSSION

The analysis of the relative importance of the comprehensive list of external variables that may influence where small firms start their exporting provided some useful insights into the main question (i.e. whether or not stage models are still useful predictors of where micro and small firms will start their exporting activity) which formed the focus of this chapter.

From the analysis, some conclusions were drawn regarding the usefulness of the traditional process theories in predicting where micro and small firms start their exporting activity.

Of all the variables that were analysed, the strength of the demand for the firm's product in the export market had the greatest impact in determining where firms start their exporting activity. The next most important variable is the ease with which the country's currency is convertible. Thirdly, the level of market growth for the firm's product followed by a good transportation system in the foreign market and the level of industrialization of the foreign market are in the top five most influential variables influencing the decision on where to start exporting. The high level of importance displayed by these variables in this study context is consistent with findings in other geographical context reported in the empirical literature on the subject[96].

The top five variables identified above seem to reflect the export market's potential. A country's market potential is considered in the wider literature of international business to be an important criterion when firms are assessing their foreign market entry strategy (Koch, 2001). Markets which possess characteristics such as limited government regulations, high end products and, demanding customers are rated as good entry targets. Indeed, these characteristics are consistent with the above results. For example, markets with limited government regulations tend to have currency that is freely convertible therefore making the location more attractive for foreign investments.

Five other variables were identified as having a medium level impact on the decision of where to start exporting. These variables include: no tariffs or quota; similar culture; population concentrated in easily identifiable area; high political stability and geographically close to home. The variables in this category show a mix of geo-cultural/political characteristics (Whitelock & Jobber, 2004). However, there are some results in this group that do not conform to theoretical expectations.

Geographical closeness is at the bottom of the ranking for variables that have a medium level of impact on the decision of where to start exporting. It is ranked at number 10. The theoretical expectation however is that this variable should have had a greater impact if indeed, stage models have any usefulness in predicting where firms will start their exporting activity. Stage theory predicts that firms will enter markets that are closer psychically and then move to more distant markets (e.g., see Welch & Loustranen, 1988, Johanson & Vahlne, 1977, 1990). One of the interpretations of this argument is that firms will enter markets that are geographically close (O'Grady & Lane, 1996). However, the findings in this analysis do not support this claim. Looking at the markets entered by Jamaican micro and small firms on their debut in exporting, the results show that almost thirty three percent (33%) or about one third of these firms entered markets that are psychically and geographically more distant from their domestic market. Table 5.6 indicates the country of initial exports for the firms.

The U.S.A. and Canada, although geographically close to the Caribbean, possess different political, regulatory, and business systems. This makes them psychically distant from the Caribbean. Europe and the Rest of the World are geographically far away from Jamaica. Culturally, there are also a lot of dissimilarities. This means that Jamaica should be

[96] For some of these results see, Koch, 2001; Whitelock & Jobber, 2004; Dimitratos, 2002; Gurau, 2002 etc.

psychically more distant from these markets. According to stage models, these should not be the first markets to enter for Jamaican firms, when starting their exporting activities[97].

The remaining seven variables were identified as having a relatively low impact on the firm's decision regarding where to start exporting. This category includes variables such as very low competition in the market, similar language, similar system of government, entrepreneur knew market personally, pure chance and, population comes from one ethnic background. These variables reflect the softer issues (but by no means least important) in international trade. In some research, they are found to be of little influence when determining which market to enter (e.g., Whitelock & Jobber, 2004). However, they become most problematic when carrying out business in the export market (Leonidou, 2004). This therefore calls for a reassessment of models which predict the firm's market entry but exclude them. Importantly, however, these factors are at the heart of the psychic distance concept thus making them relevant to the process theory of internationalization. The results however, suggest that they have the least impact on the decision of where to start exporting.

Has Stage Theory Predictions Held up in the Jamaican Context?

When the list of variables was analysed under the various conceptual themes put forward by Whitelock & Jobber, (2004), the conclusions regarding the usefulness of stage model in predicting where Jamaican small firms start exporting activity remained the same. The factor labelled *attractive market* was seen as most influential in making the decision regarding where to start exporting activity. This was followed by the factor labelled developed economy. Geo-cultural/political similarity was third. Competitive environment and cultural unity were fourth and fifth respectively.

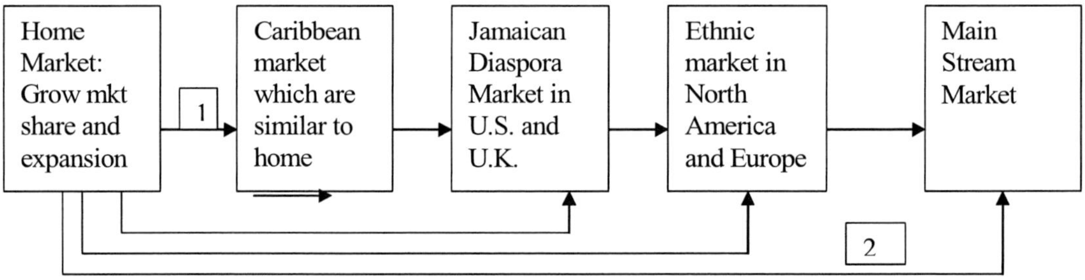

N.B. Path 1 signifies that some small firms take an incremental step to exporting. Path 2 on the other hand signifies that the other firms also take radical approach to exporting. What we haven't found is any firm that started international and then returned to home market. This indicates that "International New Ventures" may be absent in the manufacturing sector in Jamaica (Oviatt & McDougall, 1994)

Figure 5.2. The internationalization path of Jamaican small firms.

[97] Interestingly also, the theory predicts that older firms will have a larger portfolio of countries to which they export (McNaughton, 2003). However, an analysis of the data reveals otherwise. It is the younger firms which export to more than one country. These results appear to indicate that empirically the theory does not hold in this context.

The individual variables attached to the factor attractive market do not appear to have any relationship to psychic distance, a core pillar of the stage model. These variables appear to relate to the economical and behavioural perspectives on exporting. The interpretation here is that, when Jamaican small firms are making the decision regarding where to start their exporting activities, they focus more on economic factors, not geographical or cultural distance. This may not be a bad thing as it shows the entrepreneurial nature of the Jamaican firms. The entrepreneurship literature argues that entrepreneurs have no boundaries in seeking business opportunities and thus are not hindered by cultural or geographical distance (Covin & Slevin, 1991). The results here tend to support this hypothesis.

Stage models predict that firms will enter exporting in a stepwise manner. In other words, they would first go to markets that they are familiar with then, move to less familiar markets over time. However, the evidence from this research suggests that Jamaican small firms do not generally enter export markets in this step-wise manner as predicted by the stage model. The majority of Jamaican firms entered more than one market on their debut into exporting. Most of these markets are psychically distant in comparison to the Jamaican market, using the crude aggregate national definition of the concept. Further, implicit in this step-wise approach is that firms should enter familiar markets within the host country before going into main stream markets. For example, if Jamaican firms export to Great Britain, they should first export to the Jamaican Diaspora market in that country then move to main stream market over time. Incidentally, the experiences of Jamaican firms in the export market do not always identify with this process. Figure 5.2 captures the multiple path that Jamaican small firms take when they enter international markets.

There are two clear paths to internationalization. Path 1 is where the firm takes the incremental step as is predicted by the stage model while Path 2 is where the firm internationalizes rapidly. Importantly, the motivations for export initiation play a critical role in determining the path taken by these firms. For example, firms which enter exporting due to unsolicited order generally enter the mainstream market on debut. On the other hand, those firms which take a systematic planned approach to exporting generally take an incremental approach to entering mainstream markets. In some cases, because entrepreneurs are familiar with main stream markets in places such as the U.K. and U.S.A., although systematic planning is done, firms still enter mainstream markets first. This appears to be a function of the entrepreneur's network relationship (Harris & Wheeler, 2005).

The social and business networks of the entrepreneur have a lot of influence on which export market the firm actually enters (Ellis, 2000; Johanson & Vahlne, 2003). Entrepreneurs, who lived or worked outside the Caribbean before starting their own firm, are more radical in their approach on entering into international business. The firms with these types of entrepreneurs move directly into main stream markets in most cases. For example, those entrepreneurs who lived and worked in the U.S. and U.K. for long periods penetrated the main stream markets in these countries when they started their initial exporting. This occurred it seems, because they knew the business culture and had friends and business contacts there.

Another important prediction of the stage model relates to the entry mode strategy that firms employ when making the decision to start exporting. The theory argues that firms will use the least risky entry mode in their first attempt at international business and later move to riskier modes (Jones, 1999). The application to export entry mode is that, it is least risky to export directly whilst the most risky is to go through a distributor or a middleman

(Ramaseshan & Patton, 1994)[98]. An examination of the different modes used by the small firms to service the export market revealed that they used the riskiest means of entry, contrary to what the stage model predicts. Table 5.7 highlights the various modes by which these firms service their export market.

The most common export entry mode for these small firms is the use of a distributor. Indeed, of all the other methods available for export market entry, this method (exporting through a distributor) appears to be the most risky (Ramaseshan & Patton, 1994). Distributors will carry other competitors' product thus; small firms with a small volume of product may not get much attention from these distributors. Further, entrepreneurs' relationship with distributors can also make this mode very risky. For example, in Latin America, signing with a distributor is a long term business therefore; it becomes very difficult to get rid of poor performing distributors. This will no doubt impact the firm's success in the export market.

Table 5.4. Export entry modes for servicing foreign markets

Entry mode	Mean $\overline{X}$
Market directly to foreign distributors	3.95
Market directly to final users	2.50
Use of joint venture	2.32
Use of sales office	2.00

Conclusion

It appears that the predictions from stage theory of internationalization do not hold up well in the Jamaican context. The results show that micro and small firms in Jamaica tend to operate counter to what the theory predicts. For example, measures of psychic distance appear to be weak predictors of where micro and small firms in Jamaica will start their exporting activity. The results in this chapter, like most studies of the 1990s, have not found the overwhelming consensus that was reached in the early 1980s that firms enter the export market in a structured and incremental manner[99]. These findings have tremendous implications for the internationalization literature given that most studies looking at export market entry use the stage model as the main conceptual framework (Coviello & McAulley, 1999). Clearly, the findings suggest that no single model more so, the stage model, is sufficient to predict where firms start their exporting activities. Explanations from other

[98] In the internationalization literature, exporting is seen as one of the ways by which a firm can enter a foreign market. It is argued that it is the least risky of all other modes (e.g. Joint Venture, FDI etc.). However, since small businesses generally internationalize through exporting (Hatten, 1997), in this context, the mode by which the firm services the export market e.g. use of wholesaler, distributor, retailer etc. (Enet, 1977, Dudley, 1989) is seen as the entry strategy. Therefore, the predictions from stage theory regarding entry mode has to be analysed in this context and not the arms length approach to international business transactions.

[99] Importantly, it is noteworthy to mention that the results are not implying that measures of psychic distance are not important in influencing where Jamaican firms start their exporting activities. They simply imply that when the firm is deciding on which foreign market to enter, these are not the first factors to be considered. Of most importance to the Jamaican small firm in deciding which export market to enter are factors reflecting the economic conditions of those markets e.g. high demand for the product.

theoretical lens such as the network model should be used along with the stage model to predict where micro and small firms will start their exporting activity.

End of Chapter Case. Company Case- PBP Enterprise

PBP is a small manufacturing company in Jamaica. It was established over two decades ago by a chemical engineer. The firm employs 50 persons and had an annual turnover in 2003 of J$ 75M (US$ 1.25m).

The company manufactures and sells plastic bottles made from resin. In addition to producing plastic bottles, they also bottle and sell coconut water. The owner thought that since they were already making plastic bottles, it would only require them to get the coconut, so they seized that opportunity and started the coconut water business along with their plastic bottle making business.

The owner, a chemical engineer also speaks German quite fluently. This he attributes to his father's descendants, whose native language was German. He holds a B.Sc. in Chemistry from the University of Manchester and worked in the United Kingdom (U.K.) for a number of years before returning to Jamaica. His interest to start his own business came when he and one of his work colleagues in the U.K. saw a gap for their skill in the manufacturing sector in Jamaica. They decided to return home to fill that gap. This led to the establishment of PBP in 1983 as a limited liability company.

The Move into International Business

PBP first export order was initiated by the customer. The social network which the owner had while in England provided the impetus for this first order. He recalls that the customer wanted a low cost product (plastic bottles) but of a high quality. His former colleagues at his old job in England knew of his operation in Jamaica and directed the customer to PBP. The customer contacted the firm and took the first order in 1988. The owner welcomed this opportunity since the company was in need of hard currency to purchase inputs for the production of the bottles. The need to gain hard currency was the greatest motivator for PBP to fill the order. With continuous order coming from this customer, the owner confessed that he was comfortable with the export revenue and as such did not bother to look for new business in the export market.

Further Foreign Market Expansion

After the company lost its only foreign customer due to intense competition in the foreign market, the reality struck that the need for foreign exchange is still critical for the firm's survival. The firm is a heavy importer of raw material for its operations. This led to the owner to start seeking overseas business. However, market research proved to be very expensive. Therefore, the strategy used to get overseas business was to partner with supplier of raw materials (mainly resins). This relationship helped the firm to identify potential customers to whom it could sell its products. For example, the company that PBP supplies coconut water to, tells PBP of its other customers. PBP, then contacts these customers to sell them plastic bottles. This sort of networking enhances the firm's ability to win overseas business. Indeed, the owner states that it is through the network and the firm's reputation that they were able to build their export business.

Export Market Selection

In choosing the markets to enter, PBP's philosophy is: "where the customer is that's where the firm will go". This suggests that psychic distance is not the first thing that comes to mind when deciding where to start exporting. It is the demand for the firm's product in these markets that drives this decision.

However, factors such as ethnicity, cultural norms and the transportation system in the foreign market were stated as being of high importance as well. Culture is important because of the products the firm sells. Export markets with a high Jamaican population are important since they consume a lot of coconut water. Because the product is perishable, the transportation system of the destination country also becomes very critical in deciding which markets to enter.

Today, the company makes 10% of its revenue from exporting and exports its products to three markets (U.K., U.S. and Other Caribbean countries). The firm does not have a R&D department. It depends on the Scientific Research Council of Jamaica and JTI to provide it with such services.

Export Market Entry Mode

The company uses distributors to sell its products in the foreign market. It uses a direct or integrated channel of distribution, that is, the distribution network is owned by the company. This strategy the owner opines; is very useful for his firm as there is a lack of trust in using big businesses as distributors. He states clearly that his firm does not collaborate with big businesses because if they (big businesses) know the full potential of his line of business, due to their superior stock of resources, they will want to take it over.

With only 10% of revenue coming from exports and given that there is a growing demand for the firm's products, greater penetration of the export market is possible. However, PBP does not want to move too quickly into further expansion and thus lose control over its business operation.

Challenges Faced in Developing the Export Business

Indeed, exporting for PBP is not smooth sailing. It is tough business. The firm has encountered its share of problems. It is seen as being challenging because of the various barriers faced in the international business arena.

Security appears to be a major threat to the firm's export business. In one instance, hard drugs (e.g., Marijuana) were placed in one of the firm's cargo which resulted in it losing an important export contract. Because of the type of products which the firm exports, it is easy to stuff containers with drugs such as marijuana or cocaine. This vulnerability to illegal activities is a major threat as it will immediately wipe out any export contract which the firm has.

Another troubling sign for PBP is the volatility in the country's exchange rate. The firm is a heavy importer of raw material for its production process. When the exchange rate is unstable, it signals difficulty in planning and setting prices. For example, a depreciating currency means that exports will become cheaper but in the same breath, the price for imported goods will also be very high. Since the firm is a net importer, exchange rate depreciation will have an overall negative effect on the business. This situation sometimes results in the firm having to charge higher prices for it products in the export market thus, losing export orders to competitors on the basis of price.

Future Export Development

PBP thinks the need to grow the business is of utmost importance and exporting will play a significant role. The owner sees the Jamaican market as being very small and thus the need to have serious growth will demand that the firm look outside the domestic market.

To boost their export volume, PBP sees an expansion of the company's product line to include more ethnic products as being critical. They want to develop products such as ethnic alcoholic beverage, sports beverages etc. Future target market is ethnic markets in North America and the United Kingdom as these customers have been very loyal to the firm's product offering.

Conclusion

This case has shed some light on some of the main issues discussed in the body of the chapter. The demand for the firm's product is the most crucial factor in determining where it starts its exporting activities. More importantly, the case highlights the role of social network in determining where the firm exports its products. It also shows that barriers such as exchange rate instability are very critical in impacting the firm's ability to develop and sustain its export business. The fact that the owner sees exporting as being critical for the future growth of the company sends a good signal for future export growth and development.

Chapter 6

Getting Non-exporters to Start Exporting

Introduction

There are two main reasons for trying to understand exporting in micro and small firms. The first is to get those firms that are exporting to increase their export volume and, the second is to get those firms that are not exporting to start. A large body of the work on the export behaviour of the firm however, focuses only on the exporters. The rationale seems to be that; learning about obstacles exporters face will indicate why other firms do not export. This however, can be quite misleading. Understanding why non-exporters do not export from their own perspective is very important in order to reveal the true reasons behind non-exporting. However, very few studies have focused on the non-exporters[100]. An important contribution of this book therefore is the dedication of an entire chapter to non-exporters to better understand their plight in failing to become exporters. A key feature of the chapter is where it shows that non-exporters are not a homogenous group and therefore, the experiences of the different types of non-exporters are important in trying to understand their reasons for not exporting.

The remainder of the chapter will summarize as far as possible, the previous work that exists on non-exporters in trying to draw some theoretical insights on why they do not export. Following this summary, the chapter will provide some empirical insights into factors that non-exporters in the Jamaican context see as preventing them from becoming exporters. It will also highlight measures that need to be put in place to stimulate these firms to become exporters. The chapter, at the end will also highlight the plight of the different groups of non-exporters through the use of mini-case studies.

Previous Work on Non-exporters

Despite the extensive literature on the export behaviour of the firm[101], only a limited number pays specific attention to non-exporters when trying to understand why they respond

---

[100] Some of these studies include, Simpson & Kujawa, 1974; Johnston & Czinkota, 1982; Leonidou, 1995c etc.

[101] See, Bilkey, 1978; Miesenbock, 1988; Aaby & Slater, 1989; Leonidou & Katsikeas, 1996; Leonidou et al., 1998; Zou &Stan, 1998 for an update on this literature.

negatively to export stimuli and remain focused on their domestic market. For example, Leonidou et al., (1998) reviewed 46 studies looking at managers' influence on the firm's export behaviour and found that only one (1) study focused solely on non-exporters. The majority of studies which analyse the firm's export behaviour include non-exporters to the extent that there is a comparison between exporters and non-exporters based on some firm or managerial characteristics[102]. Despite these many analyses, only to a limited extent the comparison goes beyond firm and managerial characteristics to look at the subjective perception[103] of non-exporters regarding export stimuli[104]. Indeed, non-exporters' outlook on export stimuli is critical in order to fully understand why some firms choose to export while similar others remain focused on their domestic market.

While the majority of studies focus on the export behaviour of exporters[105] a few looked at non-exporters that have the potential to export but are not doing so (e.g., Wiedersheim-Paul et al., 1978; Leonidou 1995a, 1995c). The main aim was to understand from their perspective, the reasons for not exporting.

Reasons for Non-exporting

The type and quality of pre-export information and how it is disseminated seem to impact significantly on whether or not non-exporters respond positively to export stimuli. In a study of small and medium-sized enterprise in Detroit USA, Yaprak, (1985) found that non-exporters are not involved in exporting mainly because of a lack of information about foreign markets. The study also identified a number of other subjective factors which hinder the firm from being involved in exporting. Chief among them is the lack of foreign market contacts in identifying buyers for the firm's product. This factor however, speaks to the criticality of export market information in determining how firms respond to export stimuli. If firms have sufficient information about buyers in the export market, it appears that they will respond positively to export stimuli given that all other things are equal.

Small non-exporters, maybe due to their resource constraints, are very reactive in seeking information on customers in the export market. They do not carry out their own market research to find out about opportunities in the export market instead, they depend on secondary sources of information. Further, they are motivated to enter foreign markets when there is a ready buyer for their products (Yaprak, 1985). Because the cost of market research can be exorbitant (Vernon, 1966; Gumede, 2004), it may dissuade small non-exporters from gathering information about foreign markets unless they are guaranteed a buyer for their products. Although, in recent time, small firms have been using creative ways to overcome

---

102 Some examples of these studies include, Obben & Magagula, 2003; Hall & Tú, 2004; Westhead et al., 2001; Westhead, 1995; Crick & Chandaury, 1997; Burton & Schelmelgich, 1987; Ross, 1989; Daniels & Guyburo, 1976; Yaprak, 1985; Keng &Jiuan, 1989; Christensen et al., 1987 etc.

103 Subjective perception refers to the entrepreneur's personal feelings or prejudices towards exporting. The entrepreneur will attach different levels of importance to export stimuli based on the firm's idiosyncratic features and its overall vision. This therefore makes the degree of importance attached to these stimuli a very subjective issue when determining whether or not the firm enters into exporting.

104 Some of the studies that focus on this subjective perception include Keng & Jiuan, 1989; Yaprak, 1985; Christensen et al., 1987; Leonidou, 1995c.

105 See for example Uris & Czinkota, 1989; Calof & Vivers, 1995; Julian, 2003; Czinkota, 1982; Moen, 1999; Mehran & Moini,1999; Katsikeas & Piercy, 1993.

cost barriers; a number of small firms have established personal and business networks to enhance their ability to sell abroad (Ellis, 2000; Dana & Wright, 2004; Coviello & Munro, 1997).

Besides information inadequacy, other factors mentioned by small non-exporters as reasons for them not getting involved in exporting are: sufficient domestic market, not giving much thought to exporting, lack of personnel for the export operation and, products not marketable in the overseas market. A significant proportion of the sample in the Yaprak (1985) study reported that they felt the domestic market was adequate for their firm's survival and so there was no need to rush into exporting. Other studies outside of North-America also revealed that a positive outlook regarding demand in the domestic market is a critical factor influencing non-exporters' perception of export stimuli and their decision to remain focused on their domestic market (see Keng & Jiuan, 1989 for this study). It appears that non-exporters' optimistic view regarding their domestic market is a major factor influencing their negative perception of export stimuli and thus preventing them from getting involved in exporting.

In a Singaporean study by Keng & Jiuan, (1989) of non-exporters, twenty seven percent of the sampled firms suggest that they felt comfortable operating in the home market and as such are not rushing into exporting. The lack of marketability of the firm's products is considered to be the next most important reason for not exporting. A large number of entrepreneurs see their products as not marketable overseas; therefore, they do not think of exporting as a business option. The availability of information regarding the export market is considered the third most important factor. Entrepreneurs see a lack of contact in the export market as an important reason for not getting involved in exporting.

Other factors seen as critical in influencing the non-exporter to respond negatively to export stimuli are: lack of financing for the venture, difficulty in gaining market entry, insufficient operational resources (e.g., production machinery, human resource expertise etc.), lack of information about foreign market and, the need to have control over exports. The perception of difficulties in gaining market access seems to be derived from the non-exporters view that their products are of a low quality, their price is uncompetitive and the negative perception regarding government regulation and quotas (Keng & Jiuan, 1989).

From a developing country's perspective, Christensen et al., (1987) revealed that non-exporters did not get involved in exporting because of their pre-occupation with their domestic market. They also generally perceive their products to be of low quality and not marketable overseas (although this was not considered to be the most significant reason). Interestingly, the non-exporters in their study perceive exporting as less risky than the exporters. This perception however, we think, results from non-exporters not having been in the export market thus they do not know the level of risks involved. In other words, ignorance of exporting can be used to explain this perception.

Domestic market context may also play a role in determining how non-exporters respond to export stimuli. For example, the analysis of the literature reveals that the three most important reasons for Singaporean firms' non-engagement in export are different from those identified by American firms. For American firms, the number one reason for non-exporting is a lack of information regarding buyers in the export market, while for the Singaporean firms, the number one reason for non-exporting is the firm's positive view of their domestic market (i.e. domestic market is sufficient to serve their needs). The information on buyers in the export market is ranked as the third most important factor. This difference captures quite clearly the importance of context specific studies. Methodological differences are not the reason for the difference in findings since both studies used similar method (descriptive statistics e.g., frequency) to determine the relative importance of the factors identified as impacting their decision not to export. The sample size was also similar in both cases (Yaprak, 1985 had 40 non-exporters in his sample while Keng & Jiuan, 1989 had 44 non-exporters in their sample) and so could not be the reason for the difference in the findings.

Summarily, this scarce literature shows that non-exporters reject export stimuli and remained focused on their domestic market mainly as a result of a lack of information about export markets, the buyers in those markets and, their (the non-exporters) pre-occupation with their domestic market. These are not the only reasons but seem to be the most influential based on the interpretation of the extant literature. Non-exporters seem to be very passive and thus do not go out to aggressively seek foreign market information (Leonidu 1995c). This however appears to be a reflection of their positive outlook regarding the ability of their domestic market to satisfy business needs. Most domestic markets are becoming very competitive and so firms will have to seek customers in new markets. Therefore, non-exporters will have to be motivated to start exporting.

Motivating Non-exporters to Engage in Exporting

One would be inclined to perceive business decision as rational and objective. Therefore, getting involved in exporting would be considered a rational decision given the increasing integration of markets around the world. Researchers show that this decision is not always rational in the sense that normal business processes are followed[106]. The export venture may turn over a profit for the firm however, if this profit is not sufficient to offset the extra efforts that are put into the venture, the firm may choose not to get involved. To motivate non-exporters to start exporting, the venture must be seen as profitable enough to offset any extra efforts that they put into the process (Leonidou, 1995c). The literature suggests that finding successful exporters and reporting them in the press is one way in which non-exporters can be motivated to get engaged in exporting. This however, has to be done in the context where profitability is the major motivator for these non-exporters and the local market is insufficient to provide this motivation.

If non-exporters are motivated by the profit to be gained from exporting, then the cost involved in initiating the venture will become a critical factor in deciding whether to get involved. The fixed cost of exporting (e.g., shipping, negotiation, executive time, market search, product promotion etc.) can be overwhelming for small non-exporters, therefore dissuading them from taking on the activity (Hall &Tú, 2004, Mittelstaedt, 2003). To motivate these non-exporters therefore, it must be shown that the costs involved in starting the venture is not exorbitant and the revenue to be gained will outweigh the costs and make the venture profitable.

Further, Caughey & Chetty, (1994), in a study of New Zealand small firms, found that non-exporters are more likely to be motivated by forces external to their firms. Consistent with this finding, the literature points to motivating factors, which act as forces inducing the

---

[106] For a discussion on rational business process, see, Lee & Brasch, 1978; Aharoni, 1966; Harris &Wheeler, 2005; Ellis, 2000.

decision to enter exporting. Some of these motivating factors are: unsolicited order from foreign customers, communication between overseas customers and the entrepreneur, and fall off in sales in the local market (e.g., see Albaum & Peterson, 1984; Leonidou 1998; Simpson & Kujawa, 1974). These factors are consistent with those reported by current exporters as motivating their decision to enter into exporting (see, for example, Kaynak & Stevens, 1982; Ghauri & Kumar, 1989; Leonidou, 1995a).

Providing non-exporters with information regarding business opportunities in the export market will be an important factor to motivate them to become exporters. Small non-exporters devote very little attention to market research (Christensen et al., 1987) mainly due to their limited financial and human resources. However, lack of information on export market opportunities is seen as one of the major barriers inhibiting these firms from becoming exporters. Therefore, in order to motivate non-exporters to get involved in exporting, it will be critical that some programmes be put in place to provide them with market research information. The extant literature argues that non-exporters who seek pre-export information are the ones that are most likely to engage in exporting (e.g., see Wiedersheim-Paul et al., 1978). Helping these firms to gather export information will be a critical element in motivating them to become exporters.

What the discussion above shows is that a number of factors influence non-exporters to have a negative perception of export stimuli, and as such they do not engage in exporting. A number of researchers argue that it is this perception that matters most when making the final decision to sell abroad (e.g., Cavusgil et al., 1979; Cavusgil, 1984a; Shaw & Darroch, 2004 etc.). Further, the international literature points to a number of factors that prevent non-exporters from responding positively to export stimuli. However, the relative importance of these factors varies according to the domestic environment from which the firm operates. Therefore, it is important for country specific studies to be done to identify what factors are relevant in their geographical context.

Why do Micro and Small Firms in Jamaica Remain as Non-exporters?

To provide some insights into the above question, this chapter employed similar methods to those of previous work (e.g., Keng & Jiuan, 1989; Yaprak, 1985; Leonidou, 1995c etc). Descriptive statistics such as frequency, percentage and mean scores were used to analyse the relative importance of a number of subjective factors which influence non-exporters to remain focused on their domestic market. Further, mini-case studies found at the end of the chapter, are used as a powerful tool in providing empirical evidence on a number of the findings from the quantitative analysis and also reveal a better understanding of the issues under investigation. Researchers consider this to be a very powerful tool to use for analysis of this nature (see, for example, Broida, 2002).

Table 6.1. Reasons for remaining a non-exporter

Rank	Reasons	Mean $\overline{X}$
1	Home market adequate	3.68
2	Insufficient resources to win overseas business	3.65
2	Lack of financing for the venture	3.65
3	Lack of overseas contact	3.61
4	Foreign markets too competitive	3.48
5	Too much bureaucracy	3.42
6	Lack of personnel for export operation	3.32
7	Difficulty in doing business with overseas customers	3.10
8	Have not given much thought to exporting	3.06
9	Overseas technical requirements too high	2.97
9	Cost of winning overseas business too high	2.97
10	Lack of knowledge about foreign markets	2.90
11	Product not marketable overseas	2.84
12	Cost of looking for new business too high	2.74
13	Cannot maintain control over exports	2.48

Ranks are used as a proxy for level of importance. Lower numbers in the rank column imply higher level of importance while the highest number implies least importance.

Reason for Remaining a Non-exporter

After a careful analysis of the factors that the literature points to as normally preventing firms from entering into exporting, it was revealed that the most important factor is the perception that the home market is adequate to stimulate business growth and survival. This perception ranked number one (1) of the 15 reasons investigated. Table 6.1 highlights these results.

Completing the top five most important reasons (in order of importance) are: need for resources to win overseas business, lack of financing for the venture, lack of overseas contact, foreign markets too competitive and, the level of bureaucracy in the domestic market when selling overseas. The least important reason is the need to have control over the exporting business, a finding consistent with results from previous studies (e.g., Keng & Jiuan, 1989). The top five factors identified have also been cited by other researchers as major barriers to small firms' internationalization (e.g., Shaw & Darroch, 2004).

Although all the above reasons are important, the decision normally narrows down to one or two most important factors (Miesenbock, 1988). The analysis in the Jamaican context reveals that the most critical factor is the lack of financing for the exporting business. Table 6.2 summarizes the results from this analysis.

Table 6.2. Most important reason for remaining a non-exporter

Reason	Percentage
Lack of financing for the venture	25.8
Home market adequate	16.1
Have not given much thought to exporting	9.7
Insufficient resources to win overseas business	9.7
Foreign markets too competitive	6.5
Lack of overseas contact	6.5
Too much bureaucracy	6.5
Lack of knowledge about foreign market	6.5
Cost of winning overseas business too high	6.5
Product not marketable overseas	3.2
Overseas technical requirements too high	3.2
Total	**100**

The result suggests that resource availability is the most significant problem small firms in Jamaica face why they remain as non-exporters. Following closely behind the resource problem is what is termed the "mindset problem". Non-exporters have a very optimistic outlook regarding their domestic market's ability to ensure business growth and survival. This is the second most important reason small firms do not engage in exporting. These small firms it appears, are comfortable with their performance in their domestic market and therefore, do not see doing business abroad as being of immediate relevance. This finding is similar to the perception of Singaporean entrepreneurs regarding their domestic market (Keng & Jiuan, 1989).

An interesting insight from the data is that non-exporters are not a homogenous group. Within the non-exporter category, there are firms that have exported before and have withdrawn from the activity. These are labelled as *experienced non-exporters*. There are also those firms that have never exported and are not interested in exporting at all. These are labelled as *uninterested non-exporters*. Further, there are firms that have never exported but are interested in exporting in the very near future. These are labelled *international business seekers*. Indeed, the data show that the factors that prevent firms from becoming exporters differ among these groups. Table 6.3 highlights these results[107].

For international business seekers, the most significant reason for remaining a non-exporter is the lack of financing for the venture. Similarly, for un-interested non-exporters, the most significant reason for not exporting is their optimistic view of their domestic market. This indeed, reflects the very narrow mindset of these non-exporters and correctly captures their label as un-interested.

[107] There is no theoretical justification that comes to mind regarding these groupings however, for practical purposes, they will provide richer insights into the analysis (Cavusgil, 1984a). Because experienced non-exporters have already entered the export market, they are not used in this analysis to understand why they reject export stimuli.

Table 6.3. Reasons for non-exporting among different groups of non-exporters

Reasons	**Type of non-exporterS**				
	International Business Seekers (N=20)		Uninterested Non-exporters (N =11)		
	Rank	$\overline{X}$	Rank	$\overline{X}$	χ^2 Significance
Home market adequate	5	3.40	1	4.18	.47
Insufficient resources to win overseas business	3	3.80	6	3.36	.79
Lack of financing for the venture	1	3.95	8	3.09	.17
Lack of overseas contact	2	3.85	7	3.18	.53
Foreign markets too competitive	6	3.30	2	3.82	.06*
Too much bureaucracy	5	3.40	5	3.45	.81
Lack of personnel for export operation	4	3.60	10	2.82	.19
Difficulty in doing business with overseas customers	7	3.15	9	3.00	.97
Have not given much thought to exporting	10	2.80	4	3.55	.55
Overseas technical requirements too high	9	2.95	9	3.00	.47
Cost of winning overseas business too high	8	3.05	10	2.82	.08*
Lack of knowledge about foreign markets	8	3.05	11	2.64	.95
Product not marketable overseas	11	2.40	3	3.64	.22
Cost of looking for new business too high	9	2.95	12	2.36	.12
Cannot maintain control over exports	12	2.55	12	2.36	.58

Ranks are used as a proxy for level of importance. Lower numbers in the rank column imply higher level of importance while the highest number implies least importance.

* Statistically significant at the 10 % level.

Table 6.4. Factors that can stimulate non-exporters to become exporters

Rank	Factors	Mean $\overline{X}$
1	Profit to be gained from the venture	4.10
2	Low shipping cost	4.08
3	Increased communication between the firm's decision makers and overseas customers	4.02
4	Unsolicited order from abroad	3.71
5	Minimum demand on executive time	3.62
6	Increased management training of decision makers	3.47
7	Low packaging costs	3.42
8	Low insurance costs	3.40
9	Minimum demand on clerical staff time	2.81

Ranks are used as a proxy for level of importance. Lower numbers in the rank column imply higher level of importance while the highest number implies least importance.

What Can Stimulate Micro and Small Non-exporters in Jamaica to Become Exporters?

The non-exporters that are interested in exporting think that with the right stimuli, they can be motivated to become exporters. A number of factors that can motivate these firms to become exporters were analysed in this study. Table 6.4 highlights these results.

From the results, it appears that cost and profit are the most important factors that will motivate non-exporters to become exporters. If the profit to be gained from the activity is made clear and the cost of carrying out the activity is low, then it seems that these firms will be persuaded to become exporters. This finding is consistent with previous work by Leonidou, (1995c) on non-exporters in Cyprus, a small developing country with similar attributes to that of Jamaica[108].

Another group of non-exporters (experienced non-exporters), have received very little attention in the existing lliterature. This group of non-exporters can provide essential information regarding how firms build successful export business. generally does not receive a lot of attention in the extant literature. They have operated in the export market before but have withdrawn. It is therefore important to find out what led to this withdrawal and, whether or not there is a future for re-engagement.

The existing literature identifies a number of factors that can lead to a firm withdrawing from the export market (e.g., see Leonidou, 1995a, 1998; Wiedersheim-Paul et al., 1978). These factors were analysed in the Jamaican context to determine their level of importance in influencing Jamaican firms to make that decision. Table 6.5 captures these results.

The number one reason for withdrawal from the export market is the lack of resources to win business in the export market. Closely behind this factor is no repeat business from customers. Obstruction from foreign government is considered the least important reason for pulling from the export market. The increasing trend toward neo-liberal management of

[108] Cyprus is a small, open developing economy in Europe with a large export market (Greece) in close proximity. It also has agricultural and manufactured goods as major parts of its export offerings.

economic affairs have led to most governments practising a pro-business model of development therefore, it would be odd for them to be hostile to non-domestic firm's operating in their markets. As such, theoretically, this result meets expectation.

Table 6.5. Reasons for withdrawal from exporting

Rank	Reasons	Mean $\overline{X}$
1	Insufficient resources to look for new business	3.47
2	No repeat business from overseas customers	3.29
3	Required financial investments too high	3.06
4	Cost too high to look for new business	2.76
5	Ignorance of methods of doing business overseas	2.24
6	Obstruction from overseas government	2.18

Ranks are used as a proxy for level of importance. Lower numbers in the rank column imply higher level of importance while the highest number implies least importance.

DISCUSSION

The aim of this chapter was to provide insights from the non-exporters' perspective, on how they view exporting and why they are not involved in the activity. Besides the lack of absorptive capacity (which chapter 4 identified), very little is written about non-exporters subjective perception on exporting. This however, is very important as it can provide invaluable insights into how to motivate these firms to become exporters. Unlike chapter 3 which focused entirely on the views of exporters about exporting, this chapter has highlighted the views of the non-exporters themselves. The chapter provided a number of insights into the reasons for not exporting, how these firms can be motivated to become exporters and, why those that have exported before withdrew from the exporting business.

The analysis reveals that non-exporters perceive their lack of absorptive capacity to be a barrier to them becoming exporters. The general pattern shows that a lack of resources (e.g., lack of financing for the venture, lack of personnel for the activity, lack of information on overseas customers etc.) is the most important reason why these firms remain as non-exporters. Also, non-exporters view their product as not suitable for the export market and as such, are more preoccupied with their domestic market. For example, in one of the end of chapter cases, the entrepreneur clearly stated that his product is not for export and so he is more focused on growing his business in the domestic market because he thinks there is sufficient demand there for the product. Indeed, the optimism about the ability of the domestic market to provide growth for the business appeared to be a common theme among most non-exporters. This mindset resulted in a number of these firms not having an interest in exporting their product(s).

An interesting observation appeared from the analysis of these non-exporters' motivation for not becoming involved in the export trade. The idea that all non-exporters are the same and therefore the same incentives can be given to induce them to become exporters is a dangerous conclusion to reach. Non-exporters are not a homogenous group and, within the category of non-exporters, there are different perceptions on exporting. The analysis revealed that the three different types of non-exporters (*experienced non-exporters, uninterested non-exporters and international business seekers)* have different views on exporting albeit not statistically significant in most cases but differ in terms of relevance[109]. Two main factors are considered to differentiate significantly between uninterested non-exporters and the international business seekers regarding their reasons for remaining a non-exporter. These are: foreign markets too competitive and cost of winning overseas business too high. Those uninterested non-exporters see competitive export market as most important in rejecting export stimuli and remaining a non-exporter. Further, they see the cost of winning overseas business as least critical in them being a non-exporter. These results are in contrast to international business seekers and experienced non-exporters who see these factors as very important in deciding to remain non-exporters. The main lesson from this analysis is that it is not always prudent to make the assumption that non-exporters are a homogeneous group that will respond in the same way to export stimuli. Although they are all non-exporters, they have different reasons for not exporting therefore, in order to motivate them to export these reasons would have to be understood categorically (Leonidou, 1995a, 1995c).

To stimulate these non-exporters to become exporters, a number of factors were also identified. Consistent with findings from previous studies (e.g., Leonidou, 1995a, 1995c etc.), the profit to be gained from the venture is the most critical factor. This pattern was consistent across all categories of non-exporters. The only stimulus which discriminated against the various categories of non-exporters was increased communication between entrepreneurs and foreign customers. Both international business seekers and experienced non-exporters see this stimulus as being very important in determining their decision to remain a non-exporter while uninterested non-exporters see it as the least important factor. For example, in one of the end of chapter cases, the international business seekers lament the need for more information on foreign market buyers in order to stimulate their entry into the export market. This speaks to the important role of information in helping small firms to build and sustain their export business.

The reasons for firms' withdrawal from exporting are also not very well researched in the literature. To shed some light on this area, the group of non-exporters labelled experienced non-exporters was analysed separately. The analysis revealed that a lack of repeat business from customers in the export market is the single most important factor that resulted in these firms withdrawing from the export market. Insufficient resource to look for new business in the export market was the next most important factor.

This speaks to the reactive attitude that is common among non-exporters (Leonidou, 1995c). Non-exporters will have to understand that exporting is a tough business. They will have to learn to find creative ways to gain new business opportunities (both locally and internationally, as they will have to do so sooner than later) if they are to survive in an increasingly competitive market place. The strategy of dependence on customer loyalty is too fickle to provide any real competitive advantage in international or even local markets (Williams, 2007).

---

[109] When the chi-square tests of association was used to analyse the relationship between the firm's international business outlook and the reasons for non-exporting, statistically, only two factors were significant that is, they had p-value less than 0.05 (5%). However, in terms of ranking, the various groups reported different ranks in relation to the relative importance of the various factors that prevent exporting.

Conclusion

Besides insufficient absorptive capacity, non-exporters decided to remain focused on their domestic market for a number of other reasons. Some of these include but are not limited to a lack of information about foreign customers, a lack of personnel for exporting, a mindset that local market is not saturated enough . The level of importance that these reasons have in influencing the decision to remain a non-exporter varies based on the category that the non-exporter falls into. The analysis revealed that non-exporters are not a homogenous group and as such they were classified as three types a) *experienced non-exporters* b) *uninterested non-exporters and* c) *international business seekers).*

Non-exporters (especially the uninterested non-exporters) however, are not irredeemable in terms of their hope of becoming exporters. The analysis highlights a number of factors that can motivate them to become exporters. Chief among these factors is the reward for profit from exporting. It is important therefore that policy makers who are stimulating non-exporters to become exporters show them how they can make money from exporting[110].

This chapter has extended the empirical literature on non-exporters' perception about exporting. The lessons learned from the Jamaican cases can provide valuable insights to owners/managers of small non-exporting enterprises and export policymakers in other geographical jurisdictions on how to motivate non-exporters to become exporters. There is no doubt that firms in small, open economies will have to get engaged in the international market for the size of their domestic market is just too small to ensure any long term future survival of their enterprises. For the small firm, the best method is through exporting.

End of Chapter Cases

International Business Seekers

International business seekers are non-exporters that have a strong interest in exporting and are seeking opportunities to become exporters in the near future. The case below highlights one such firm. Before the case, some insights into the nature of international business seekers are given through their global profile.

Global Profile of International Business Seekers

From this group of firms, 25 percent of entrepreneurs hold a university degree compared to 35 percent for the overall study sample. The majority (45%) has secondary level education in relation to 35 percent for the study sample. Entrepreneurs are in the older age group category with over 40 percent having had more than 20 years work experience in a business environment before starting their own firm. A large percentage (75%) of these entrepreneurs had some previous work experience in an exporting company before starting their own firm. The majority of entrepreneurs are not proficient in a foreign language with only five percent being able to speak Spanish and French at a level which can help them to carry out business in those markets.

[110] See, Deschampsneufs (1984) for a good description of how to make money from exporting.

Generally, the firms in this category are quite young. Over 60 percent of the firms began operation in the 1980s. The majority of firms do not consider their product to be standardized. That is, if an order was to be made from an overseas customer, the firm would have to make major changes to its product before selling it in the export market. The majority of firms (75%) also see their product as the most likely alternative to their competitors' product therefore; they do not perceive the product to have any unique capabilities. There is also a feature of low technological capability and low quality product among these firms. Technological capability as measured by the amount of revenue spent on R&D revealed that 85 percent of the firms do not carry out such activity. Ninety percent (90%) of the firms also do not have any quality certification which is a measure of the quality of the firm's product. Firms in this category are mainly located in the agricultural sector (farming- fishing, tea and vegetables) accounting for 34 percent, 20 percent in garment manufacturing and 20 percent in furniture and fixtures a sub-sector of the manufacturing sector. The remaining 26 percent is spread across other activities in agriculture and manufacturing. These characteristics reflect the distribution of the sample.

Case- ILP

ILP is a small manufacturing company which produces and sells chemicals. The owner holds a bachelors degree in Chemistry. He has been operating in the business environment for 25 years and considers himself to be a visionary. Before starting his own firm, the entrepreneur worked in a major exporting company as Head of Department (HOD) which is a senior management position. He does not speak another language besides English, his native language and, he has never lived or worked in a foreign country before starting his own firm. Like most entrepreneurs, his major motivation for starting his own business is the freedom to do things his way and in the interim create wealth.

The firm started operation in 1996 with its major product being household chemicals. It produces and sells a range of household chemicals such as bleach, floor polish and other cleaning agents. In 2004 the company employed 42 employees and turned over J$ 110m (US$ 1.8m) in sales. Although the company does not have a direct R&D department or any quality certification, the entrepreneur thinks that its marketing strategy is what contributes to such strong performance in 2004.

The bulk of the customer base is from the low income segment of the population. Customers generally walk into the store with their own packaging container and purchase chemicals. The firm does not have to do packaging which is very costly thus it passes this saving on to customers in the form of lower price. This has resulted in their low price strategy. Although the company has a huge bulk of residential customers, they account for a small share of its total revenue. The bulk of the revenue comes from its business customers. The company sells large volumes of chemical to business customers in various parishes across the island who, then resell to local residential customers. This strategy has resulted in savings in terms of marketing expenses.

Since inception, the company has diversified its product offering from merely household chemicals to industrial sewage treatment chemicals. The company now produces chemicals for treating large sewage plants and swimming pools at hotels, guest houses etc. Using marketing jargon, the firm's products can be considered as fast moving consumer goods. This means that they are used by everyone everywhere in the world. Given the size of the Jamaican market and the level of competition that exists in the chemical business, there are serious threats to the firm's long term survival. However, given this reality, the firm remains committed to the domestic market.

Reasons for Non-exporting

The entrepreneur sees exporting as necessary if the firm is to grow and survive. However, the firm is not yet involved in the activity. The lack of information about foreign market operation and customers seem to be the most important reasons for it not being in exporting. Instead, the firm is busily concentrating its effort on growing in the domestic market. This emphasis on domestic growth is driven by a trip the entrepreneur made to a foreign country to seek export business. He recalls that he was asked by a buyer what percentage of the domestic market he serves. Due to the low market share he reported, the firm was not able to get the contract in the export market. The importers' rationale according to the entrepreneur; is that, if ILP cannot service a small local market, then it may be difficult for it to service a larger market. This experience has resulted in the firm refocusing its expansion strategy by focusing on expanding in the home market first so as to achieve a reasonable market share before moving into the export market.

ILP also sees the cost involved in exporting as a significant hindrance to getting involved in that line of business at present. Based on the nature of the firm's product, the cost of shipping and packaging becomes very important in influencing its entry into exporting. If these costs are not exorbitant, it will motivate the firm to get into exporting. Executive time is also another critical factor impacting the decision. The company is small with only 42 employees who are all managed by the owner. As a result, he sees any activity that will require serious dedication of his time as a non-alternative unless he gets a more formal business structure and delegate some responsibilities.

Another reason for the firm not considering exporting at present has to do with capacity and resource. The firm's present location is very small and does not allow it to produce the volume that will enable it to successfully service the export market. To gain this volume, it will require the firm to get a bigger working area and also more modern equipment. This expansion will also require extra financial capital. However, financing is not the most significant problem as the firm's relationship with its suppliers allows it some leverage in managing its working capital. This therefore allows it an opportunity to find extra capital for expansion purposes.

Future Prospects for ILP

ILP is positioning itself to take advantage of the many opportunities which lie ahead. Within the Caribbean, with the CSME coming into being, the owner opines that there will be tremendous opportunities to expand in other Caribbean markets. Given the firm's product offering and the level of per capita income in the Caribbean, the owner thinks he can take advantage of the low income market that exists in most of the other Caribbean Islands. As such, the firm is now making preparations to start exporting in the next 3-5 years.

Besides expansion in the domestic market, the owner is in serious dialogue with the Export/Import Bank (Ex-IM Bank) regarding assistance for entry into exporting. He is also in dialogue with quality agencies such as the SRCJ to provide assistance for improving product quality to export market standards. There is also dialogue with the country's marketing agency JTI in terms of getting customers abroad and added information about the export market.

For ILP, initial export market entry is aimed at the Haitian market where the majority of the population is poor and thus would have a high demand for its products. The firm wants to use the Haitian market as its launch pad into international business and as such is working assiduously to get into that market in the near future. The entrepreneur however, seems very concerned about the level of violence in that market and the unethical business practices which are reported by other firms in that market.

Conclusion

The firm seems cognisant of the need for exporting and as such is making the preparations to do so. The entrepreneur seems to have a grasp of the challenges which lie ahead for his line of business and is thus making necessary preparations from now to cushion these effects. It remains a non-exporter due to a lack of information about foreign market customers and limited resources in terms of space and equipment. However, it is making efforts to overcome these barriers and enter the export market in the near future. This is indeed a trait of an international business seeker.

Uninterested Non-exporters

These are firms that do not show an interest in exporting. They are solely pre-occupied with growing business in their domestic market. Before the company case, a global profile of these firms will be presented in order to give some insights into the nature of these firms.

Global Profile of Uninterested Non-exporters

From the total sample of non-exporters, 11 firms were considered as uninterested non-exporters. The majority (46%) of entrepreneurs in this group have vocational training as their highest educational qualification. Only a mere 18 percent hold a university degree. These entrepreneurs are generally young, with over 63 percent having below 20 years of work experience in a business environment. Ninety percent (90%) of them do not speak another language besides English, their native language. Only a limited number (9%) have ever worked in the export sector at a senior management position.

Generally, firms are located in the agricultural sector (54%) with the next most frequent activity (18% of firms) being manufacturing specifically, chemical and rubber. The majority (54%) of firms started in the 1980s. Over 50 percent of firms consider their product to be the most likely alternative to their competitor suggesting they do not have a unique product. Seventy two percent (72%) of these firms do not have a department dedicated to R&D. Also, over ninety percent (90%) of the firms do not have quality accreditation, indicating that they have a low quality product based on exporting standard.

Case- FGB

FGB is a small firm in the agricultural sector specializing in cut flowers such as heliconias, anthuriums and birds of paradise. The entrepreneur has over 30 years of business experience. Besides English, his native language, he is able to communicate in Spanish as well. He has never lived or worked abroad before starting his own firm. His highest educational qualification is a high school certificate. However, he has some experience in the export sector as a result of his work as a supervisor in a major exporting company before starting his own firm.

FGB started in 1978 as a sole proprietorship and presently employs nine (9) full time employees. The company's main product is cut flowers. It grows various types of flowers and packages them in baskets for gifts, wreath and sells to the domestic market. The entrepreneur considers his product to be unique. This perception is driven by the tropical nature of the flowers and also the methods which are used to grow and store them after harvesting. FGB grows its flowers in areas that are not highly saturated with water and where flooding is not a problem. This is because excess water will reduce production yields and provides the right conditions for diseases to thrive. Most of the firms' flowers are grown in a housing environment to ensure plants are not exposed to excess water from rainfall and farmers have control over irrigation. FGB recycles its water continually, with some treatment, to ensure higher yield for its plants. This strategy also helps to reduce the cost of water, a significant cost in the growing of cut flowers.

The entrepreneur thinks his methods of growing flowers produces better yield and higher quality plants therefore, making his product unique relative to his competitors. In addition, FGB uses only organic fertilizer, thus increasing the longevity of the products. When chemical fertilizers are used, they sometimes burn the plants and also destroy the nutrients in the soil resulting in stunted growth. The firm also carries out proper post harvest management through cold storage and the use of high quality packaging material.

The company does not have a formal R&D department and so no budget is in place for this activity. The entrepreneur however points out that he carries out his own R&D by keeping up to date with the readings from the industry. This ensures that he is aware of diseases which impact the industry and also the most current planting and harvesting techniques. Although the firm does not have quality accreditation, there is the perception that its product is of a high quality. Repeat business and the methods and techniques used to grow and preserve the plants are evidence used to justify this claim. Interestingly, although the firm's product is perceived to be of high quality, exploiting this advantage in international market through exporting is not seen as important by the entrepreneur.

Reasons for Non-exporting

"My product is not for export", is the first response that the entrepreneur gave when asked about reasons for not getting involved in the exporting business. The entrepreneur thinks that although his product is of a high quality, no one in the export market would be willing to buy cut flowers from Jamaica. When prodded to find out why the perception that the firm's product is not marketable overseas, it was revealed that there is no serious scientific evidence to support the claim. The entrepreneur remarks that he does not think that anybody overseas would want to buy cut flowers from Jamaica since they can get it cheaply in their home market. Further, the entrepreneur seems not to be aware of the potential for cut flower exports on the world market. He was not even aware that Jamaican cut flower exporters sell to export markets such as Lebanon and Saudi Arabia. The view that is expressed by this entrepreneur is that those firms that enter the export market have "big connections" which allow them to get ready buyers for their products. In other words, the assumption is that business and social networks are the drivers for selling cut flowers in the export market. He does not see this as proactive business but what he calls "network selling". Further, because of his limited networks, he just does not give any thought to exporting his product abroad.

The domestic market mindset was also very evident in FGB's case. The entrepreneur is very optimistic about the potential of the domestic market in meeting the firm's goals for growth and profitability. Comments such as "satisfaction with returns from the local market", and "local market not yet saturated" show that he is indeed, very happy operating domestically.

Future Directions for FGB

FGB does not see exporting as vital for the future survival of the business. Instead, it is concerned with expanding services in the domestic market. In this regard, the firm is planning to develop more attractive offerings for domestic customers and also diversifying into other areas of agriculture. Giving domestic customers more choice is a high priority. For example, when customers buy a basket of cut flowers, they can compliment it with fruits such as: oranges and mangoes. This sort of packaging, FGB thinks will improve its competitive edge locally.

The company also sees expanding its outlets into other parishes outside of the Kingston metropolitan region as a future plan. Having shops in some of the main plazas in the town centres of most parishes and servicing these shops from its own farm in Kingston is of priority for FGB, not exporting. The entrepreneur thinks that these plans are more realistic than trying to sell to the export market where he will possibly have to spend a lot of money to get into and, is not guaranteed any buyers for his product.

Conclusion

FGB does not see any future for exporting. The pre-occupation with the domestic market and the entrepreneur's limited information set about export market opportunities are some of the driving factors. To stimulate a firm such as FGB to become an exporter, the entrepreneur's mindset about exporting will definitely have to be changed. Increasing his information set about export market opportunities through trade fairs, export marketing conference must be high on the agenda of any policy initiative aimed at stimulating this firm to initiate exporting.

Experienced Non-exporters

These are non-exporters who have carried out exporting before but have withdrawn from the activity. They will provide a good source of information on some of the mistakes that other firms should avoid in order to be successful in the export business. Before the case, a global profile of the non-exporters is given below.

Global Profile of Experienced Non-exporters

There are 17 firms of the 48 non-exporters that are classified as experienced non-exporters. Among the non-exporters, this category had the most highly academically qualified entrepreneurs. Approximately fifty nine percent (59%) of entrepreneurs hold a university degree compared to thirty five percent (35%) for the entire study sample. The majority of entrepreneurs could be considered as part of the older generation of entrepreneurs. Fifty two percent (52%) have more than 20 years of business experience. Eighty two percent (82%) of entrepreneurs have also worked in a company that operates in the export sector before starting their own firm. The majority of entrepreneurs in this category do not speak any other language besides their native language, English. Of those who speak a foreign language, fifty eight percent (58%) speak German.

Most of the firms in this category started in the 1980s with over forty percent (40%) starting between 1980 and 2004. The majority (88%) does not have quality accreditation. Most of these firms are also not technologically oriented, with seventy one percent (71%) not having a research and development department or any spending on R&D. The majority however, considers their product to be standardized i.e. no major changes will have to be made if they were to fill an order from an overseas customer immediately. The firms in this category generally belong to the agricultural sector (29.4%) with printing and publishing (17.6%) in the manufacturing sector being the next most popular activity.

Case-ACS

ACS is a small, garment manufacturing firm specializing in school uniforms, office uniforms and individual custom made clothing. The entrepreneur, having achieved a diploma in entrepreneurship, decided to start her own business in order to have personal management of her time and to put her theoretical knowledge into practice. Though working in the business environment for over 24 years, she has never lived or worked outside her home country. She does not speak any other language besides English, her native language. Although working in the business environment for almost a quarter of a century, she has never worked in an organisation that is engaged in exporting.

The firm started operation in 1980 as a sole proprietorship. In 2004 it employed five full time employees and two on a temporary basis. With this staff complement, it turned over J$8m (US$ 133,333) in sales in 2004. The company's core product since its inception has not changed. It continues to manufacture uniforms for schools and suits for business executives.

The entrepreneur attributes the strong financial performance of the company to the increased demand from the local market and the company's customer service. There is a strong perception that the local market is not yet saturated and as such, there is still great potential for the company to increase its revenue. The company also tries to have a good personal relationship with its customers in order to encourage repeat business and also new business through recommendation from existing customers. Personal data on each customer such as their birthday is kept. The entrepreneur sends birthday cards to them and sometimes a phone call is also made. This personal marketing strategy helps the firm to be competitive in what is considered by the entrepreneur to be a highly competitive market place.

The firm does not have a department dedicated to Research & Development. However, it carries out this activity informally and sets aside one percent of its revenue for this purpose. It gets information on market trends by visiting fashion shows, surfing the internet, subscribing to magazines and eye shopping at "name brand" stores. The entrepreneur also credits feedback from the firm's customers as a major tool for coming up with new designs and the latest trends in the industry.

Unlike the other non-exporters, ACS has operated in the export market before but has now withdrawn from the activity. There are a number of factors that motivated this decision. This experience however, seems to have helped ACS to think more strategically about the future of the business.

Withdrawal from Exporting

In the early 1990s, ACS exported (uniforms) to markets in other Caribbean countries (mainly Barbados and Antigua). The firm has since withdrawn from this activity mainly due to the high cost involved in carrying out the task. The high cost of looking for new business in those markets pushed ACS to concentrate more on its operation in the local market. The firm lost its major customers in the export market and so had to find new customers in order to survive. It started carrying out market research to find new customers but recognised that for serious and diligent research, the cost would be exorbitant. This became prohibitive for ACS therefore it decided not to continue with the export side of the business. The entrepreneur also thinks that because her firm did not form the right networks while operating in the export market, it has increased the cost of gaining new customers. Having a strong network she thinks, would possibly give ACS additional jobs, so when the first set of customers left, there would still be a market for ACS in the export market.

Besides the high cost of looking for new business, ACS's decision to withdraw from the export market was made easier because of the entrepreneur's perception of the domestic market. From her interpretation, the domestic market is not yet saturated although very competitive, and therefore, the firm can remain local and still meet its goals. The entrepreneur thinks that ACS is operating below capacity. This was also evident from the machines and other equipment lying idle during the interview for this case. The entrepreneur thinks that although the market is competitive, there is still an untapped market for her line of business and therefore, she can fill this gap if the idle capacity can be converted to productive use.

Future Directions for ACS

Although exporting is not at the forefront of the firm's strategic direction, there are indications that it will return to the market in the future. The entrepreneur thinks that exporting will become relevant once the "comfort zone" in the local market is disrupted. Because the firm is doing well financially in the local market, there is no great desire to move overseas at present. However, the advent of the CSME will mean greater competition and so the market will become saturated forcing us to look outside of Jamaica to survive, the entrepreneur stated. In the meantime, the firm is positioning itself locally to take advantage of the benefits that will be derived from the regional trade agreement.

Importantly, ACS believes that having a reasonably large share of the local market is critical before servicing the export market. The firm is planning on expanding into other parishes throughout the country (it currently operates in the Kingston metropolitan region) and improving staff training and customer service delivery. According to the owner, staff training is vital if the firm is to get back into exporting and be successful. Training is seen as a tool to increase the firm's chance of getting better jobs in the export market through improved business and social networks. These networks will result in a reduction in the cost of search for new businesses. Highly qualified staff will better help in the firm's decision making and also increase the firm's attractiveness to customers through better service delivery. Improved qualification means broader horizons and therefore, more creative thinking.

Conclusion

The lack of repeat business seems to be the major reason for ACS exiting the export market. Again, this speaks to small firms' heavy dependence on customer loyalty to remain in export markets. However, what seems to be even more significant was the lack of financial resources to seek the new business. This is a very critical factor that can prevent small, resource poor firms from getting into exporting.

The entrepreneur at ACS seems to have a reasonably good understanding of the global challenges which her firm will face and as such is not totally oblivious of the need for exporting in order to gain new customers. Now that the firm is doing well financially, this should be sufficient motivation for the entrepreneur to reinvest in the business so as to have adequate resources to take on exporting in the future. The firm should learn from the mistakes it made in its first attempt at exporting and use these lessons as learning experiences in making its second attempt to enter into exporting.

Chapter 7

RESEARCH SUMMARY AND IMPLICATIONS

INTRODUCTION

It is conclusive that micro and small enterprises collectively, have a significant impact on all economies. Economies all over the world have reported that small enterprises have a significant impact on employment generation in these economies. In Jamaica for example, it is reported that about sixty percent (60%) of the employed labour force work in enterprises that have fewer than ten (10) workers[111]. Further, a recent study done in Canada which looked at firms that operated continuously between 1993-2003 showed that of all the firms, micro firms (those with less than 100 employees) contributed 77.3% of all the jobs that were created during this period[112]. These statistics show that the survival of micro and small enterprises is critical for the economic and social stability of all economies. In a globalized world economy, this survival rests on the successful operations of these enterprises in international markets. This is especially true for those enterprises that are from small, open developing economies. As chapter 1 of this book highlights, the markets in these economies are too small to facilitate the long term growth of these enterprises. The long term survival of these enterprises will require continuous upgrading of technology and the renewal of internationally competitive production, both of which will require firms to realize economies of scale and scope. Given the small size of these markets, this can only occur through exports. Firms will begin to increase in size as they begin to expand their exports which will eventually lead to economies of scale.

The arguments presented in this book aim to help government policymakers and entrepreneurs who manage small firms, especially firms from small, open economies to design effective strategies to better assist these firms to integrate into the global economy[113].

---

[111] See, Anderson, (2001) for statistics on the labour market in Jamaica in the 1990s. The PIOJ flagship publication, Economic and Social Survey Jamaica (2004) also reports this statistic.

[112] See, Halabisky, D. (2007) *Growth Firms Project: Key Findings from Phase IV, Firm Survival and Job Creation by Firm Age*, Industry Canada. Website: http://www.ic.gc.ca/epic/site/sbrp-rppe.nsf/en/rd02102e.html accessed July, 25 2008.

[113] The managers in these firms need to be able to mobilize the right resources to improve the firm's absorptive capacity while the government policy makers need to ensure that the enabling external environment is sophisticated enough to supply the firm with the necessary resources to compete internationally. This will

The strategies and policies should aim to facilitate non-exporters to become exporters and current exporters to increase the volume and variety of their exports. The SOR model presented in chapter 2 serves as a very important tool for policymakers and managers to use in assessing the readiness of their firms for exports. The export model will provide managers and policy makers with insights into what needs to be done in order to improve the firm's ability to become an exporter and, or expand its export capacity.

The next section of the chapter will present a summary of the research in this volume. Here, the main research questions investigated and the conclusions from these investigations will be highlighted. Following this discussion, the chapter examines the implications of the findings for managers in small firms, export policymakers, especially those concerned with stimulating more small firms to become exporters and, researchers interested in this stream of work. The chapter will end with some conclusions on the subject of study.

RESEARCH SUMMARY

The aim of the research presented in this book was to understand why, of the population of micro and small firms, some chose to sell a portion of their sales abroad while similar others, facing like market conditions, remained focused on their domestic market. This is a problem that the literature on the internationalization of the firm, the export behaviour of the firm and, international entrepreneurship has been grappling with over many decades[114]. Despite the progress that has been made in improving our understanding of this problem, our knowledge of why and how small firms internationalize is still limited (Westhead, 2005). This is particularly true in relation to small firms from small, developing economies where socio-economic context is different from the developed economies in North-America and Europe. Indeed, other researchers have stated that our understanding of this critical issue in the developing world is quite limited (e.g., see Oviatt, 2005; Leonidou, 1995a, 1998). The work presented in this volume extends the empirical literature in the field by focusing on a geographical context that has received little or no attention in the extant literature. This is important for theoreticians in the field as it will help them to better advance the development of a general theory on the export behaviour of micro and small firms (see Fillis, 2001; Leonidou, 2004; Oviatt, 2005 for this insight).

The major thrust of the research reported in this volume rests on empirically validating the integrative conceptual model (the SOR model) articulated in chapter 2 of the book. There is a great need to have an integrative model of this nature, because, the piecemeal manner in which most of the previous works were carried out, produced fragmented findings and, lacked a sound theoretical base for grounding their arguments (see,for example, Zahra et al., 2004; Dhanaraj & Beamish, 2003 for this critique of previous work).

For example, some researchers argue that there are several hundreds of independent variables and several dozens of indicators measuring export performance of the firm (Zou & Stan, 1998). However, most of the previous studies investigate only a limited number of

include the supply of an educated workforce, proper infrastructure and macro stability i.e. economic, social, regulatory etc.

[114] See, for example, O'Farrel et al., 1998a, 1998b; Majocchi & Zucchella, 2003; Westhead, 2005; Oviatt & McDougall, 2005, 1994; Coviello & Jones, 2004; Jones & Coviello, 2005; Dimitratos & Jones, 2005; Rialp et al., 2005 for evidence of this claim.

variables that relate to the firm's export performance. For example, Williams & Chatson, (2004) focused on the impact of language on export performance, Obben & Magagula, (2003) focused on language and education, Andersson et al., (2004) focused on age, size, industry environment, Leonidou, (1998) focused on stimuli inducing the export decision, Ellis & Pecotich, (2001) focused on the role of social networks, and Westhead et al., (2001) focused on human capital resources such as: professional experience of the entrepreneur. As such, a theoretically rigorous but parsimonious model of the firm's export behaviour is not well defined (Dhanaraj & Beamish, 2003). This book has attempted to fill this gap by providing such a model.

The SOR model in chapter 2 has applied the resource–based theory along with other theoretical insights from international business, strategy and economics as the guiding framework for grounding its arguments on exporting in the small firm. Indeed, this provides a strong theoretical base for the model. In addition, the resource-based theory is very helpful in the geographical context in which the study was done because; it allowed us to identify resources that are important in the context of developing countries versus those from developed countries. The resource stock in the developed world is different (both in terms of quantity and quality) from that of the developing world (Chan, 2005), and so will play a major role in moderating which firms become exporters. For example, literacy level in the developed world is higher compared to the developing world where universal access to basic schooling such as the primary level is not always available (World Bank, 2000). In fact, the resource stock in external environment will impact the quality and quantity of internal resources which the firm possesses and therefore impact on its absorptive capacity to respond to export stimuli (Vante, 1995). Certainly, this model can provide a basis for future research on the subject in the developing world, especially small, open developing economies. Indeed, scholars have called for a model with a strong theoretical base which can be tested across a range of countries (e.g., Dhanaraj & Beamish, 2003; Cavusgil & Zou, 1994 etc.). The model in this book has provided a step in that direction. Further, it can also offer government export policymakers profiles of which firms to target for export assistance so as to improve their country's export performance.

In providing empirical support to the theoretical model, the book has answered a number of research questions which are still inconclusive in the extant literature. The discussion below will summarize the major findings and conclusions from the empirical investigation into these questions.

Major Findings

The book began with an introduction which basically laid the foundation for the reporting of the rest of the research. The introductory chapter is important as it puts into perspective, the rationale for writing this book in the first place. Among other things, the introduction raised the debate as to the relevance of the subject through the research questions asked and the objectives of the book. Importantly, the discussion showed that although some progress has been made on the subject, because of the fragmented nature of the conclusions drawn and the limited geographical focus of most studies, there is still a gap in our understanding as to why some small firms export while similar others remained focused on their domestic market.

Chapter 1, provided a contextual background for the study. The main aim was to show the importance of the enabling external environment in stimulating the export behaviour of firms, especially micro and small firms which make up the bulk of enterprises in almost all economies but are most vulnerable and need support from the state in order to survive. The evidence revealed that for Jamaica, the study context and, indeed, other small, open developing economies; their enabling environment is not sophisticated enough to enable firms to launch out into international business successfully and therefore, there is an important need for state support[115]. Further, the chapter shows that an audit of Jamaica's export performance, especially merchandise exports, makes for an uncomfortable reading. For the decade of the 1990s, the country's export growth was miniscule with growth heavily driven by the services sector (World Bank, 2000). The merchandise sector has performed poorly, especially the non-traditional exports. Although there was a rise in demand on the world market for non-traditional exports, Jamaican firms, especially the small firms that are mostly responsible for the production of non-traditional exports, did not seize the opportunity to exploit this market. Despite the various incentives and support that were provided by government and the private sector to stimulate exporting among these firms, a large number of them appeared not to be motivated. This, it appears, resulted from the wrong stimulus being applied and the improper targeting of firms for export assistance. Clearly, the designers of these programmes did not have profiles of firms that have a greater proclivity to become exporters. This book has provided some assistance in this regard.

Chapter 2 of the book chronicles a theoretical model that will provide export policy makers and managers in small firms with profiles of firms that have a greater proclivity towards exporting. Drawing on various theoretical and empirical literature, as well as using analogy from the natural sciences, the chapter articulates a Stimuli, Organism, Response (SOR) model as one explanation for some small firms becoming exporters while similar others facing like market conditions do not. This integrative model helps to extend the empirical work in the area especially as it relates to firms from small, developing economies. The testing of the model formed the basis for the rest of the work that was reported in the book.

Chapter 3, the first of the chapters that seek to provide empirical support for the theoretical model articulated in chapter 2, dealt specifically with the stimuli aspect of the model. The main thrust of the work in that chapter was to determine whether or not export initiation is a systematic investigation of foreign market opportunities or, if it results merely from fortuitous circumstances. Investigating the relative importance of the range of stimuli that trigger exporting in the firm has helped us to shed some light on this issue. The results from this investigation revealed that stimuli internal to the firm were more important in triggering export decision than those external. This is in contrast to most studies in the developed world which argue that external stimulus such as unsolicited order from foreign customers is most important in triggering export decision in the firm.

This difference, it is argued, may result from the unsophisticated nature of the enabling environment in the developing world which prevents external stimuli from reaching the firm. For example, if firms are to get unsolicited orders from overseas customers, there has to be a functioning website with a directory of firms so that customers can solicit these orders. Also, the telephone systems in these firms must be working properly; the firms should have

[115] See, Wint, (2003) chapter 10 for a very good review of the rationale for supporting micro enterprises.

adequate facility for customers to make payments; there has to be adequate transportation facilities to deliver the order; among a number of other factors. Without these, then it is the owners in these firms who will have to consciously decide to go out and seek export opportunities for their businesses. In essence, it appears from the analysis that the export initiation decision is driven by a systematic investigation for foreign market opportunities and not a mere response to fortuitous orders[116]. Indeed, it is highly recognised in the literature that firms which initiate exporting because of proactive motivations are more likely to be successful than those which enter by reactive means such as a response to an unsolicited order (Leonidou, 1995a; Albaum, et al., 1989; Welch & Wiedershiem- Paul, 1980).

Despite the importance of export stimuli in the export development process, the SOR model acknowledges that they by themselves will not result in the firm becoming an exporter. What will make the difference is the absorptive capacity in these firms. The absorptive capacity as measured by the quality and quantity of resources in the firm will determine whether or not entrepreneurs in the small firm respond positively or negatively to export stimuli. With this acknowledgement, chapter 4, focuses on these resources in the firm that will increase its chance of becoming an exporter.

In chapter 4, the book presents a logistic regression model to determine the odds of the firm becoming an exporter given the quantity and quality of a number of resources which it possesses. These resources were proxied by various variables which the extant literature identifies as suitable proxies for resources. These variables were detailed in chapter 2 of the book. Consistent with the resource-based theory, variables reflecting the human capital[117] and physical capital[118] resources of the firm were identified and their theoretical relationship with the firm's exporter performance established.

The analysis revealed that five of the theoretical relationships established are supported by the empirical data. In order words, the resources that are more amenable to getting the firm to become an exporter are: *the foreign travel experience of the entrepreneur, the previous export experience of the entrepreneur, the number of employees in the firm, the quality of the firm's product and, the degree of standardization of the product.* Further, it was demonstrated that the degree of standardization of the product is the most important resource that will improve the firm's absorptive capacity to respond positively to export stimuli.

The practical realities of the adaptation of the firm's product to the export market are critical when small, resource poor firms are thinking about foreign market entry. To make alteration to products before selling them in the export market may require investments in machinery, training for staff, new variations in packaging, style, and colour. This investment can be quite exorbitant for small, resource poor firms. Moreover, the export orders which these small firms receive are normally small, thus inadequate to offset the cost involved in adaptation. Because of the cost savings to be gained from having a standardized product, small firms that possess this resource will have more confidence in trying to exploit market opportunities abroad. In other words, firms with a standardized product are more likely to

---

[116] The result shows that the small firms from the research sample have some entrepreneurial characteristics and are not just a set of internationalized small firms. This makes it worthwhile to look at these firms when addressing issues in international entrepreneurship (Dimitratos & Jones, 2005, Dimitratos & Plakoyiannaki, 2003).

[117] See for example Becker, 1964; Pena, 2002; Cooper et al., 1994; Westhead et al., 2001 for arguments to support these variables.

[118] See for example, Williamson, 1975; Barney, 1991; Amit & Schoemaker, 1993; Chan, 2005; Penrose, 1980 for a description of these resources.

respond positively to export stimuli and enter foreign markets. This finding is consistent with other studies in the area (e.g., Tookey, 1964; Vernon, 1966; McNaughton & Brown, 2004)[119].

The five theoretical relationships not supported also indicated counter intuitive signs from what the theoretical arguments postulate. However, they find some support in the extant empirical literature. For example, educational level of the entrepreneur, the entrepreneur's age and the entrepreneur's proficiency in a foreign language all had negative signs on their coefficients. However, studies carried out in other geographical context found similar signs regarding the relationship between these variables and export propensity[120]. Theoretically, these results also make sense given that the quantity and quality of the internal resource stock are also determined by their external environment (Vatne, 1995). We have also argued in earlier chapters that the enabling environment in developing economies are less sophisticated than that of developed economy. Therefore, you will expect certain resources to be of a lower quality and thus their negative relationship with export performance.

The main thrust of the argument in this chapter is that resources will determine the competitive advantage the firm has or can achieve, and these advantages will give it added confidence to exploit its unique bundle of resources abroad. It is this added confidence which provides the reason for a positive response to export stimuli.

Both chapters 3 & 4 by focusing on export stimuli and the firm's resources respectively have provided one explanation as to why some firms export while similar others remain focused on their domestic market. After the decision is made to enter exporting, the small firm is still confronted with another difficult decision, that is, where to start its exporting activity. In other words, there is a market entry decision to make. Chapter 5 of the book provides some insights to help managers in these small firms to make this difficult decision.

Using the stage theory of internationalization as the lens for conceptualizing the arguments on market entry decision, chapter 5 of the book highlights the major factors that impact the decision regarding which market to start exporting the firm's product. The discussions and analyses revealed that the attractiveness of the export market was the most important factor that determines where the small firm starts its exporting activity. Attractiveness is measured by the strong demand for the firm's product in the export market, a growing market and pure chance. Importantly, the analyses point out that stage theory of internationalization is a weak predictor of where Jamaican small firms will start their exporting activity. Policy makers therefore, cannot rely solely on the predictions of the stage model to formulate policies that will help Jamaican small firms to select export markets. The networks that the entrepreneurs in these firms plug into are very important in determining where these firms start their exporting activity.

Chapter 6, the final of the empirical chapters, presented a rather interesting perspective from non-exporters on why their firms do not export. This analysis is unique in the sense that only a limited number of studies in the extensive literature on the firm's export behaviour focus on non-exporters when trying to understand why firms do not export. The analysis in this chapter will go a far way in extending the empirical work in this area. Specifically, the chapter aimed at understanding from the non-exporters perspective, what other factors besides absorptive capacity, casue them to reject export stimuli and what can be done to

---

[119] It must be noted that standardization might not explain export market entry for firms which operate in markets where innovativeness and flexibility are needed, due to the need for customized production.

[120] For example, see Obben & Magagula, 2003; Daniels & Guyburo, 1976; McConnel, 1979; Dichtl et al., 1990; Andersson et al., 2004 etc.

stimulate them to export in the future. The results in the chapter revealed that non-exporters remain focused on their domestic market because they view the market as unsaturated and therefore, the firm can achieve its goals by operating locally. Further, they see exporting as costly and argue that they lack sufficient financing for such activity. These firms however, can be persuaded to become exporters if exporting is seen as a profitable business activity.

Interestingly, this chapter found that non-exporters are not a homogeneous group as implied by the line of argument in most of the literature (see, for example, Leonidou, 1995a). The analyses showed that non-exporters could be classified as three types. These are *experienced non-exporters* (those non-exporters that have exported before but have withdrawn from the export market), *international business seekers* (those non-exporters that are not exporting currently but are actively seeking export opportunities abroad) and, *uninterested non-exporters*(those non-exporters that are not seeking export opportunities and have no interest in seeking such opportunities in the future). Indeed, this classification will have considerable implications for policies that are geared towards stimulating non-exporters to become exporters.

IMPLICATIONS OF THE FINDINGS

The research reported in this volume has far reaching implications for entrepreneurs (owners)/managers in these small firms, export policy makers who are interested in stimulating small firms to export and, future researchers interested in the subject. Further, the findings will have implications for export stimulation in other geographical context with similar characteristics to Jamaica. Some of these economies include countries such as Fiji, Cyprus, Mauritius, Malta, Seychelles and, other members of Caricom.

Implications for Managers

If micro and small firms are to become exporters and be successful in international markets, the managers in these firms will have to cultivate an internal environment conducive to exporting. Exporting will have to be viewed as an important business activity that is essential to the firm's survival. It cannot be viewed as just an activity on the periphery of the firm's operation. With the increased integration of markets and the rapid evolution in technology, unless ludditism overtakes the world, the current course of market integration will not be reversed. It therefore means that all firms, irrespective of size, will have to participate in the global economy, especially those from small economies where market size is just too small to ensure long-term survival. In other words, for the small firm, it will be "export or die".

The research in this book has provided some insights into how managers can create, in their firms, an environment conducive to exporting. Owners will need to increase their travel experiences abroad, send more staff on overseas trips to trade fairs, send staff to exporting seminars locally and internationally. Managers should also try to employ, in their recruitment process, persons who have worked in organisations that have done exporting successfully or in the export sector generally. Besides the international mindset that these employees will bring to the firm, they may also improve the firm's networking capabilities. Further, entrepreneurs should improve their relationship management by attending special courses to help them to effectively handle their relationships with foreign buyers. This will also help them to plug into business and social networks that can allow them to solicit export orders.

Implications for Government Export Policy Makers

Governments in small economies generally use scare resources to provide assistance for firms to become exporters. This is because they often see exporting as a public good which generates positive externalities and therefore the entire society benefits when firms export their goods and services abroad. However, with the low levels of exports from these economies, especially in Jamaica's case, it appears that a large number of firms are not motivated by these assistance programmes. Indeed, with most small economies struggling to balance government budgets and deal with other social issues such as crime, education, and healthcare the big issue is, how best these scare resources can be used to support firms to become exporters and prevent wastage. This study has provided in chapter 4, some profiles of firms that make them more amenable to exporting. These profiles should be used as a basis for providing assistance to the large number of firms that generally come to government for assistance to engage in exporting. Firms that have the profiles outlined are the first that should be targeted for assistance as they show a greater proclivity toward exporting[121]. It will also help export policy makers to better assess the risks associated with individual firms that come with proposal for export assistance therefore, preventing inefficient and improper use of limited resources.

Policy makers should help to facilitate unsolicited order for small firms through the establishment of programmes that will generate contacts between foreign buyers and domestic suppliers. The cost of doing market research is definitely too exorbitant for small firms but, it is an important activity for export information. Policy markers should ensure that facilities are in place where, these small firms can plug into for information on foreign buyers. Further, an important element in ensuring that firms gain unsolicited order is visibility. One way in which policy makers can help is to ensure that a database exists of all firms that have something to sell to the world. This way, potential foreign customers can have access to this information and if they require a product in the future, they can contact these firms.

These measures to stimulate unsolicited order in Jamaica can also be applied in other small developing economies where unsolicited order is not forthcoming. There is no doubt that unsolicited orders will serve as an important trigger for exporting in most small firms. But, to generate these orders, the enabling environment in which these firms operate will have to be sophisticated enough to ensure that the firms get sufficient visibility so that potential customers can call on them for goods and/or services in the future. Indeed, this will require a stable macroeconomic, social and regulatory environment as well. For example, foreign customers tend not to look for products in markets that are socially unstable (i.e. high crime

[121] We are not saying that these profiles alone should be used to determine who gets export assistance. Other subjective measures should also be used e.g. how the assistance officer views the firms' networks. However, the profiles should serve as the tool for selecting which firms are targeted. This is because they are easily identifiable and transparent.

rate, poor health facilities) because they may think that this instability will undermine the quality of the product they get. Further, they will want to know that there is a strong regulatory structure in place so that if anything goes wrong with the product or services bought, they will have some sort of recourse. Also, with macroeconomic stability, they will be better able to predict prices and determine how much the intended goods or services will cost in the future. Under these conditions, there is a greater likelihood that firms will get unsolicited orders than if the reverse were true. Export policy makers therefore, will have to bear these things in mind when trying to stimulate firms to enter exporting.

Further, it is also important that export policy makers understand that non-exporters are not a homogeneous group and therefore should not be treated as such when export stimulation assistance is given. This study has shown that there are three types of non-exporters and that they have different interests in exporting and therefore, view export stimuli differently. As such, when trying to stimulate these firms into exporting, policy makers have to first understand the type of non-exporter they are dealing with before they can determine the type of assistance to provide. This will prevent wastage of resources and also ensure that the correct stimuli are given to motivate these firms to become exporters.

Implications for Future Research

The results from the research in this volume have no doubt extended the empirical literature in the field of export behaviour of the small firm. Further, the articulation of the theoretical model in chapter 2 is very helpful as a lens for conceptualizing the issue and arguments surrounding the export behaviour of the firm. Other researchers can test this model in other geographical context with similar characteristics to Jamaica. There is no doubt that there is a great need for comparative studies on the export behaviour of the firm. This will not only extend the literature but provide stronger evidence for theorists in the field to develop a general theory on the export behaviour of the firm.

The findings from this study have provoked the intellectual foundations of some fundamental concepts in this area of research. For example, the research in this volume has not found very strong evidence to support the thesis of stage models as a valid predictor of where small firms will start their exporting activity. The implication is that researchers will have to revisit the tenets of this theory and make modifications to its major assumptions to take in the new realities and characteristics of firms. Further, researchers must be cautious when applying this theory to explain the internationalization behaviour of firms from across various geographical locations. These are issues that future researchers will want to address.

Getting into exporting is an important decision and must be taken seriously. However, more significantly, in an increasingly competitive global market; is the need to sustain the export business once they have started. More research is needed, especially in small developing economies, on the strategies used by successful exporters to export successfully abroad. This will require serious qualitative exploration as quantitative models will not be able to identify the nuances involved in strategy development. In-depth case studies and cross case analyses will serve as good tools to use for these issues.

Indeed, there is also a need for more longitudinal studies on the small firm's export behaviour. This can be a very expensive and time consuming activity but, it is necessary if ever there will be a general theory on small firms' export behaviour. Exporting from the small firms is very dynamic and so the snapshot view that is gained from cross sectional studies will not give a full understanding of the process. However, this snapshot is very important to advance policies on export stimulation because the firm still has to survive while the longitudinal study is being under taken.

Conclusion

Stimulating micro and small firms to initiate exporting is not an option for export policy makers and entrepreneurs in small, developing economies. They will have to do it whether now or in the very near future. These economies are just too small to ensure the survival of all firms and economic sectors. Interaction with the international markets is inevitable. Additionally, with the "creative destruction" (Schumpeter, 1961) brought on by the liberalization of markets and improvements in information and communications technology, this will further force small firms to look for markets outside of their domestic base in order to sell their goods and services. Certainly, this "Schumpeterian shock"[122] will continue for a long time to come therefore, it will be either export or die for small firms from small, open developing economies like Jamaica.

[122] This phrase is used to describe the sort of changes that fundamentally restructure an industry sector. There is no doubt that liberalization of markets and technology have restructured almost all industries worldwide. For a view on this see Porter, 2008.

APPENDIX

Edu Dropped

Variables	β	Wald	Sig.	Exp(B)
EA	-.015	.309	.578	.985
EFL	-1.229	1.613	.204	.293
EFT*	1.912	4.780	.029	6.768
EPEE*	1.515	6.674	.010	4.551
YCS	-.041	.060	.806	.960
NEC*	.041	6.406	.011	1.042
SDP*	1.831	9.051	.003	6.242
PQ*	1.487	3.807	.051	4.424
TS	-.603	2.024	.155	.547
Constant	-1.844	2.045	.153	.158

* = significant variables.

EA dropped

Variables	β	Wald	Sig.	Exp(B)
EFL	-1.235	1.655	.198	.291
EFT*	1.821	4.638	.031	6.180
EPEE*	1.488	6.473	.011	4.427
YCS	.000	.000	.999	1.000
NEC*	.043	7.424	.006	1.044
SDP*	1.821	8.937	.003	6.179
PQ*	1.557	4.240	.039	4.745
TS	-.577	1.878	.171	.561
EDU	-.032	.018	.894	.969
Constant	-2.237	3.314	.069	.107

* = significant variables.

Efl dropped

Variables	β	Wald	Sig.	Exp(B)
EFT*	1.454	3.491	.062	4.280
EPEE*	1.433	6.193	.013	4.192
YCS	-.047	.081	.777	.954
NEC*	.036	5.368	.021	1.037
SDP*	1.802	9.014	.003	6.063
PQ*	1.516	4.065	.044	4.555
TS	-.588	1.984	.159	.555
EDU	-.061	.067	.796	.941
EA	-.018	.408	.523	.982
Constant	-1.500	1.022	.312	.223

* = significant variables.

Eft dropped

Variables	β	Wald	Sig.	Exp(B)
EPEE*	1.327	5.695	.017	3.769
YCS	.021	.018	.894	1.021
NEC*	.043	7.522	.006	1.044
SDP*	1.652	8.217	.004	5.216
PQ*	1.657	4.959	.026	5.245
TS	-.545	1.749	.186	.580
EDU	-.032	.020	.887	.968
EA	-.005	.039	.843	.995
EFL	-.276	.133	.716	.759
Constant	-1.946	1.806	.179	.143

*= significant variables.

Epee dropped

Variables	β	Wald	Sig.	Exp(B)
YCS	-.003	.000	.983	.997
NEC*	.039	6.919	.009	1.040
SDP*	1.749	9.161	.002	5.750
PQ*	1.565	4.568	.033	4.784
TS	-.582	2.072	.150	.559
EDU	-.049	.046	.831	.952
EA	-.009	.105	.746	.991
EFL	-.981	1.089	.297	.375
EFT*	1.673	3.785	.052	5.326
Constant	-1.355	.869	.351	.258

*= significant variables.

Ycs dropped

Variables	β	Wald	Sig.	Exp(B)
NEC*	.043	8.156	.004	1.044
SDP*	1.828	9.003	.003	6.224
PQ*	1.508	3.895	.048	4.516
TS	-.605	2.049	.152	.546
EDU	-.029	.014	.905	.972
EA	-.012	.247	.619	.988
EFL	-1.224	1.580	.209	.294
EFT*	1.876	4.764	.029	6.526
EPEE*	1.504	6.569	.010	4.501
Constant	-1.988	2.959	.085	.137

* = significant variables.

Nec dropped

Variables	β	Wald	Sig.	Exp(B)
SDP*	1.472	6.951	.008	4.359
PQ*	1.522	4.213	.040	4.583
TS	-.441	1.172	.279	.643
EDU	-.050	.047	.829	.951
EA	-.036	1.782	.182	.965
EFL	-.548	.411	.521	.578
EFT*	2.106	6.095	.014	8.214
EPEE*	1.485	7.499	.006	4.416
YCS	-.217	2.213	.137	.805
Constant	.260	.042	.838	1.297

* = significant variables.

Spd dropped

Variables	β	Wald	Sig.	Exp(B)
PQ*	1.827	6.380	.012	6.216
TS*	-.765	3.475	.062	.465
EDU	-.003	.000	.989	.997
EA	-.011	.169	.681	.989
EFL	-1.127	1.553	.213	.324
EFT*	1.627	3.829	.050	5.089
EPEE*	1.393	6.869	.009	4.028
YCS	-.017	.011	.915	.984
NEC*	.030	4.368	.037	1.031
Constant	-.874	.394	.530	.417

* = significant variables.

Pq dropped

Variables	β	Wald	Sig.	Exp(B)
TS	-.272	.528	.467	.762
EDU	.014	.004	.951	1.015
EA	-.024	.791	.374	.976
EFL	-1.325	1.816	.178	.266
EFT*	2.203	5.840	.016	9.055
EPEE*	1.548	7.491	.006	4.701
YCS	-.062	.150	.698	.940
NEC*	.040	6.619	.010	1.041
SDP*	1.981	11.338	.001	7.246
Constant	-1.693	1.277	.258	.184

* = significant variables.

Ts dropped

Variables	β	Wald	Sig.	Exp(B)
EDU	-.056	.055	.814	.946
EA	-.012	.192	.661	.988
EFL	-1.186	1.591	.207	.305
EFT*	1.868	4.519	.034	6.476
EPEE*	1.508	6.754	.009	4.517
YCS	-.059	.134	.714	.943
NEC*	.038	5.725	.017	1.039
SDP*	1.926	10.292	.001	6.860
PQ	1.077	2.499	.114	2.936
Constant	-2.045	1.860	.173	.129

* = significant variables.

Model Diagnostics

To test the goodness of fit of the model, a number of diagnostic tests were carried out. These tests give us some idea of how well our model can predict the odds of the small firm becoming an exporter given its possession of a combination of physical and human resources. They will also provide insights into how far the model can predict the outcome of the firm being an exporter outside of the given data set. The following tests are looked at below.

Significance of the Model

In logistic regression, the goodness of fit of the model can be determined by any of the following: a) the Model chi-square, b) R^2 (e.g., McFadden R^2, Nagelkerke R^2, Cox & Snell R^2 etc.) c) Log likelihood statistic and d) Hosmer & Lemeshow statistic. The model chi-square tells us whether a significant relationship exists between all the independent variables and the dependent variable. A significant model chi-square shows that a significant relationship exists between the dependent and independent variables. In other words, it tells us that all the independent variables combined have parameters different from zero. From this analysis, the Model chi-square ($\chi^2 = 41.24$) is highly significant at the 5 percent level ($p = 0.000$), thus suggesting a high level goodness of fit for the model.

The Hosmer & Lemeshow statistic tests the hypothesis that the actual data in the model is different from the predicted data. In this case, a non-significant statistic would be deemed appropriate for a good fitting model. It would allow us to test the null hypothesis that the observed and predicted data are not different. The value of this statistic is non-significant ($p = 0.17$) at the 5 percent level, thus suggesting a good fit for the model. That is, the model is predicting real world data fairly well.

The log likelihood statistic helps to predict the amount of unexplained variation in the data. In logistic regression, it is multiplied by -2 (Field, 2000). It is stated that the lower the log likelihood statistic, the better the fit of the model, simply because there exists less unexplained variation in the model. In this analysis, when the model was estimated with only the constant included, the -2 log likelihood is 127.37. When the independent variables were added, the -2 log likelihood was reduced to 86.13. This shows that when the independent variables are added to the model, it better explains the dependent variable than without them. Again this result shows a good fit for our model.

Similar to multiple regression, the model R^2 (McFadden R^2) can help us to predict the goodness of fit of the model. It explains how much of the variation in the dependent variable is explained by the independent variables. In this analysis, it shows that 32 percent of the variation in the dependent variable is explained by the model. Other alternatives to the model R^2 are also used to measure goodness of fit (e.g., Nagelkerke R^2 or Cox & Snell R^2). However, Cox & Snell is reported less frequently because it cannot reach the maximum value of 1 (Hair et al., 1998). Nagelkerke R^2 is most frequently used. In this analysis, we achieved a fairly high Nagelkerke R^2 (.48). This value is in line with previous studies and in some cases surpasses them, (e.g., Andersson et al., 2004, Hall & Tú, 2004, Tú, 2003).

Generally, all the diagnostics investigated so far show a reasonably well fitted model. However, these are not the only diagnostics which should be analysed to determine the goodness of fit of the model. It is pertinent in any regression analysis to also look at the model residuals as a measure of its goodness of fit.

Residual Analysis

Residual analysis is done in order to identify and possibly eliminate points which do not fit the data properly and those which exert undue influence on the model (Field, 2000). Models which have good fit will normally have small residuals while those with poor fit will have large residuals. The model unstandardized residual will give an idea of how large or small residuals are. This however is very subjective since there exists no standard as to what is large or small. To overcome this level of subjectivity, statisticians recommend that the standardized residuals be observed instead.

In a normally distributed sample, it is observed that 95 percent of residual cases lie between -2 and +2 deviation from the mean, 99 percent lie between -2.5 and +2.5 deviation from the mean. For good fitting models, it is stated that under no circumstance should any standardized residual be greater than +/- 3, moreover, more than 5 percent of the data should not have standardized residual above +/- 2.5.

In this analysis, 94 percent of the residuals fall within +/- 2 deviation from the mean and 100 percent fall within +/- 2.5. These figures are within the conventional statistical guidelines and thus show a reasonably good fitting model. The table below shows those residual cases which fall outside +/- 2 deviation of the mean.

Residuals outside of +/- 2 standard deviation of the mean

Cases	Observed Group	Predicted Group	Predicted Probability	Standardized Residual Value
24	E	N	.10	2.19
39	E	N	.19	2.05
51	N	E	.95	-2.54
69	N	E	.93	-2.39
71	N	E	.83	-2.09
83	N	E	.84	-2.06

Influential Cases

Although our model does not show signs of unacceptable levels of error from the residual analysis, and only six cases are misclassified (Hair et al., 1998), it is still critical to discover whether certain cases are putting undue influence on the parameters. This will help us to determine whether the model is stable across the sample of small firms or, if it is being influenced by a few cases.

To test for influential cases a number of statistics are available. This include: Cook's distance statistic, leverage statistic and the standardized version of Cook's distance, DFBeta. Cook's distance gives an indication of a single case influence on the overall fit of the model, while leverage and DFBeta indicate the influence of a single case on individual coefficients. The Cook's distance statistic is an unstandardized measure and as such no absolute value exits to determine whether or not a case is influential. However, statisticians suggest that values greater than 1 show signs of influential cases (Stevens, 1992). In some cases, DFBeta is seen as a standardized version to Cook's distance thus having an absolute value for influential cases (Field, 2000). For residuals with DFBeta values greater than +/-1 or +/-2, it implies cases with strong influence on individual coefficients in the model. Alternatively, there is the leverage statistic (hat value). This statistic lies between 0 and 1 (i.e. cases with 0 have no influence and cases with 1 have high influence). Some statisticians recommend that cases with twice the average value of the statistic be observed (Hoaglin & Welsch, 1978) while others recommend that cases three times the value be observed (Stevens, 1992).

From the analysis of these statistics, our model reveals that all the residuals fall in the recommended statistical limits. There are a few cases (Cases: 33,39,51,69,71) where the Cook's distance is above 1 (but have not reached 2 in any instance), however, their DFBeta values are less than 1 and in no instance is the leverage statistic above 2 or 3 times the average statistic (0.12). Examining these cases for errors in data entry showed none. None of the cases are unrepresentative of the general population therefore they are not eliminated from the model. Moreover, Hair et al., (1998) stated that six misclassified cases provide an inadequate basis for further analysis.

Multicollinearity

Multicollinearity is a significant problem in any regression analysis because it can lead to the rejection of a rather good predictor when indeed it is a significant variable in the model. This is the classical Type II error in statistics. The Pearson Product Moment Correlation (Pearson R) is used to check for the existence of first order correlation among the variables.

Pearson R correlation among independent variables

	EP	EA	EFL	EFT	EPEE	YCS	NEC	SDP	PQ	TS	EDU
EP	1										
EA	-.09	1									
EFL	.11	.03	1								
EFT	.24*	.07	.60**	1							
EPEE	.33**	_.03	.14	.07	1						
YCS	-.02	_.36**	-.03	.06	.09	1					
NEC	.31**	-.11	.28**	.28**	.16	_.22**	1				
SDP	.30**	.00	-.05	-.06	.11	.11	.17	1			
PQ	.33**	-.25*	.09	.17	.19	.08	.22*	.17	1		
TS	.01	-.18	.13	.21*	.02	.00	.26*	-.13	.38*	1	
EDU	.04	-.02	.10	.08	.01	-.05	.07	.05	.18	.13	1

N.B. * Correlation significant at the 0.05 level of significance (2-tailed).
** Correlation significant at the 0.01 level of significance (2-tailed).
All figures in the table are rounded up to 2 decimal places.

Although 15 significant correlations are observed among the variables, the magnitudes of the correlations are not strong enough to merit a threat of multicollinearity. From the research literature, it is suggested that correlation coefficient above 0.9 is cause for concern of multicollinearity (Ramaseshan & Patton, 1994). Globally, the correlation coefficients in this analysis are highest at 0.6. Hence, multicollinearity does not appear to be a problem. However, because Pearson R only shows first order correlations (macro level), there may exist more subtle forms of correlations which it misses. As such, alternative techniques are used to test for multicollinearity.

Following the advice of Myers (1990) and Menard (1995), the Variance Inflation Factor (VIF) and the Tolerance Statistics of the variables are examined. The table below shows the results of this analysis.

Correlation using Tolerance and VIF statistics

Variables	Collinearity Statistic	
	Tolerance	VIF
Educational qualification	.951	1.052
Entrepreneur's age	.753	1.328
Entrepreneur's foreign language proficiency	.614	1.629
Entrepreneur's foreign travel experience	.581	1.722
Entrepreneur's previous export experience	.904	1.106
Year company started operation	.751	1.331
Number of employees in the company	.728	1.373
Standardized product	.878	1.139
Product quality	.708	1.413
Technology	.770	1.298

Statisticians suggest that VIF above 10 and Tolerance statistic below 0.1 are signs of multicollinearity in the independent variables. From the analysis, all the variables have VIF below 10 and tolerance value above 0.1. This suggests that no threat of multicollinearity in its subtlest form exists in the model.

Predictive Accuracy of the Model

Hair et al. (1998) argued that the main objective of logistic regression is to achieve the highest predictive accuracy of the outcome for the dependent variable given a set of predictors. To do this, the model requires certain assumptions:

a. The expected value of the error is equal to zero
b. Errors are not correlated with each other
c. Errors are not correlated with independent variables
d. No perfect multicollinearity between independent variables

It is also argued that the logit model requires fewer assumptions than Ordinary Least Square models to produce high predictive accuracy. This is one benefit of the logit model over other similar techniques.

From the analysis, the predictive accuracy for exporters and non-exporters are: 85.4 percent and 80 percent respectively. This gives an overall predictive accuracy of 82.6 percent.

Predictive accuracy of the model

Export Performance	Export Performance		Percentage correct
	Exporter	Non-exporter	
Exporter	35	9	80
Non-exporter	7	41	85.4
Overall percentage			82.6

Again, this predictive accuracy falls in line with those of previous work (e.g., Obben & Magagula, 2003, Hall & Tú, 2004, Tú, 2003, Westhead et al., 2001, Philp, 1998 etc.).

REFERENCES

Aaby, N. E., & Slater, S. F. (1989). Management influence on export performance: A review of the empirical literature 1978-88. *International Marketing Review,* 6, 4, pp 7- 26.

Acs, Z., Dana, L.P., & Jones, M. (2003). Toward new horizons: The internationalization of entrepreneurship. *Journal of International Entrepreneurship,* 1, 1, pp 5-12.

Adams, G., & Hall, G. (1993). Influences on the growth of SMEs: An international comparison. *Entrepreneurship & Regional Development, 5*, 1, pp 73-84.

Adjibolosoo, S. (1999). *Rethinking Development Theory and Policy: A Human Factor Critique.* New York: Praeger Books

Aharoni, Y. (1966). *The foreign investment decision process.* Boston, Mass: Harvard University.

Albaum, G., Strandskov, J., Duerr, E., & Dowd, J. (1989). *International marketing and export management.* Great Britain: Addison-Wesley Inc.

Albaum, G., & Peterson, R.A. (1984). Empirical research in international marketing: 1976-1982. *Journal of International Business Studies,* (Pre 1986), spring/summer, 15, 1, pp 161-173.

Al-Laham, A., & Souitaris, V. (2008). Network embeddedness and new-venture internationalization: Analysing international linkages in the German biotech industry. *Journal of Business Venturing,* 23, 5, pp 567- 586.

Alon, A. (2004). International market selection for small enterprise: A case study in international entrepreneurship. *SAM Advanced Management Journal,* 69, 1, pp 25 -33.

Alon, I., & McIntyre, J.R. (2008). *Globalization of Chinese enterprises.* New York: Palgrave Macmillan.

Amit, R., & Schoemaker, P.J.H. (1993). Strategic assets and organisational rent. *Strategic Management Journal,* 14, pp 33-46.

Andersen, O. (1993). On the internationalization process of firms: A critical analysis. *Journal of International Business Studies,* 2nd Quarter, 24, 2, pp 209 -231.

Andersen, P.H. (1995). *Collaborative internationalization of small and medium- sized enterprises: SMEs participation in the international division of labour.* Copenhagen: Jurist-og Økonomforbundets Forlag DJØF Publishing.

Anderson, P. (2001). The changing role of self-employment: A review of the Jamaican labour market during the nineties and prospects for growth. *UWI Research Day Forum on Private Sector Perspectives on Economic Growth.* Kingston: Jamaica, 18th October.

Andersen, O., & Kheam, L.S. (1998). Resource-based theory and international growth strategies: An exploratory study. *International Business Review,* 7, 2, pp 71-82.

Andersson, S., Gabrielsson, J., & Wictor, I.(2004). International activities in small firms: Examining factors influencing the internationalization and export growth of small firms. *Canadian Journal of Administrative Sciences,* 21, 1, pp 22- 31.

Autio, E., Yli-Renko, H., & Salonen, A. (1997). International growth of young technology-based firms: A Resource-based network model. *Journal of Enterprising Culture,* 5, 1, pp 57-73.

Autio, E. (2005). Creative tension: The significance of Ben Oviatt's and Patricia Mc Dougall's article a theory of international ventures. *Journal of International Business Studies,* 36, 1, pp 9-20.

Autio, E., Sapienza, H.J., & Almeida, J.G. (2000). Effects of age at entry, knowledge intensity and imitability on international growth. *Academy of Management Journal,* 43, 5, pp 909-924.

Axinn, C.N., & Matthyssens, P. (2002). Limits of internationalization theories in an unlimited world. *International Marketing Review,* 19, 4/5, pp 436- 449.

Ayub, M.A. (1981). *Made in Jamaica: The development of the manufacturing sector.* Baltimore: The John Hopkins University Press.

Babbie, E. R. (2001). T*he practice of social research 9th Edition.* London: Wadsworth Thomas Learning.

Balabanis, G., Theodious, M., & Katsikea, E.S. (2004). Export marketing: developments and research agenda. *International Marketing Review* 21, 4/5, pp 353- 377.

Baker, A. T., & Kaynak, E. (1992). An empirical investigation of the differences between initiating and continuing exporters. *European Journal of Marketing,* 26, 3 pp 27-36.

Bank of Jamaica -BOJ (1997, 2002), *"Balance of payment statistics*", Kingston: Jamaica.

Bank of Jamaica -BOJ (2002). *Balance of payment statistics.* Kingston: Jamaica.

Barney, J. B. (1991). Firm resources and sustained competitive advantage. *Journal of Management,* 17, 1, pp 99 -120.

Barrow, C. (1998). The Barriers to Growth that Small Firms Face. Paper for Rent X11, Research in Entrepreneurship and Small Business, Lyon, France.

Beamish, P.W. (1987). Joint ventures in LDCs: Partner selection and performance. *Management International Review, 27*, 1, pp 123- 37.

Beamish, P.W. (1990). The internationalization process of smaller Ontario firms: A Research agenda. In Rugman, A.M. (ed) *Research in global strategy management- international business research for the twenty- first century: Canada's New Research Agenda* (pp 77-92). Greenwich: JIA Press Inc.

Beaver, G. (2002). *Small business entrepreneurship and enterprise development.* Harlow: Prentice Hall.

Becker, G.S. (1964). *Human capital.* New York: Columbia.

Bell, J., Crick, D., & Young, S. (2004). Small firm internationalization and business strategy. *International Small Business Journal,* 22, 1, pp 23-56.

Bernal, R. L. (2006). Nano-firms, integration and international competitiveness: The experience and dilemma of the CSME. In Denis Benn and Kenneth Hall (Eds.), *Production integration in CARICOM: From theory to action* (pp90-115). Kingston: Ian Randle Publishers.

Bijmolt, T.H.A., & Zwart, S.P. (1994). The impact of internal factors on the export success of Dutch small and medium- sized firms. *Journal of Small Business Management,* 32, 2, pp. 69-83.

Bilkey, W. J., & Tesar, G. (1977). The export behaviour of smaller-sized Wisconsin manufacturing firms. *Journal of International Business Studies* (Pre- 1986), Spring, 8, 1, pp 93- 98.

Bilkey, W.J. (1978). An attempted integration of the literature on the export behaviour of firms. *Journal of International Business Studies,* 9, 1, (Spring / Summer), pp 33-46.

Bilkey, W. J. (1982). Variables associated with export profitability. *Journal of International Business Studies,* (pre- 1986), 13, 2, pp 39-55.

Bloodgood, J.M., Sapienza, H.J., & Almeida, J.G. (1996). The internationalization of high-potential U.S. ventures: Antecedents and outcomes. *Entrepreneurship Theory and Practice,* Summer, pp 61- 76.

Blumentritt, T. (2003). Does Small and mature have to mean dull?: Defying the ho-hum at SMEs. *Journal of Business Strategy,* 25, 1, pp 27-33.

Bonaccorsi, A. (1992). On the relationship between firm size and export intensity. *Journal of International Business Studies,* Fourth Quarter, 23, 4, pp 605 -635.

Buckley, P.J., & Ghauri, P.N. (2004). Globalization, economic geography and the strategy of the multinational enterprise. *Journal of International Business Studies*, 35, 2, pp 81- 9.

Buckle, P.J., & Ghauri, P. N. (1999). *The internationalization of the firm: A Reader"* 2nd Edition. London: International Thomson Business Press.

Bulcke, D.V. (2004). Critical perspectives on internationalization. *Journal of International Business Studies,* 35, 3, pp 251-254.

Burpitt, W. J., & Rondinelli, D. (2000). Small firms' motivations for exporting: To earn and learn? *Journal of Small Business Management,* October, 38, 1, pp 1- 14.

Burton, F. N., & Schlegelmilch, B.B. (1987). Profile analyses of non-exporters versus exporters grouped by export involvement. *Management International Review,* 27, 1, pp 38-49.

Brewer, P.A. (2007). Operationalizing psychic distance: a revised approach. *Journal of International Marketing.* 15,1, pp 44-66.

Brooks, M. R., & Rosson, P. J. (1982). A study of export behaviour of small and medium-sized manufacturing firms in three Canadian provinces. in Michael R. Czinkota and George Tesar (Ed), *Export management in an international context* (, pp 39-54). New York: Praeger.

Broida, M.S.(2002). *Using the mini case as an educational tool.* Unpublished Paper presented at the ICSB World Conference Washington D.C. U.S.A.

Brouthers, L.E., & Nakos, G. (2005). The role of systematic international market selection on small firms' export performance. *Journal of Small Business Management,* 43, 4, pp 363-381.

Calof, J. L. (1993). The impact of size on internationalization. *Journal of Small Business Management,* 31, 4 pp 60-69.

Calof, J. L. (1994). The relationship between firm size and export behaviour revisited. *Journal of International Business Studies,* Second Quarter, pp 367- 388.

Calof, J. L., & Viviers, V. (1995). Internationalization behaviour of small and medium –sized South African enterprises. *Journal of Small Business Management*, October, 33, 4, pp 71 – 79.

Caughey, M., & Chetty, S. (1994). Pre-export behaviour of small manufacturing firms in New Zealand. *International Small Business Journal,* April- June, 12, 3, pp 62-68.

Cavusgil, S. T., Bilkey, W.J. & Tesar, G. (1979). A note on the export behaviour of firms: Exporter profile. *Journal of International Business Studies,* 10, Spring/ Summer, pp 91-97.

Cavusgil, S. T. (1980). *On the internationalization process of firms.* European Research, pp 273- 280.

Cavusgil, S. T., & Nevin, J.R. (1981). Internal determinants of export marketing behaviour: An empirical investigation. *Journal of Market Research,* February. 18, 1, pp 114- 119.

Cavusgil, S.T. (1982). Some observations on the relevance of critical variables for internationalization stages. In Michael R. Czinkota and George Tesar (Ed), *Export management in an international context* (pp 276-286) New York: Praeger,.

Cavusgil, S.T. (1984a). Organisational characteristics associated with export activity. *Journal of Management Studies,* 21, 1, pp 3-22.

Cavusgil, S.T. (1984b). Differences among exporting firm based on their degree of internationalization. *Journal of Business Research,* 12, pp 195-208.

Cavusgil, S. T. & Zou, S. (1994). Marketing strategy performance relationship: An investigation of the empirical link in export market ventures. *Journal of Marketing,* January, 58, 1, pp 1-21.

Chan, R.Y.K. (2005). Does the natural resource-based view of the firm apply in an emerging economy?: A survey of foreign invested enterprises in china. *Journal of Management Studies,* 42, 3, pp 625-672.

Chatterjee, S., & Wernerfelt, B. (1991). The link between resources and type of diversification: Theory and evidence. *Strategic Management Journal,* 12, pp 33- 48.

Chiara, A.D., & Minguzzi, A. (2002). Success factors in SME's internationalization process: An Italian investigation. *Journal of Small Business Management*, 40, 2, pp 144- 153.

Christensen, C. H., Coppead, A., & Coppead, R. (1987). An empirical investigation of the factors influencing exporting success of Brazilian firms. *Journal of International Business Studies,* Fall, 18, 3, pp 61-77.

Christensen, R. C. (1979). *Management succession in small and growing enterprises.* New York: Arno Press.

Chetty, S.K., & Hamilton, R.T. (1993). Firm-level determinant of export performance: A meta- analysis. *International Marketing Review,* 10, 3, pp 26-34.

Contractor, F.J., Kundu, S.K., & Hsu, C. (2003). A three stage theory of international expansion: the link between multinationality and performance in the service sector. *Journal of International Business Studies,* 34, 1, pp 5-18.

Contractor, F.J. (1984). Choosing between direct investment and licensing: theoretical considerations and empirical tests. *Journal of International Business Studies,* Winter, pp 167-188.

Cooper, A.C.,Gimeno-Gascon, F.J., & Woo, C.Y. (1994). Initial human and financial capital as predictors of new venture performance. *Journal of Business Venturing,* 9, 5, pp 371-395.

Coviello, N.E., Ghauri, P.N. & Martin, K.A-M. (1998). International competitiveness: Empirical findings from SME service firms. *Journal of International Marketing,* 6, 2, pp 8-27.

Coviello, N.E., & Mc Auley, A. (1999). Internationalization and the smaller firm: A review of contemporary empirical research. *Management International Review,* 3rd Quarter, 39, 3, pp 223- 256.

Coviello, N., & Munro, H. (1997). Network relationships and the internationalization process of small software firms. *International Business Review,* 6, 4, pp 361-386.

Coviello, N.E., & Jones, M.V. (2004). Methodological issues in international entrepreneurship. *Journal of Business Venturing,* 19, 4, pp 485-508.

Covin, J.G., & Slevin, D.P. (1991). A conceptual model of entrepreneurship as firm behaviour. *Entrepreneurship Theory and Practice, 1*6, 1, pp 7- 25.

Crick, D. (2002). The decision to discontinue exporting: SMEs in two U.K. trade sectors. *Journal of Small Business Management, Milwaukee,* 40, 1, pp 66-77.

Crick, D. (2004). The internationalization process of firms in the United Kingdom. In Léo - Paul Dana (Ed), *Handbook of Research on International Entrepreneurshi*p (pp 580- 595). Cheltenham U.K: Edward Elgar.

Crick, D., & Chaudhry, S. (1997). Small businesses' motives for exporting; the effect of internationalization. *Journal of Marketing Practice* 3, 3, pp 156.

Curran, J., & Blackburn, R. (2001). *Researching the small enterprise.* London: Sage.

Czinkota, M. R. (1982). *Export development strategies: US promotion policy.* New York: Praeger Publishers.

Czinkota, M. R., & Johnston, W. J. (1983). Exporting: does sales volume make a difference? *Journal of International Business Studies* (Pre-1986), Spring / Summer, 14, 1, pp 147-153.

Czinkota, M. R., & Ricks, D. A. (1983). The use of a multi- measurement approach in the determination of company export priorities. *Academy of Marketing Science Journal* (Pre-1986), Summer, 11, 3, pp 283-291.

Czinkota, M.R., & Ursic, M. (1991). Classification of exporting firms according to sales and growth into a share matrix. *Journal of Business Research,* May 22, 3, pp 234- 253.

Czaba, L. (2003). The role of financing in the growth of the SME sector: The case of Hungary. In Robert J. McIntyre and Bruno Dallago (Ed), *Small and Medium Enterprises in Transitional Economies* (pp 185-205).United Nations University, New York: Plagrave. pp 185- 205.

Dana, L – P. (2004). *Handbook of Research on International Entrepreneurship.* Cheltenham U.K: Edward Elgar.

Dana, L-P. & Wright, R.W.(2004). Emerging paradigms of international entrepreneurship. In Léo - Paul Dana (Ed), *Handbook of Research on International Entrepreneurship* (pp 3-15). Cheltenham U.K.: Edward Elgar.

Daniels, J. D., & Goyburo, J. (1976). The exporter-non-exporter interface: A search for variables. *Foreign Trade Review,* 3, pp 258-282.

Dar*ling, J. R., & Postnikoff, J. F. (1985). Strategic export information for small business. Journal of Small Business Management,* (Pre- 1986), 23, 4, pp 28-37.

Das, M. (1994). Successful and unsuccessful exporters from developing countries: Some preliminary findings. *European Journal of Marketing,* 28, 12, pp 19-3.

Davies, O., Fissha, Y., & Kirton, C. (1980). Small-scale, non-farm enterprises in Jamaica: Initial survey results. *Social and Economic Studies,* 29, 1, pp 1-39.

Davies, O., & Witter, M. (1989). The development of the Jamaican economy since independence. In Rex, Nettleford (Ed.), Jamaica in Independence: *Essays on the Early Years* (pp75-101). Kingston: Heinemann.

Demer, J. (2001). Exploring new markets. *CMA Management,* 75, 5, pp 52-53.

Demick, D.H., & O'Reilly, A. (2000). Supporting SME internationalization: A collaborative project for export development. *Irish Marketing Review,* 13, 1, pp 34-45.

Deng, P. (2008). Resources, capability and outbound FDI from Chinese companies. In Alon, I and McIntyre, J.R. (Ed) *Globalization of Chinese enterprises* (pp17-30). New York: Palgrave Macmillan.

Deschampsneufs, H. (1984). *Export for the small business.* London: Kogan Page.

Dhanaraj, C., & Beamish, P. (2003). A resource-base approach to the study of export performance. *Journal of Small Business Management,* 14, pp 242 – 261.

Diamantopoulos, A., & Inglis, K. (1988). Identifying differences between high and low involvement exporters. *International Marketing Review,* 5, Summer, pp 52-60.

Dichtl, E., Koeglmayr, H-G., & Mueller, S. (1990). International orientation as a precondition for export success. *Journal of International Business Studies,* 21, 1, pp 23- 40.

Dimitratos, P. (2002). The firm's location in the home country and internationalization: Some evidence from Greek small firms. *Intereconomics,* 37, 2, pp 91-100.

Dimitratos, P., & Plakoyiannaki, E. (2003). Theoretical foundations of an international entrepreneurial culture. *Journal of International Entrepreneurship,* 1, 2, pp 187-215.

Dimitratos, P., & Lioukas, S. (2004).Greek perspectives of international entrepreneurship. In Léo - Paul Dana (Ed), *Handbook of Research on International Entrepreneurship* (pp455-480). Cheltenham U.K.: Edward Elgar.

Dimitratos, P., & Jones, M. (2005). Future directions for international entrepreneurship research. *International Business Review,* 14, 2, pp 119- 128.

Dudley, J. (1989). *Exporting.* London: Pitman Publishing.

Dunning, J.H. (1988). The eclectic paradigm of international production: a restatement and some possible extension. *Journal of International Business Studies* 19, 1, pp 1-31.

Dominguez, L.V., & Sequeira, C.G. (1993). Determinants of LDC exporters' performance: A cross national study. *Journal of International Business Studies,* First Quarter, 24, 1, pp 19- 40.

Ellis, P., & Pecotich, A. (2001). Social factors influencing export initiation in small and medium-sized enterprises. *Journal of Marketing Research,* February, 38, 1, pp 119-129.

Ellis, P. (2000). Social ties and foreign market entry. *Journal of International Business Studies,* 31, 3, pp 443-470.

Enet, D. (1977). *Exporting for small and medium-sized firms.* United Kingdom: Business Books Ltd.

Eriksson, K., Majkgard, A., & Deo Sharma, D. (2000). Path dependence and knowledge development in the internationalization process. *Management International Review,* 40, 4, pp 307- 328.

Erramilli, M.K. (1991). The experience factor in foreign market behaviour of service firms. *Journal of International Business Studies,* 22, 3, pp 479-501.

Eshgi, A. (1992). Attitude-behaviour inconsistency in exporting. *International Journal of Marketing,* 9, 3, pp 40- 61.

Etgar, M., & McConnel, J.E. (1976). *International marketing as a decision-making behaviour of business organisations.* unpublished, cited in Bilkey, (1978).

Etemad, H., & Wright, R.W. (1999). Internationalization of SMEs: Management responses to a changing environment. *Journal of International Marketing,* 7, 4, pp 4- 10.

Etemad, H. (2004). The emerging context of international entrepreneurship; an overview, interrelations and extensions. In Hamid Etemad (Ed.) *International entrepreneurship in small and medium size enterprises* (pp 1-15). Cheltenham, U.K.: Edward Elgar.

Fadahunsi, A., Smallbone, D, & Salinder, S (1999). Networking in ethnic minority enterprise: An analysis of small minority –owned firms in North London. 22nd ISBA National Small Firms Policy and Research Conference. *Conference Proceedings* Vol.1 pp 491-512.

Field, A. (2000). *Discovering statistics for SPS*. New York: Sage.

Fillis, I. (2001). Small firm internationalization: An investigative survey and future research directions. *Management Decision*, 39, 9, pp 767- 783.

Fillis, I. (2002). The internationalization process of the craft micro-enterprise. *Journal of Developmental Entrepreneurship*, Apr, 7, 1, pp 25-43.

Gankema, H.G.J., Snuif, H.R., & Zwart, P.S. (2000). The internationalization process of small and medium-sized enterprises: An evaluation of stage theory. *Journal of Small Business Management,* 38, 4, pp 15- 27.

Garnier, G. (1982). Comparative export behaviour of small Canadian firms in the printing and electrical industries. In Michael R. Czinkota and George Tesar (Ed), *Export management in an international context* (pp 113-131). New York: Praeger.

Garvey, M. (2002). *Jamaica's international business performance: Managerial mindsets and export outcomes*. Kingston: Arawak Publications.

Gereffi, G. (1999). International trade and industrial upgrading in the apparel commodity chain. *Journal of International Economics* 48, pp 37-70.

Ghauri, P.N., & GrØnhaug, K. (2002). *Research methods in business studies* 2nd Edition. Edinburgh: Prentice Hall.

Ghauri, P.N., & Kumar, P.(1989). A empirical investigation of factors influencing export behaviour of small Swedish firms. In Avlonitis,G., Papavasilou, N.K., & Kouremenos, K.G.(Eds), *Marketing thought and practice in the 1990s*(pp355-372). EMAC Proceedings, Athens.

Gill, J., & Johnson, P. (1997). *Research methods for managers* 2nd Edition. London: Paul Chapman Publishing Ltd.

Goodnow, J.D., & Hansz, J.E. (1972). Environmental determinants of overseas market entry strategies. *Journal of International Business Studies,* 3, 1, pp 33-50.

Gujarati, D.N. (2003). Basic econometrics 4th Edition. New York: Mc Graw Hill.

Gumede, V. (2004). Export propensities and intensities of small and medium manufacturing enterprises in South Africa. *Small Business Economics,* 22, pp 379-389.

Gurau, C. (2002). The internationalization process of U.K. biopharmaceutical SMEs. Journal of American Academy of Business, 2, 1, pp 241- 247.

Hall, G. (1995). *Surviving and prospering in the small firm sector*. London: Routledge.

Hall, G. & Tú, C. (2004). Internationalization and size, age and profitability in the United Kingdom. In Léo - Paul Dana (Ed), *Handbook of Research on International Entrepreneurship* (pp596-613). Cheltenham U.K.: Edward Elgar.

Hall, G., Tu, C., & Cook, M. (2005). Factors influencing the export propensity of UK SMEs. Unpublished, *Manchester Business School* U.K. pp 1-23.

Hakim, C. (1989). *Research design: Strategies and choices in the design of social research.* London: Routledge.

*Hair, J.F. et al., (1998). *Multivariate data analysis* 5th Edition. New York: Prentice Hall.

Harris, D. (1997). *Jamaica's export economy: Towards a strategy of export- led growth.* Kingston: Ian Randle Publishers.

Harris, S., & Wheeler, C. (2005). Entrepreneurs' relationship for internationalization: functions, origins and strategies. *International Business Review*, 14, 2, pp 187- 207.

Hatten, T.S. (1997). Small business: Entrepreneurship and beyond. New Jersey: Prentice – Hall, Inc.

Hinttu, S. Forsman, M., & Kock, S. (2004). A network perspective on international entrepreneurship. In Léo -Paul Dana (Ed), *Handbook of Research on International Entrepreneurship* (pp715-731). Cheltenham U.K.: Edward Elgar.

Hoaglin, D., & Welsch, R. (1978). The hat matrix in regression and ANOVA. *American Statistician,* 32, 1, pp 17-22.

Holzmüller, H.H., & Kasper, H. (1990). The decision-maker and export activity: A cross national comparison of foreign orientation of Austrian managers. *Management International Review,* 30, 3, pp 217-230.

Hymer, S. (1976). *The international operations of national firms: A study of foreign direct investment.* Cambridge Mass: MIT Press.

Ibrahim, B.A. (2004). Internationalization: motive and process. In Léo–Paul Dana (Ed), *Handbook of Research on International Entrepreneurship* (pp129-136) Cheltenham U.K.: Edward Elgar.

Ifju, P.A., & Bush, R.J. (1993). Export barriers and incentive in the eastern lumber industry. *Forest Products Journal,* 43, 3, pp 45-48. www.ilocarib.org.tt/infsources/sme/definition. html.

IMF (1997). *Balance of payment statistics year book:* Parts 2&3. Washington D.C.

IMF (2002). *Balance of payment statistics year book:* Parts 2&3. Washington D.C.

IMF (2004). *Balance of payment statistics: Country Tables*. Washington D.C.

Jaffe, E., Pasternak, D.H. & Nebenzahl, I.(1988). The export behaviour of small and medium-sized Israeli manufacturers. *Journal of Global Marketing,* 2, 2, pp 27-49.

Johanson, J., & Wiedershiem-Paul, F. (1975). The internationalization of the firm: Four Swedish cases. *Journal of Management Studies,* October, 12, 3, pp 305-322.

Johanson, J. & Vahlne, J-E. (1977). The internationalization process of the firm - A model of knowledge development and increasing foreign market commitments. *Journal of International Business Studies* (pre- 1986), Spring, 8, 1, pp 23-32.

Johanson, J. & Vahlne, J-E. (1990). The mechanism of internationalization. *International Marketing Review,* 7, 4, pp 11-25.

Johanson, J., & Vahlne, J.E. (2003). Business relationship learning and commitment in the internationalization process. *Journal of International Entrepreneurship,* 1, 1, pp 83-101.

Jones, M. (1999). The internationalization of small high-technology firms. *Journal of International Marketing,* 7, 4, pp 15- 41.

Jones, M.V., & Coviello, N.E. (2005). Internationalization: conceptualizing an entrepreneurial process of behaviour in time. *Journal of International Business Studies,* 36, 3, pp 284-303.

Jonhston, W.J., & Czinkota, M.R. (1982). Managerial motivations as determinants of industrial export behaviour. In Michael R. Czinkota and George Tesar (Ed), *Export management in an international context*(pp3-17). New York: Praeger.

Joynt, P. (1982). An empirical study of Norwegian export behaviour. In Michael R. Czinkota and George Tesar (Ed), *Export management in an international context* (pp55-69). New York: Praeger, pp 55-69.

Jovanovic, B. (1982). Selection and evolution of industry. econometrica, 50, 3, pp 649-670.

Julian, C. C. (2003). Export marketing performance: A study of Thailand firms. *Journal of Small Business Management,* 41, 2, pp 213- 221.

Karafakiouglu, M. (1986). Export activities of Turkish manufacturers. *International Marketing Review,* 3, 4, winter, pp 34-43.

Katsikeas, C. S., & Morgan, R. E. (1994). Differences in perceptions of exporting problems based on firm size and export market experience. *European Journal of Marketing,* 28, 5, pp 17- 35.

Katsikeas, C.S., & Piercy, N.F. (1993). Long-term export stimuli and firm characteristics in a European LDC. *Journal of International Marketing,* 1, 3, pp 23-47.

Katsikeas, C.S. (1996). Ongoing export motivation: Differences between regular and sporadic exporters. *International Marketing Review,* 13, 2, pp 4-19.

Kaynak, E. (1978). Difficulties of undertaking marketing research in the developing countries. *European Research,* 6, 6, pp 251.

Kaynak, E., & Stevenson, L. (1982). Export orientation of Nova Scotia manufacturers. In Michael R. Czinkota and George Tesar (Ed), *Export management in an international context* (pp132-145). New York: Praeger.

Kaynak, E., & Kothari, V. (1984). Export behaviour of small and medium-sized manufacturers: Some policy guidelines for international marketers. *Management International Review,* 24, 2, pp 61-69.

Kaynak, E., Ghauri, P.N., & Olofsson-Bredenlow, T. (1987). Export behaviour of small Swedish firms. *Journal of Small Business Management,* April, 25, 2, pp 26- 32.

Kaynak, E. (1990). A cross regional study of export performance: Atlantic provinces and Prairie region manufacturers contrasted. *Developments in marketing science*, XIII, pp 161-165.

Kaynak, E. (1992). A cross regional comparison of export performance of firms in two Canadian regions. *Management International Review,* 2nd Quarter, 32, 2, pp. 163-180.

Keng, K. A., & Jiuan, T.S. (1989).Differences between small and medium sized exporting and non- exporting firms: Nature or nurture. *International Marketing Review,* 6, 4, pp 27-40.

Kingsley, G., & Malecki, E.J. (2004). Networking for competitiveness. *Small Business Economics,* 23, pp 71-84.

King, D. (2001). The evolution of structural adjustment and stabilisation policy in Jamaica. *Social and Economic Studies,* 50, (1): 1-53.

Kirpalani, V. H., & McIntosh, N.B. (1980). International marketing effectiveness of technology –oriented small firms. *Journal of International Business Studies,* Winter, pp 81-90.

Knight, G.A., & Cavusgil, S.T. (1996). The born global firm: A challenge to traditional internationalization theory. *Advances in International Marketing,* 8, pp 11-26.

Knight, G.A., & Cavusgil, S.T. (2004). Innovation, organisational capabilities and the born-global firm. *Journal of International Studies,* 35, 2, pp 124-141.

Koch, A. (2001). Factors influencing market and entry mode selection: developing the MEMs model. *Marketing intelligence and planning,* 19, 5, pp 351-361.

Kotabe, M., & Czinkota, M. R. (1992). State government promotion of manufacturing exports: A gap analysis. *Journal of International Business Studies,* 4th Quarter, 23, 4, pp 637-658.

Kothari, V. (1989). Overseas strategies of small business- A longitudinal study. In Avlonitis, Papavasiliou, N.K. & Kouremenos, A.G. (Eds), *Marketing thought and practice in the 1990s* (PP153-167). EMAC Proceedings: Athens.

Krugman, P., & Obstfeld, M. (2003). International economics: *Theory and policy* 9th Edition. New York: Addison- Wesley.

Kumar, N., & Siddharthan, N.S. (1994). Technology, firm size and export behaviour in developing countries: The case of Indian enterprise. *Journal of Development Studies,* 31, 2, pp 289- 309.

Lado, A.A., Boyd, N.G., Wright, P. & Kroll, M. (2006). Paradox and theorizing within the Resource-Based View. *Academy of Management Review,* 31, 1, pp. 115-131.

Lamb, P. W., & Liesch, P. W. (2002). The internationalization process of the smaller firm: Re-framing the relationships between market commitment, knowledge and involvement. *Management International Review,* 1st Quarter, 42, 1, pp 7- 26.

Lashley, J. (2003). Small and micro business issues in Barbados: Investigating the contingent environment. P*aper presented at SALISES fourth annual conference*, Sherbourne Centre, Barbados, 15- 17th January, pp. 1-24.

Lautanen, T. (2000). Modelling small firms' decisions to export- Evidence from manufacturing firms in Finland, 1995. *Small Business Economics,* 14,2, pp 107 -124.

Lee, W-Y., & Brasch, J. J. (1978). The adoption of export as an innovative strategy. *Journal of International Business Studies,* 9, 1, (Spring/Summer), pp 85-93.

Leonidou, L.C. (1995a). Export stimulation research: Review, evaluation and integration. *International Business Review,* 4, 2, pp 133-156.

Leonidou, L.C. (1995b). Empirical research on export barriers: Review, assessment, and synthesis. *Journal of International Marketing,* 3, 1, pp 29-43.

Leonidou, L.C. (1995c). Export stimulation: A non-exporter's perspective. *European Journal of Marketing,* 29, 8, pp17-36.

Leonidou, L. C. & Katsikeas, C. S. (1996). The export development process: An integrative review of the empirical models. *Journal of International Business Studies,* 3rd Quarter, 27, 3, pp 517-551.

Leonidou, L.C. (1998). Factors stimulating export business: An empirical investigation. *Journal of Applied Business Research,* Spring, 14, 2, pp 43- 68.

Leonidou, L.C., Katsikeas, C.S., & Piercy, N.F. (1998). Identifying managerial influences on exporting: Past research and future directions. *Journal of International Marketing,* 6, 2, pp 74- 102.

Leonidou, L.C., Katsikeas,C.S., & Hadjimarcou, J (2002). Executive insights- building successful export business relationships: A behavioural perspective. *Journal of International Marketing",* 10, 3, pp 96- 115.

Leonidou, L.C. (2004). An analysis of the barriers hindering small business export development. *Journal of Small Business Management,* 42, 3, pp 279-302.

Lewis, W.A. (1954). Economic development with unlimited supplies of labour. *The Manchester School,* vol 22 pp 139.

Li, L, Li, D., & Dalgic, T. (2004). Internationalization process of the small and medium-sized enterprises: Towards a hybrid model of experiential learning and planning. *Management International Review,* 44, 1, pp 93-116.

Lipparini, A., & Lorenzo, G. (1999). The leveraging of interfirm relationship as a distinctive organisational capability: A longitudinal study. *Strategic Management Journal,* 20, pp 317-338.

Madsen, T. K., & Servias, P. (1997). The internationalization of born globals: An evolutionary process? *International Business Review,* 6, 6, pp 561- 583.

Majocchi, A., & Zucchella, A. (2003). Internationalization and performance: Findings from a set of Italian SMEs. *International Small Business Journal,* August, 21, 3, pp 249-266.

Malekzaden, A.R., & Rabino, S. (1986). Manufacturers' export strategies. *International Marketing Review, 3,* 4, pp 27-33.

Manolova, T., Brush, C.G., Edelman, L.F., & Greene, P.G. (2002). Internationalization of small firms: Personal factors revisited. *International Small Business Journal,* 20, 1, pp 9-30.

Masurel, E. (2001). Export behaviour of service sector SMEs. *International Small Business Journal,* 19, 2, pp 80 – 84.

Mathur, V.K. (1999). Human capital base strategy for regional economic development. *Economic Development Quarterly,* 13, 3, pp 203.

McConnell, J. (1979). The export decision: An empirical study of firm behaviour. *Economic Geography,* 55, 3, pp171-183.

McDougall, P.P., Shane, S, & Oviatt, B.J.(1994). Explaining the formation of international new ventures: The limits of theories from international business research. *Journal of Business Venturing,* 9, 6, pp 469-487.

McDougall, P.P., & Oviatt, B.J. (2000). International entrepreneurship: The intersection of two research paths. *Academy of Management Journal*, 43, 5, pp 902-906.

McIntyre, A., (1995). *Trade and economic development in small open economies: The case of Caribbean countries*. Connecticut: Praeger.

McNaughton, R. B. (2003). The number of export markets that a firm serves: Process models versus the born global phenomenon. *Journal of International Entrepreneurship,* 1, 3, pp 297-311.

McNaughton, R.B., & Brown, P.(2004). The case of Canadian computer software firms. In Léo – Paul Dana (Ed), *Handbook of Research on International Entrepreneurship*(pp 338-351) Cheltenham U.K.: Edward Elgar.

Mehran, J., & Moini, A. H. (1999). Firms' export behaviour. *American Business Review,* Jan, 17, 1, pp 86-93.

Miles, M., & Huberman, M. (1994). *Qualitative data analysis: An expanded source book.* London: Sage.

Misenbock, K. J. (1988). *Small business and exporting: A literature review. International Small Business Journal,* 6, 2, pp 42-61.

Mission Report (1985). *Jamaica: An integrated development programme for pre-micro, micro and small business.* Kingston: Jamaica.

Mittelstaedt, J.D., Harben, G.N., & Ward, W.A. (2003). How small is too small? Firm size as barrier to exporting from the United States. *Journal of Small Business Management,* 41, 1, pp 68-84.

Moen, O. (1999). The relationship between firm size, competitive advantages and export performance revisited. *International Small Business Journal,* 18, 1, pp 53- 72.

Moen, O., & Servias, P. (2002). Born global or gradual? Examining the export behaviour of small and medium -sized enterprises. *Journal of International Marketing,* 10, 3, pp 49-72.

Morgan, R.E., & Katsikeas, C.S. (1997). Obstacles to export initiation and expansion. *International Journal of Management Science,* 25, pp 677-690.

Nicholls, J.A.F., Lyn-Cook, M., & Roslow, S. (1989). Strategies for export marketing of non-traditional products. *International Marketing Review,* 6, 4, pp 58- 72.

Obben, J., & Magagula, P. (2003). Firm and managerial determinants of the export propensity of small and medium-sized enterprises in Swaziland. *International Small Business Journal,* Feb, 21, 1, pp 73- 89.

Ocompo, J. A. (2002). Small economies in the face of globalization. *Third William G. Demas Lecture at the Caribbean Development Bank,* Barbados, pp1-25.

O'Farrell, P. N., Wood, P.A., & Zheng, J. (1998a). Internationalization by business service SMEs: An inter- industry analysis. *International Small Business Journal,* 16, 2, pp 13-33.

O'Farrell, P.N., Wood, P.A., & Zheng, J.(1998b). Regional influences on foreign market development by business service companies: Elements of a strategic context explanation. *Regional Studies,* 32, 1, pp 31-48.

O'Grady, S., & Lane, H.W. (1996). The psychic distance paradox. *Journal of International Business Studies, Second Quarter,* 27, 2, pp 309-333.

Ogram, E.W. Jr. (1982). Exporters and Non-exporters: A profile of small manufacturing firms in Georgia. In Michael R. Czinkota and George Tesar (Eds), *Export management in an international context,*(pp 70-84). New York: Praeger.

Oviatt, B. M., & Mc Dougall, P. P. (1994). Toward a theory of international new ventures. *Journal of International Business Studies,* 1st quarter, 25, 1, pp 45- 64.

Oviatt, B. M., & Mc Dougall, P. P. (1997). Challenges for internationalization process theory: The case of international new venture. *Management International Review,* 37, 2, pp 85-99.

Oviatt, B., & Mc Dougall, P. (2005). The internationalization of entrepreneurship. *Journal of International Business Studies,* 36, 1, pp 2-8.

Oviatt, B. (2005), Book reviews - The handbook of research on international entrepreneurship and emerging paradigms in international entrepreneurship. *Journal of International Business Studies,* 36, 4, pp 484-487.

Pena, I. (2002). Intellectual capital and business start-up success. *Journal of Intellectual Capital,* 3, 2, pp180-198.

Peng, M.W. (2004). Identifying the big questions in international business research. *Journal of International Business Studies,* 35, 2, pp 99-108.

Penrose, E. (1980). *The theory of the growth of the firm. 2nd Edition.* Oxford: Basil Blackwell Publisher.

Philp, N.E. (1998). The export propensity of the very small enterprise (VSE). *International Small Business Journal,* 16, 4, pp 79-93.

Pindyck, R.S., & Rubinfeld, D.L. (1998). *Econometric models and economic forecasts. 5th Edition.* New York: Mc Graw Hill.

PIOJ (2000). *Economic and social survey Jamaica.* Kingston: Jamaica.

PIOJ (2004). *Economic and social survey Jamaica.* Kingston: Jamaica.

PIOJ (2007). *Economic and social survey Jamaica*. Kingston: Jamaica.

Pla-Barber, J., & Alegre, J. (2007). Analysing the link between export intensity, innovation and firm size in a science-based industry. *International Business Review,* 16, pp275-293.

Pope, R. A. (2002). Why small firms export: Another look. *Journal of Small Business Management,* 40, 1, pp 17- 26.

Popper, K.R. (1963). *Conjectures and refutations: The growth of scientific knowledge.* London: Routledge & Kegan Paul.

Porter, M.E. (1990). *The competitive advantage of nations.* New York: Free Press.

Porter, M.E. (2008). *The five competitive forces that shape strategy.* Harvard Business Review, January.

PSOJ (2004). Small states in transition- from vulnerability to competitiveness. *Paper presented at the ITC Executive Forum,* Port of Spain, Trinidad & Tobago, pp1-10.

Rabino, S. (1980). An examination of barriers to exporting encountered by small manufacturing firm. *Management International Review,* 20, 1, pp 67- 73.

Ramaseshan, B., & Patton, M. A. (1994). Factors influencing international channel choice of small business exporters. *International Marketing Review,* 11, 4, pp 19-34.

Rasheed, H.S. (2005). Foreign entry mode and performance: the moderating effects of environment. *Journal of Small Business Management,* 43, 1, pp 41-54.

Reid, S. D. (1981). The decision-maker and export entry and expansion. *Journal of International Business Studies,* 12, 2, pp 101- 112.

Reid. S.D. (1982). The impact of size on export behaviour in small firms. In Michael R Czinkota and George Tesar (Eds), *Export management in an international context,* (pp18-38). New York: Praeger.

Reid, S. D. (1983). Export trilogy sets research agenda. *Journal of International Business Studies,* (pre-1986), Fall, 14, 2, pp 153-155.

Reid, S. (1986). Is technology linked with export performance in small firms. In Hubner (Ed), *The art and science of innovation management.* Amsterdam: Elsevier Science Publishers, pp 273- 283.

Rennie, M. (1993). Born global. McKinsey Quarterly, no. 4. pp 4-52.

Rhee, H.J. (2002). An exploratory examination of propensity and performance in new venture internationalization. *New England Journal of Entrepreneurship,* 5, 1, pp 51 66.

Rialp, A., & Rialp, J. (2001). Conceptual frameworks on SMEs' internationalization: Past, present and future trends of research. *Reassessing the internationalization of the firm,* Volume 11, pp 49-78.

Rialp, A., Rialp, J., & Knight, G.A. (2005). The phenomenon of early internationalizing firms: what do we know after a decade (1993-2003) of scientific inquiry? *International Business Review,* 14, 2, pp 147-166.

Roberts, C. (2000). Breaking through the barriers to sustainable development. Enterprise 2000 Report, Kingston: Jamaica.

Rodriguez, J.L., & Rodriguez, R.M.G. (2005). Technology and export behaviour: A resource-based view approach. *International Business Review,* 14, 5, pp 539-557.

Rogers, E.M. (1962). *Diffusion of innovation.* New York: Free Press of Glencoe.

Rosa, P., & McAlpine, A.(1991). Graduate career orientation towards enterprise. In L.Davies & A. Gibbs(Ed), *Recent research in entrepreneurship*(pp 73-105). Alder-shot: Gower.

Rosa, P. (1993). Family background and entrepreneurial activity in British graduates. In R. Atkin, E/ Chell and C. Mason (Eds), *New directions in small business research(*pp36-55). Aldershot: Avebury/ Gower.

Rosa, P. (2003). Hardly likely to make the Japanese tremble: The businesses of recently graduated university and college entrepreneurs. *International Small Business Journal,* 21, 4, pp 435- 459.

Ross, C.A. (1989). Exporters and non-exporters of manufactured products: The case of Jamaica. *Journal of Global Marketing,* 3, 2, pp 77-103.

Root, F.R. (1994). *Entry strategies for international markets.* New York: Lexington Books.

Rugman, A. M., & Verbeke, A. (2004). A perspective on regional and global strategies of multinational enterprises. *Journal of International Business Studies,* 35, 1, pp3-17.

Russow, L.C., & Okoroafo, S.C. (1996).On the way towards developing a global screening model. *International Marketing Review,* 13, 1, pp 46-64.

Samiee, S., Walters, P.G.P., & Dubois, F.L. (1993). Exporting as an innovative behaviour: An empirical investigation. *International Market Review,* 10, 3, pp 5-25.

Sayer, A. (1992). *Methods in social science: A realist approach* 2nd Edition. London: Routledge.

Schumpeter, J.A. (1961). *The theory of economic development.* Cambridge MA: Harvard University Press.

Seringhaus, R.F.H., & Rosson, P.H. (1990). *Government export promotion: A global perspective.* London: Routledge.

Seyoum, B. (2006). US trade preferences and export performance of developing countries: Evidence from the generalized system of preferences. *International Business Review,* 15, 1, pp 68-83.

Shankar, O. (2004). One more time: International business in a global economy. *Journal of International Business Studies,* 35, 2, pp 161-17.

Shaw, V., & Darroch, J. (2004). Barriers to internationalization: A study of entrepreneurial new ventures in New Zealand. *Journal of International Entrepreneurship,* 2, 4, pp 327-343.

Simpson, C.L. Jr., and Kujawa, D. (1974). The export decision process: An empirical inquiry. *Journal of International Business Studies,* (pre-1986) Spring, 5, 1, pp 107-117.

Simmonds, K., & Smith, H. (1968).The first export order- a marketing innovation. British *Journal of Marketing Science,* XVIII, pp 93- 100.

Snowdon, B. & Vane, H. (1999). *Conversations with Leading Economists: Interpreting Macroeconomics.* U.K.: Edward Elgar

Söderbom, M. (2002). What drives manufacturing exports in Africa? Evidence from Ghana, Kenya and Zimbabwe. *CASE- UNIDO Working Paper No.2,* pp 1-10.

STATIN, (2002). *External Trade.* Kingston: Jamaica.

Stimchcombe, A.L. (1965). Social structure of organisation. In J.M. March (Ed), *Handbook of Organisation* (pp142-193). Chicago: Rand Mc Nally Publishers.

Stlyes, C. (1998). Export performance measures in Australia and the United Kingdom. *Journal of International Marketing,* 6, 3, pp12-36.

Stevens, J.P. (1992). *Applied multivariate statistics for social sciences* 2nd Edition. New York: Academic Press.

Storey, D.J. (1994). *Understanding the small business sector.* London: Routledge.

Tesar, G., & Tarleton, J.S. (1982). Comparison of Wisconsin and Virginia small and medium –sized exporters: Aggressive and passive exporters. In Michael R. Czinkota and George Tesar (Eds), *Export management in an international context* (pp85-112). New York: Praeger.

Terpstra, V., & Yu, C.M. (1988). Determinants of foreign investment of US advertising agencies. *Journal of International Business Studies,* 19, 1, Spring, pp 33-46.

Thomas, M.J., & Araujo, L. (1985). Theories of export behaviour: A critical analysis. *European Journal of Marketing,* 19, 2, pp 42- 52.

Tindigarukayo, J. (2001). *Challenges in conducting sample surveys in the Caribbean. Social and Economic Studies*, 50, 2, pp 167-188.

Tookey, D.A. (1964). Factors associated with success in exporting. *Journal of Management Studies,* 1, March, pp 48-66.

Tseng, C-H., Tansuhaj, P.S. & Rose, J (2004). Are strategic assets contributions or constraints for SMEs to go international? An empirical study of the US manufacturing sector. *Journal of American Academy of Business,* 5, 1-2, pp 246-254.

Tú, C. (2003). *The internationalization process of small and medium- sized enterprises.* Unpublished Ph.D. Dissertation, Manchester Business School, U.K.

Tyebjee, T.T. (1994). Internationalization of high tech firms: initial vs. extended involvement. *Journal of Global Marketing,* 7, 4, pp 59- 78.

Ursic, M.L,. & Czinkota, M.R. (1989). The relationship between managerial characteristics and exporting behaviour. *Developments in Marketing Science,* 12, pp 208-210.

UNCTAD, (1996/97). *Handbook of international trade and development statistics.* New York & Geneva: United Nations.

UNCTAD, (1999). *Trade and development report.* New York & Geneva: United Nations.

UNCTAD, (2004). *Hand Book of Statistics.* New York & Geneva: United Nations.

US Department of Commerce (2004). Trade stats express-national trade data: http://tse.export.gov/MapFrameset.

Vatne, E. (1995). Local resource mobilization and internationalization strategies in small and medium sized enterprises. *Environment and Planning,*, 27, 1, pp 63-80.

Verbeek, M. (2001). *A Guide to modern econometrics.* U.S.A: John Wiley & Sons.

Vernon, R. (1966). International investment and international trade in the product life cycle. *Quarterly Journal of Economics,* 80, pp 190-207.

Welch, L.S., & Loustarinen, R. (1988). Internationalization: Evolution of a concept. *Journal of General Management,* 14, 2, pp 36-64.

Welch, L.S. (2004). International entrepreneurship and internationalization: common threads. In Léo-Paul Dana (Ed), *Handbook of Research on International Entrepreneurship* (pp137-149). Cheltenham U.K.: Edward Elgar.

Welch, L.S., & Wiedersheim-Paul, F. (1980). Initial exports: A marketing failure? *Journal of Management Studies*, 17, 3, pp 333-344.

Westhead, P. (1995). Exporting and non-exporting small firms in Great Britain A matched pairs comparison. *International Journal of Entrepreneurial Behaviour and Research,* 1, 2, pp 6- 36.

Westhead, P., Wright, M., & Ucbasaran, D. (2001). The internationalization of new and small firms: A Resource-based view. *Journal of Business Venturing,* 16, 4, pp 333-358.

Westhead, P., Wright, M., & Ucbasaran, D. (2004). Internationalization of private firms: environmental turbulence and organisational strategies and resources. *Entrepreneurship & Regional Development,* 6, pp 501-522.

Westhead, P. (2005). Léo-Dana (ed.) Handbook of Research on International Entrepreneurship, Cheltenham: Edward Elgar, 2004. 864pp. *International Small Business Journal,* 23, 5, pp 577-581.

Whitelock, J., & Jobber, D. (2004). The evaluation of external factors in the decision of UK industrial firms to enter a new non- domestic market: An exploratory study. *European Journal of Marketing,* 34. 11/12, pp 1437- 1455.

Whitey, J.J. (1980). Differences between exporters and non-exporters: some hypotheses concerning small manufacturing business. *American Journal of Small Business,* Vol 4, pp. 29- 37.

Wiedersheim-Paul, F., Olson, H.C., & Welch, L.S. (1978). Pre-export activity: The first step in internationalization. *Journal of International Business Studies* 9, 1, (Spring/ Summer), pp 47-58.

Williams, D. A. (2007). Competitiveness of small enterprises: Insights from a developing economy. *The Round Table,* 96, 390, pp 347-363.

Williams, J.E.M., & Chaston, I. (2004). Links between the linguistic ability and international experience of export managers and their export marketing intelligence behaviour. *International Small Business Journal,* 22, 5, pp 463-486.

Williamson, O.E. (1975). *Markets and hierarchies*. New York: Free Press.

Wint, A. G. (1995). *Corporate management in developing countries: The challenge of international competitiveness.* Westport, Connecticut: Quorum Books.

Wint, A. (1997). *Managing Towards International Competitiveness: Cases and Lessons from the Caribbean, Kingston:* Ian Randle Publishers

Wint, A.G. (1998). The role of government in enhancing the competitiveness of developing economies: selective functional intervention in the Caribbean. *International Journal of Public Sector Management,* 11, 4, pp. 281-299.

Wint, A.G. (2003). *Competitiveness in small developing economies: Insights from the Caribbean.* Kingston: UWI Press.

Witter, M., & Anderson, P.Y. (1991). *Distribution of the social cost of Jamaica's structural adjustment 1977- 1989.* Prepared for research project on the impact of structural adjustment on the social debt in Jamaica. Sponsored by the International Labour Organisation and the Planning Institute of Jamaica. Pp 1-102.

Wolff, J. A., and Pett, T. L. (2000). Internationalization of small firms: An examination of export competitive patterns, firm size and export performance. *Journal of Small Business Management,* April, 38, 2, pp 34- 47.

Wonnacott, T. H., & Wonnacott, R.J. (1990). *Introductory statistics for business and economics.* 4th Edition. U.S. A.: John Wiley & Sons, Inc.

World Bank (2000). *Entering the twenty-first century. In World Development Report,* New York: Oxford University Press.

World Bank (2005). *A time to choose: Caribbean Development in the 21st Century",* New York: Oxford University Press.

Wortzel, L.H., & Wortzel, H.V. (1981). Export strategies of NIC and LDC based firms. *Columbia Journal of World Business,* Spring, pp 51-60.

WTO (2001). *International trade statistics.* France.

WTO (2004). *International trade statistics.* Switzerland.

Yaprak, A. (1985). A empirical study of the differences between small exporting and non-exporting US firms. *International Marketing Review,* Summer, 2, 2, pp 72- 83.

Young, S., Hammil, J., Wheeler,C., & Davies, J.R. (1989). *International market entry and development: Strategies and development.* Hemel Hempstead: Harvester Wheatsheaf.

Young, S., Dimitratos, P. Dana, L-P. (2003). International entrepreneurship research: What scope for international business theories? *Journal of International Entrepreneurship,* 1, 1, pp 31-42.

Yin, R.K (2003). *Case study research: design and methods* 3rd Edition. London: Sage.

Zarah, S.A. Cloninger, P., FENA, J & Choi, Y (2004). Emerging research issues in international entrepreneurship. In Léo -Paul Dana (Ed), *Handbook of Research on International Entrepreneurship* (pp732-743) Cheltenham U.K.: Edward Elgar.

Zou, S., & Stan, S. (1998). The determinants of export performance: A review of the empirical literature between 1987 and 1997. *International Marketing Review,* 15, 5, pp 333- 356.

Zou, S., Fang, E., & Zhoa, S. (2003). The effect of export marketing capabilities on export performance: An investigation of Chinese exporters. *Journal of International Marketing,* 11, 4, pp 32-55.

About the Author

Densil A. Williams is a lecturer of International Business in the Department of Management Studies at UWI, Mona in Jamaica. His research interests include strategy of firms, economic development and international business. He has served as consultant on a number of projects dealing with the competitiveness of firms in small economies. His current research is also focused on the international activities of the small firm. Densil's works appear in major journals in Europe and North-America. He has also presented his works at major international conferences in Europe and North-America.

INDEX

C

D

E

F

G

N

O

P

Q

R

S

T

U

V

W

Y

Z